TEACHING MUSIC CREATIVELY

Second edition

Pamela Burnard and Regina Murphy

with James Biddulph,
Deborah Blair,
Jenny Boyack,
Marcelo Giglio,
Gillian Howell,
Elizabeth Mackinlay,
Kathryn Marsh,
Emily Okuno,
Alex Ruthmann,
Rena Upitis, and
Jane Wheeler

Routledge
Taylor & Francis Group

LONDON AND NEW YORK

Second edition published 2017
by Routledge
2 Park Square, Milton Park, Abingdon, Oxon OX14 4RN

and by Routledge
711 Third Avenue, New York, NY 10017

Routledge is an imprint of the Taylor & Francis Group, an informa business

First edition published by Routledge 2013

British Library Cataloguing-in-Publication Data
A catalogue record for this book is available from the British Library

Library of Congress Cataloguing-in-Publication Data
Names: Burnard, Pamela. | Murphy, Regina.
Title: Teaching music creatively / Pamela Burnard and Regina Murphy.
Description: Second edition. | Abingdon, Oxon ; New York, NY : Routledge,
    2017. | Includes bibliographical references and index.
Identifiers: LCCN 2016057693| ISBN 9781138187184 (hardback) |
    ISBN 9781138187207 (pbk.) | ISBN 9781315643298 (ebook)
Subjects: LCSH: School music—Instruction and study. | Education, Primary.
Classification: LCC MT1 .B866 2017 | DDC 372.87/044—dc23
LC record available at https://lccn.loc.gov/2016057693

ISBN: 978-1-138-18718-4 (hbk)
ISBN: 978-1-138-18720-7 (pbk)
ISBN: 978-1-315-64329-8 (ebk)

Typeset in Times New Roman and Helvetica Neue
by Apex Covantage, LLC

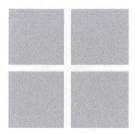

CONTENTS

CONTENTS ▪ ▪ ▪ ▪

CONTRIBUTORS

Pamela Burnard (England) is Professor of Arts, Creativities and Education at the University of Cambridge, UK, where she manages Higher Degree courses in Arts, Creativity, Education and Culture (ACEC) and Educational Research. She is internationally known for her work in the areas of creative learning and creative teaching and diverse creativities in professional and educational practice. Pamela has always been concerned with developing teaching strategies and aids to encourage teachers to examine their own understandings of creativity in order to foster the creative engagement of both teachers and children. Pamela believes that all teachers need to examine their own understandings of creativity in order to help children to develop their own creativity in music and that all teachers are creative practitioners and musicians themselves. Pamela has published widely in the fields of music education and creativities research.

Regina Murphy (Ireland) is Head of School of Arts Education and Movement at the Institute of Education, Dublin City University, Ireland, where she teaches and directs postgraduate courses. She has presented numerous workshops and papers nationally and internationally. As a former primary teacher, she has taught in schools in Ireland, England and New Zealand. She also worked as a primary principal before entering higher education. Regina was one of the key personnel in the development of the primary school music curriculum in Ireland and in the subsequent national professional development programme for primary teachers. Amongst her publications are a set of comprehensive resources to support music making in primary schools for children aged 4 to 12. Curriculum and assessment in music education, and the expertise of the generalist primary teacher in particular, continue to motivate her research interests. She is co-editor of the *British Journal of Music Education* and a past board member of the International Society for Music Education (ISME) 2008–2012. She is also a founding member of the Society for Music Education in Ireland.

James Biddulph (England) has been a primary school teacher since 2001 and is now the Head Teacher of Avanti Court Primary School in East London. In 2002 his creative and successful approach to teaching gained him Advanced Skills Teachers

(AST) status in Music and in 2003 he was awarded Outstanding New Teacher of the Year for London. He successfully develops partnerships with a number of local schools and Creative Partnerships, developing the arts to enrich the curriculum and share good practice. His two master's degrees focus on children's and teachers' perceptions of creative learning experiences. He is on the review board for the *British Journal of Music Education* and is a trustee of Stratford Circus (a theatre and arts space in East London). Since April 2010 he has been working on his PhD at Cambridge University focussed on creative learning in multicultural contexts.

Jenny Boyack, PhD (New Zealand), is a primary school music specialist in Palmerston North, New Zealand. Jenny has had many years of experience as a primary school teacher, adviser to schools and music teacher educator, and is a choir director and church organist. Her research interests include vocal development, singing self-efficacy, music leadership in the primary school and music education for generalist teachers, and she is passionate about inclusive music education practices.

Gillian Howell (Australia) is a PhD candidate at Griffith University and lecturer in Community Music Leadership at Melbourne Polytechnic. Her research investigates community music in war-torn and post-conflict countries, among newly arrived refugees in Australia, and intercultural community music leadership. She has worked as a music leader and researcher in post-conflict settings in Europe, South Asia, and South-East Asia, and in 2016 was awarded a prestigious Endeavour Research Fellowship to research music and reconciliation in Sri Lanka and Norway. Gillian is also an award-winning musician and teaching artist, working with many of Australia's leading symphony orchestras and arts organisations. She was the founding creative director of the Melbourne Symphony Orchestra's Community Engagement Program, drawing the orchestra into challenging new community collaborations, and creating some of its most enduring community engagement programs. She serves on several national and international boards, including as a Commissioner of the Community Music Activity Commission of the International Society for Music Education, and Board member of Community Music Victoria. She maintains a blog exploring music leadership and practice at gillianhowell.com.au.

Elizabeth Mackinlay (Australia) is Associate Professor in the School of Education at the University of Queensland where she teaches Arts Education, Indigenous Education, Qualitative Research Methods and Women's Studies. Elizabeth completed her PhD in Ethnomusicology in 1998 and continues her work with Aboriginal women at Burrulula in the Northern Territory of Australia. She also completed a PhD in Education at the University of Queensland in 2003 and has a primary education degree from Charles Darwin University. Her book, *Disturbances and Dislocations: Teaching and Learning Aboriginal Women's Music and Dance*, was published in 2007 by Peter Lang. She has co-edited a number of books with Cambridge Scholars Press, including *Aesthetics and Experience in Music Performance* (2005), *Musical Islands* (2009) and *Applied Ethnomusicology: Historical Approaches and New Perspectives* (2011). Elizabeth has published many chapters and articles in the fields of ethnomusicology, indigenous education, music and arts education and feminist studies. She has most recently worked on a book titled *Teaching and Learning Like a Feminist: Stories of*

Experience in Higher Education, published by Sense Publishers in 2016. Elizabeth is currently involved in a number of different research projects which include drumming circles for primary students, the politics and pedagogies of indigenous Australian studies in primary and tertiary education contexts, programs for mentoring indigenous pre-service teachers, music and mothering and feminism in higher education. She is currently the editor of *Music Education Research and Innovation* (MERI) and co-editor of the *Australian Journal of Indigenous Education* (AJIE).

Kathryn Marsh (Australia) is former Chair of Music Education at the Sydney Conservatorium of Music, University of Sydney, where, as Associate Professor, she teaches subjects relating to primary music education, cultural diversity in music education and music education research methods. She has a PhD in Ethnomusicology and a professional background as a primary generalist teacher, music specialist and teacher of English as a Second Language. Her research interests include children's musical play, children's creativity and cultural diversity in music education, most recently exploring the role of music in the lives of refugee children. She has written numerous scholarly and professional publications, including her recent book, *The Musical Playground: Global Tradition and Change in Children's Songs and Games*, published by Oxford University Press and winner of the Folklore Society's 2009 Katherine Briggs Award. She has been actively involved in curriculum development and teacher training for many years and has presented internationally on a regular basis. She has been the recipient of major national research grants which have involved large-scale international cross-cultural collaborative research into children's musical play in Australia, Europe, the UK, USA and Korea and, as a member of an interdisciplinary research team, conducted the National Review of School Music Education in Australia.

Alex Ruthmann (USA) is Associate Professor of Music Education and Music Technology and Director of the Music Experience Design Lab (MusEDLab) at NYU Steinhardt in New York City. He currently serves as Associate Editor of the *Journal of Music, Technology & Education*, and is Co-Editor of the forthcoming *Oxford Handbook of Technology and Music Education* with Roger Mantie and the *Routledge Companion to Music, Technology & Education* with Andrew King and Evangelos Himonides. He is a Coordinating Principal Investigator on a Digital Media & Learning Competition 6 grant with Evan Tobias from Arizona State University designing music learning playlists for the LRNG platform. His current research explores co-design methods for developing new technologies and experiences for music making, learning and engagement with end users and audiences. He recently co-founded MusED-Works, a music experience design and development studio to commercialize IP coming from the MusEDLab into playful apps and technologies that lower barriers to creative expression.

Rena Upitis (Canada) is Professor of Arts Education at Queen's University in Canada, and a former Dean of Education at Queen's. She is also President and CEO of Wintergreen Studios, an education and retreat centre founded in 2007. Rena served a six-year term as National Research Co-director of Learning Through the Arts, a multi-year project that brings artists to the classrooms of over 100,000 Canadian students. Her current research explores how web-based technologies can support student-centred learning, especially in the arts. She has worked as a music teacher in Canada and the United States and has been a studio teacher of piano and music theory for over thirty-five years. Rena's research has been recognized by several awards, including the George C. Metcalf Research Award (2002) and the Canadian Association for Curriculum Studies Publication Award (2005).

Jane Wheeler (England) is passionate about teacher continuing professional development and motivating all young people to find their 'voice' in music making, whatever it is. She has recently become a freelance music education artist and consultant and has set up her own company Living Song (http://www.livingsong.co.uk), having spent the past three years setting up the music programme for ARK Schools (2008–2011). This included developing the One Voice choirs programme across ARK Schools and the advanced choir, SPARK (Singing Pathways ARK), and leading on the London Sing Up partnership, with iGospel, British Gospel Arts and Newham Young People's Chorus (NYPC). She also established a primary and secondary network and teacher training programme for music education. Prior to this she was the music advisor for the London Borough of Newham at which time she set up and directed the borough-wide choral singing programme, teacher training programme and music engagement strategies for primary and secondary children. She was appointed in April 2005 after working for two years at Newham VIth Form FE College (NewVIc) and University of East London as part of the music team and as an Advanced Skills Teacher, working centrally for the 'Learning and Schools' in Newham. She continues to work at NewVIc directing and facilitating Solid Harmony Youth Community Choir, which has been running for ten years (http://www.solidharmony.co.uk). She continues to work as musical director with NewYVC (https://www.youtube.com/watch?v=Svek8YtnSNs) as part of the portfolio of Living Song's work.

CLASSROOM CASE AND ACTIVITY CONTRIBUTORS

Deborah Blair (USA) is Associate Professor of Music Education at Oakland University (Rochester, MI) where she teaches undergraduate and graduate courses in educational psychology and qualitative research and a wide variety of methods courses for general and choral music settings. Her research interests focus on the application of constructivism theories of learning and teaching across K–12 classrooms, teacher education and learners with exceptionalities.

Marcelo Giglio, PhD (Switzerland), is Professor and Head of Research Projects at University of Teacher Education BEJUNE, Switzerland. His research focuses on the relationship between teachers and pupils in innovative and creative pedagogical situations. He has published in Spanish, French and English. He is author of *Cuando la colaboración creative cambia la forma de enseñar* (translated 'When collaborative creativity changes the form of teaching') (University of Cantabria, Spain, 2013).

Emily Okuno (Kenya) is Associate Professor of Music at the Kenya Polytechnic University College in Nairobi, Kenya, where she also serves as Director of the Centre for

Creative and Cultural Industries. She has taught music at kindergarten, primary, secondary and tertiary levels of education in Kenya. Her current research interest and focus are on music education that is culturally relevant for learners' identity formation and for appropriate utilisation of local music resources as learning material. She is the author of *Issues in Music Education in Kenya: A Handbook for Teachers* and *Indigenous Kenyan Children's Songs: An Anthology*.

SERIES EDITOR'S FOREWORD

Teresa Cremin

Over the last two decades, teachers in England, working in a culture of accountability and target setting, have experienced a high level of specification both of curriculum content and pedagogy. Positioned as recipients of the prescribed agenda, it could be argued that practitioners have had their hands tied, their voices quietened and their professional autonomy constrained. Research reveals that during this time some professionals have short-changed their understanding of pedagogy and practice (Burns and Myhill, 2004; English, Hargreaves and Hislam, 2002) in order to deliver the required curriculum. The relentless quest for higher standards and 'coverage' may well have obscured the personal and affective dimensions of teaching and learning, fostering a mindset characterised more by compliance and conformity than curiosity and creativity.

However, alongside the standards agenda, creativity and creative policies and practices also became prominent and a focus on creative teaching and learning developed. Heralded by the publication *All Our Futures: Creativity, Culture and Education* (NACCCE, 1999), this shift was exemplified in the Creative Partnerships initiative, in the Qualifications and Curriculum Authority's creativity framework (QCA, 2005) and in a plethora of reports (e.g. CapeUK, 2006; DfES, 2003; OFSTED, 2003; Roberts, 2006). It was also evident in the development of the Curriculum for Excellence in Scotland. The definition of creativity frequently employed was creativity is 'imaginative activity fashioned so as to produce outcomes that are both original and of value' (NACCCE, 1999: 30). Many schools sought to develop more innovative curricula, and many teachers found renewed energy through teaching creatively and teaching for creativity.

Yet tensions persist, not only because the dual policies of performativity and creativity appear contradictory, but also because the new National Curriculum draft programmes of study in England at least afford a high degree of specificity and profile the knowledge needed to be taught and tested. We need to be concerned if teachers are positioned more as technically competent curriculum deliverers, rather than artistically engaged, research-informed curriculum developers. I believe, alongside Eisner (2003) and others, that teaching is an art form and that teachers benefit from viewing themselves as versatile artists in the classroom, drawing on their personal passions and creativity as they research and develop practice. As Joubert observes:

> Creative teaching is an art. One cannot teach teachers didactically how to be creative; there is no fail safe recipe or routines. Some strategies may help to promote creative thinking, but teachers need to develop a full repertoire of skills which they can adapt to different situations.
>
> (Joubert, 2001, p. 21)

However, creative teaching is only part of the picture, since teaching for creativity also needs to be acknowledged and their mutual dependency recognised. The former focuses more on teachers using imaginative approaches in the classroom in order to make learning more interesting and effective, the latter, more on the development of children's creativity (NACCCE, 1999). Both rely upon an understanding of the notion of 'creativity' and demand that professionals confront the myths and mantras which surround the word. These include the commonly held misconceptions that creativity is connected only to participation in the arts and that it is confined to particular individuals, a competence of a few specially gifted children.

Nonetheless, creativity is an elusive concept; it has been multiply defined by educationalists, psychologists and neurologists, as well as by policy makers in different countries and cultural contexts. Debates resound about its individual and/or collaborative nature, the degree to which it is generic or domain specific, and the difference between the 'Big C' creativity of genius and the 'little c' creativity of the everyday. Notwithstanding these issues, most scholars in the field perceive it involves the capacity to generate, reason and critically evaluate novel ideas and/or imaginary scenarios. As such, I perceive it encompasses thinking through and solving problems, making connections, inventing and reinventing and flexing one's imaginative muscles in all aspects of learning and life.

In the primary classroom, creative teaching and learning have been associated with innovation, originality, ownership and control (Jeffrey and Woods, 2009) and creative teachers have been seen, in their planning and teaching and in the ethos which they create, to afford high value to curiosity and risk-taking, to ownership, autonomy and making connections (Cremin, 2009; Cremin, Barnes and Scoffham, 2009). Such teachers, it has been posited, often work in partnership with others: with children, other teachers and experts from beyond the school gates (Cochrane and Cockett, 2007). Additionally, in research exploring possibility thinking, which it is argued is at the heart of creativity in education (Craft, 2000), an intriguing interplay between teachers and children has been observed; both are involved in possibility, thinking their ways forwards, and in immersing themselves in playful contexts, posing questions, being imaginative, showing self-determination, taking risks and innovating (Burnard, Craft and Cremin, 2006; Craft, McConnon and Mathews, 2012; Cremin, Burnard and Craft, 2006). A new pedagogy of possibility beckons.

This series *Learning to Teach in the Primary School*, which accompanies and complements the edited textbook *Learning to Teach in the Primary School* (Arthur and Cremin, 2010), seeks to support teachers in developing as creative practitioners, assisting them in exploring the synergies and potential of teaching creatively and teaching for creativity. The series does not merely offer practical strategies for use in the classroom, though these abound, but more importantly seeks to widen teachers' and student teachers' knowledge and understanding of the principles underpinning a creative approach to teaching – principles based on research. It seeks to mediate the wealth of research evidence and make accessible and engaging the diverse theoretical perspectives and scholarly arguments available, demonstrating their practical relevance and value to the profession. Those who aspire to develop further as creative and curious educators will, I trust, find much of value to support their own professional learning journeys and enrich their pedagogy and practice and children's creative learning right across the curriculum.

ABOUT THE SERIES EDITOR

Teresa Cremin (Grainger) is a Professor of Education (Literacy) at the Open University and a past President of UKRA (2001–2002) and UKLA (2007–2009). She is currently co-convenor of the BERA Creativity SIG and a trustee of Booktrust, The Poetry Archive and UKLA. She is also a Fellow of the English Association and an Academician of the Academy of Social Sciences. Her work involves research, publication and consultancy in literacy and creativity. Her current projects seek to explore children's make believe play in the context of storytelling and storyacting, their everyday lives and literacy practices and the nature of literary discussions in extracurricular reading groups. Additionally, Teresa is interested in teachers' identities as readers and writers and the characteristics and associated pedagogy that fosters possibility thinking within creative learning in the primary years. Teresa has published widely, writing and co-editing a variety of books including *Writing Voices: Creating Communities of Writers* (Routledge, 2012); *Teaching English Creatively* (Routledge, 2009); *Learning to Teach in the Primary School* (Routledge 2010); *Jumpstart Drama* (David Fulton, 2009); *Documenting Creative Learning 5–11* (Trentham, 2007); *Creativity and Writing: Developing Voice and Verve* (Routledge, 2005); *Teaching English in Higher Education* (NATE and UKLA, 2007); *Creative Activities for Character, Setting and Plot, 5–7, 7–9, 9–11* (Scholastic, 2004); and *Language and Literacy: A Routledge Reader* (Routledge, 2001).

REFERENCES

Arthur, J. and Cremin, T. (eds.) (2010) *Learning to Teach in the Primary School* (2nd edition). London: Routledge.

Burnard, P., Craft, A. and Cremin, T. (2006) Possibility thinking. *International Journal of Early Years Education*, 14(3), 243–62.

Burns, C. and Myhill, D. (2004) Interactive or inactive? A consideration of the nature of interaction in whole class teaching. *Cambridge Journal of Education*, 34, 35–49.

CapeUK. (2006) *Building Creative Futures: The Story of Creative Action Research Awards, 2004–2005*. London: Arts Council.

Cochrane, P. and Cockett, M. (2007) *Building a Creative School: A Dynamic Approach to School Development*. London: Trentham.

Craft, A. (2000) *Creativity Across the Primary Curriculum*. London: Routledge.

Craft, A., McConnon, L. and Mathews, A. (2012) Creativity and child-initiated play. *Thinking Skills and Creativity*, 7(1), 48–61.

Cremin, T. (2009) Creative teaching and creative teachers. In A. Wilson (ed.) *Creativity in Primary Education*. Exeter: Learning Matters, pp. 36–46.

Cremin, T., Barnes, J. and Scoffham, S. (2009) *Creative Teaching for Tomorrow: Fostering a Creative State of Mind*. Deal: Future Creative.

Cremin, T., Burnard, P. and Craft, A. (2006) Pedagogy and possibility thinking in the early years. *International Journal of Thinking Skills and Creativity*, 1(2), 108–19.

Department for Education and Skills (DfES). (2003) *Excellence and Enjoyment: A Strategy for Primary Schools*. Nottingham: DfES.

Eisner, E. (2003) Artistry in education. *Scandinavian Journal of Educational Research*, 47(3), 373–84.

English, E., Hargreaves, L. and Hislam, J. (2002) Pedagogical dilemmas in the National Literacy Strategy: Primary teachers' perceptions, reflections and classroom behaviour. *Cambridge Journal of Education*, 32(1), 9–26.

Jeffrey, B. and Woods, P. (2009) *Creative Learning in the Primary School*. London: Routledge.

Joubert, M. M. (2001) The art of creative teaching: NACCCE and beyond. In A. Craft, B. Jeffrey and M. Liebling (eds.) *Creativity in Education*. London: Continuum, pp. 21–38.

National Advisory Committee on Creative and Cultural Education (NACCCE). (1999) *All Our Futures: Creativity, Culture and Education*. London: Department for Education and Employment.

OFSTED (Office for Standards in Education). (2003) *Expecting the Unexpected: Developing Creativity in Primary and Secondary Schools*. HMI 1612. E-publication. Available at www.ofsted.gov.uk (accessed 9 November 2007).

Qualifications and Curriculum Authority (QCA). (2005) *Creativity: Find It, Promote It! – Promoting Pupils' Creative Thinking and Behaviour Across the Curriculum at Key Stages 1, 2 and 3 – Practical Materials for Schools*. London: QCA.

Roberts, P. (2006) *Nurturing Creativity in Young People: A Report to Government to Inform Future Policy*. London: DCMS.

ACKNOWLEDGEMENTS

The editors would like to thank the series editor Teresa Cremin as well as Helen Pritt from Routledge, who have been an invaluable support in undertaking this second edition. We are delighted to introduce the second edition of this book, which sets out to offer an updated and substantial new edition with co-authoring of new chapters in response to current primary phase concerns. There is even a new author, Elizabeth Mackinlay, whose new chapter on 'teaching interculturally' offers an open and equal way to support children so as to reach their full creative potential and not be constrained by cultural stereotyping. These chapters offer further alternatives to mechanical approaches to more creative ways of teaching music in which teachers look at children's music making and creating, strive to understand it and then put their understanding to creative use in the classroom where children are given both trust and freedom to be creative with music.

This book reports on the latest research and development, on theory and practice, and reflects on observations and conversations, debates and discussions and collaborations with colleagues and children in classrooms, in initial teacher training and professional development contexts and courses, in universities, community music and arts organisations and in policy contexts. We would like particularly to thank Teresa Cremin for her keen interest and encouragement to produce this second edition book on music in the *Learning to Teach in the Primary School* series. We would also like to express our gratitude to the community of educators, artists and scholars who have contributed to this book, each of whom, with experiences drawn from diverse settings and contexts, share a passion for teaching and learning music in primary education, and for examining and translating what, how and why creativity is so important and central to classroom practice. These colleagues have taken their fine-coloured threads of creative practice and woven a vivid tapestry of case studies and activities rich in creativity that are well worth a tired teacher's spare time. The hope is that readers will go on to be inspired and empowered to make a reality of teaching music creatively in their own classrooms.

We also acknowledge the valuable assistance of Brian Richards from the University of Reading, who generated several illustrative models, and to Liz Tray for her diligent editing and typesetting of chapters.

Finally, thanks go to Suzanne Richardson and Helen Pritt from Routledge for their patience and support.

Particular thanks are also due to all the schools and arts communities involved in the cases and activities shared, and in addition to those here:

Primary and Early Years teacher education students at Massey University, Palmerston North, New Zealand.

Sagam Primary School in Siaya County, Western Kenya, and the Kenya Music Festival Foundation, Kenya.

Newham Sixth Form College, Prince Regent Lane, London.

Lifelong Kindergarten Group at the MIT Media Lab, and Eric Rosenbaum and Jay Silver, developers of Singing Fingers, USA.

Students and staff at ArtPlay, Western English Language School, Collingwood English Language School and The Song Room, Melbourne, Australia.

Magne Espeland, Norway, for kind permission to use adaptations from *Upbeat* (Murphy and Espeland [2007] Dublin: Gill and MacMillan).

Social Sciences and Humanities Research Council of Canada Learning Through the Arts, The Royal Conservatory Hennigan School, Canada.

And to all the children for their music.

This book is unique in that it is not simply a collection of chapters by individuals, but the product of a collaborative learning community.

INTRODUCTION

Pamela Burnard and Regina Murphy

ABOUT THIS BOOK

This second edition book in this series stems from the conviction that all those who are concerned with primary education should have a deep interest in creativity, children, music and the creative endeavour of teaching and learning music. Readers will also be interested in what can be done to help teachers feel more confident to teach music more creatively, not only in their classrooms but to be celebrated throughout the school (with, we hope, appropriate openness, understanding and enthusiasm). While this book draws on research and theory, and is aware of the latest developments in policy, each chapter is written in a style which is intended to support, stimulate and speak to all readers; its audience being made up of an amalgam of teacher trainees, practising specialist and generalist teachers, school leaders and parents, students and teacher educators, as well as researchers and policy makers.

The leitmotif of the book is a particular approach to thinking about creativity and the practice of teaching music creatively. This includes the ways in which, in our everyday practice, we strive to teach creatively, to listen and see what children's creativity in music looks like, and to be ready for anything and everything.

This book is based on a cornucopia of convictions about creativity and in so doing provides a range of theory-informed practices whereby teachers in diverse settings can explore the effective teaching and worthwhile learning of music. These practices are expressed at the intersection of multiple dimensions, which are referred to as **themes** relating to teaching for creativity in music and **threads** for teaching music creatively. Teaching music creatively involves teachers putting into practice their commitment to children's music practices in developing a culture of creative opportunities, ensuring their own musical involvement and creative participation alongside the children and building a learning community characterised by trust and openness where both teachers and children feel confident and secure working with and learning in music. Teaching for creativity in music, by contrast, focuses on developing children's creativity in music, their capacity to make connections, work with the unexpected, value openness, ask questions, participate collaboratively and experiment with ideas alone and with others. The argument of this book is that at the heart of teaching, and a participatory learning culture, is the power of teachers to think, not just about pedagogical issues, but to recognise both their innate ability to be musical and to teach music as a positive force that guides their pedagogical choices. In addition, creating, sharing, listening, performing, notating and assessing music constitute a common purpose of the learning community. Consequently, this gives the members of the community (for both teachers and children) a strong sense of ownership, adding to their will to commit themselves to the community whose creative practice with music is socially and culturally co-constructed as well as mutually defining identities. Also importantly, policy makers and school leaders, who hold value-rich beliefs about, or choose not to notice, the effects of music on children's learning, and who exercise a constraining influence and control over creative teachers' confidence and security in their undertakings with music, fail to see the connections between children's interests and how creative teachers make sound choices in the classroom about what is in the creative and musical interests of children. Teaching music creatively requires teachers to see, to understand and to apply their understanding of each child's music and music learning.

The aim of the book is to prompt action as well as thought, by teachers and other educators, in order to prompt a readiness to ask what is, and how best can we go about, teaching music creatively in primary school education. We hope teachers simply cannot resist but adopt the ideas for working with children offered in each chapter, in order to further develop an understanding of creativity and of children's musical learning – rather than simply exchanging practice – spurred on by the possibilities and spaces for teaching music creatively. We have tried not to suggest that there is only one possible set of ways or recipes for creative practice in teaching primary music but rather to reject deterministic views of teachers' thinking on their own music ability and considering ways teachers might become more confident and secure in their undertakings when teaching music creatively.

This book is designed to appeal to *all* those who are interested in teaching music more creatively and who take it as axiomatic that anyone concerned with children's music – as well as in creativity – is interested in teaching music creatively in a primary school setting.

Each chapter is based on the principle that *the conceptual considerations of creativity stand alongside the teacher's value system in the formation of teaching music creatively.* To recognise that we cannot achieve absolute perfection or a professional performing artist or musician's level in teaching music is a first step towards recognising other characteristics of the process.

Chapter 1 (Teaching music creatively) discusses the way we think about teaching music in the context of primary practice itself and the changes needed if children's music is to be placed at the centre of the music curriculum and the life of the school community. Written by an international expert in children's play pedagogy, Chapter 2 (Sounding children's (inter-)cultural practices through musical play) illustrates how play creates meaning and offers a dynamic entry into teaching for creativity.

Chapter 3 (Engaging interactively with children's group improvisations) and Chapter 4 (Children composing) offer ways of creating learning communities of practice where the pluralism of children's improvising and composing sits in a creatively embedded place within the curriculum and where pedagogical strategies are built to avoid underestimating what children and their teachers are capable of. Case studies and class activities are shared by primary teachers and teacher educators, who then give a diverse collection of practical ideas on how best teaching music creatively can be managed in the primary school classroom. These chapters would be a good introduction to any primary school class teacher who is working in music with children for the first time.

Collaborative performance practices are characterised and illustrated in Chapter 5 (Becoming performers), which argues that music plays a large part in the primary school community. Music performance is a collaborative enterprise, one which capitalises on creative work and enables children to foster creative qualities such as teamwork, commitment, play and engagement, risk-taking and agency, and contributes to a group's sense of identity and to an individual's sense of belonging to a group. Becoming a performer is a way of coming together musically to experience collaborative creative work. Interactions between children and teacher, whether turn-taking, joining in, handing over and following on as part of the music, can illuminate a framework for understanding children as active learners who take responsibility for and manage their own learning through participatory acts of meaning-making and enquiry.

Making music with children offers opportunities for developing voice games, singing and song-making, as Chapter 6 (Singing the primary curriculum) brilliantly illustrates. We know that radical changes in technology are fundamentally changing how children communicate and express themselves. In Chapter 7 (Exploring new media musically and creatively), unique and exciting resources and activities are explored for engaging children in learning activities that encourage them to enhance their musical skills and creativity awareness.

A suite of chapters – Chapter 8 (Enhancing creativity through listening to music), Chapter 9 (Celebrating children's invented notations) and Chapter 10 (Integrating the primary curriculum) – look at how listening, reading and writing music can be creatively integrated events which connect to children's musical, literacy and numeracy skills and other thematic practices. It has been a fundamental tenet of primary practice that the teacher should engage children in activities which involve a number of skills simultaneously. These chapters offer all kinds of possibilities for music to be at the centre or at least part of a creatively planned and integrated curriculum.

Chapter 11 (Assessing creatively) looks at rethinking how we approach assessing children's music and music learning creatively. It gives the opportunity to look reflectively at children's needs and teachers' choices in order to assess creatively, and examines why we need to question the statutory forms of testing which unduly constrain children's creativity in and through which the child grows in their desire to make meaning through music.

Chapter 12 (Using a whole-music approach creatively) shares a vision of what a whole-school approach in primary schools can be if music is at the heart of education in terms of children's interests and teachers' choices.

Chapter 13 (Teaching music interculturally) draws upon the author's own work as an ethnomusicologist and primary music intercultural educator. In particular, this chapter defines what we mean by 'intercultural', and the intercultural music classroom as a contact zone. The centrality of relationship to intercultural music education and the pedagogical possibilities of adopting a whole school, classroom and personal ethos to intercultural music education are introduced.

Chapter 14 (Teaching creatively in creative learning communities) introduces a way of engaging with and guiding teachers in the development of an effective professional creative learning community.

TEACHING MUSIC CREATIVELY

Pamela Burnard

INTRODUCTION

Creativities in childhood and education have long been seen as central pedagogical principles in the primary curriculum. Music, too, is a vital part of childhood. It is a subject which deserves to be taught with skill and depth as part of the primary curriculum and should be a vital part of what children learn as part of their primary schooling entitlement. Today's primary teachers need not feel divided and unsure of their individual capacities for teaching music because they are, in reality, well positioned to provide unprecedented opportunities for nurturing the musical and creative capacities of children. We now have a spectrum of research evidence, which is firmly aligned with the UN Convention on the Rights of the Child (i.e., that all children can and should benefit from receiving a wide-ranging, adventurous and creative cultural education). It describes the purposes which the primary phase of education should serve and the values which it should espouse, and suggests a primary curriculum and learning environment that places arts and creativity generally, and music specifically (whether statutory or non-statutory elements), at the 'heart' of effective primary education (Alexander, 2010).

Teaching music, whether discretely or in combination with other subjects, and fitting it into the life of the school as a whole, requires the confidence to develop a pedagogy of repertoire rather than recipe, and of principle rather than prescription; this should be implemented in a flexible and creative way that is specific to children's needs as they move through the primary phase. It should provide a broad and balanced education that involves the school community and engages with the environment.

While no one will argue that at the heart of the educational process lies the child, the evidence tells another story. While there should be no hierarchy of subjects, the reality is that not every subject will receive as much time as others. The most conspicuous casualty is music. However, building capacity to ensure that the entitlement to music in the primary curriculum, and its inclusion into the life of the primary school as a whole, becomes a reality for children in the primary sector is paramount. Music matters because children find immense pleasure in musical participation. Children's culture matters and culture is what defines them (Campbell, 2002).

Children find immense pleasure in musical participation, whether in formal roles as performers, composers, improvisers, song makers, notators and audiences or in the multiple forms of children's musical play genres (exemplified in the chapter by Marsh and Young on 'Musical play', in McPherson, 2006, as a central principle of teaching creatively) that constitute part of an oral tradition (such as singing games that are owned, spontaneously performed and orally transmitted by children, and incorporate the elements of text, music and movement). Whether their music is made alone or in the company of others, children use music to help maintain emotional and social well-being and celebrate culture and community in ways which involve entertaining or understanding themselves and making sense of the world around them. Children initiate musical activities for themselves, exciting the imagination either as an individual or within a friendship group, community or family setting in their varied daily experiences. Yet, despite such childhood experiences, there are many adults around the world who have trained as primary teachers for whom the associations between music and creativity are not positive. It is the aim of this book to encourage and enable teachers to review and adopt a more creative approach to the teaching of music in the primary phase.

THERE IS ANOTHER WAY

In this increasingly digital age, exposure to music is everywhere, both by design and by accident. Children download files from the Internet and engage with the Wii and Play-Station games, they watch and hear music videos online, attend concerts, overhear music in shopping centres and play music games in the community playground or in recreational settings. They may even participate in musical practices in diverse communities within their wider socio-cultural environment. Music permeates children's lives; from lullabies at bedtime to the sung and chanted games in the playground, from the attraction they feel for novelty and their capacity to create and innovate to the popular phenomena of iPhones, iPads, video games and mainstream technology that can be found in the living rooms of millions of homes worldwide. Research indicates that we are all 'wired' for music from birth and that musical ability, like creativity, is not the preserve of the gifted few (Barrett, 2006). For all of us (not just some people) music manifests itself in our lives in a variety of ways and significantly enhances and enriches our understanding of ourselves and the world. For everyone, music has the power to lift us out of the ordinary, to elevate our experience beyond the everyday and the commonplace. Another aim of this book is to invite readers to question their own cultural assumptions and the stereotypical views that divide learners (and teachers) into distinct categories: those who are 'musical' and those who are not, and those who are 'creative' and those who are not.

At the outset, then, we need to question some of the myths underlying views of who can and cannot teach music; we need to explore why teachers should develop and be empowered by an understanding of what constitutes teaching music creatively in primary school; and we need to examine the many interacting influences that can enable them to use their powers as educators to transform children's learning. As with other aspects of the primary curriculum, the ability to teach music and teach it creatively is neither fixed nor measurable in terms of a so-called 'ability' (a label which deterministically views learning and ability as a fixed internal capacity, which one either has or does not have). On the contrary, children's musical learning capacity can be enabled and expanded in all its rich variety and complexity (through building their skills, confidence, imagination, curiosity and inventiveness in music), by teaching music creatively and planning experiences and opportunities that promote deep engagement – experiences that fill children with a sense of agency, that endow them with creativity, motivation, courage and belief in their own capacity as musical thinkers, makers and creators. In this book we argue that teaching music creatively has to do with the creative involvement of the teacher working collaboratively alongside children and how best to set about educating children unfettered by labels (Robinson and Azzam, 2009).

We know, thanks to research, what children need in their primary schooling. They need the opportunity to build their social skills, their language and their confidence. They do this best through structured play and talk, by interacting with each other and with interested and stimulating adults. Teachers can facilitate teaching music creatively, while fostering children's creativity in music, by working together and learning alongside children as active co-learners, making choices and decisions together about how to expand opportunities for expressing themselves effectively as performers, song makers, composers, improvisers and listeners, in a creative context where music is at the core. Teachers need to foster a strong positive sense of themselves as competent, complex, creative people, each capable of playing a full part within a collaborative learning community and recognising that they have the power to transform themselves by building a community of powerful professional learners. Teachers need to become innovative leaders of exploration in an environment of possibility. To achieve this, they need to dispel myths and confront long-held beliefs, both individually and collectively, as the whole staff of a school work together day by day to create their vision of a primary curriculum that includes the development of educational practices and specific pedagogies for teaching music creatively – practices and pedagogies in which teachers and children are engaged imaginatively, making connections, taking risks and innovating together. In a lecture called 'What can education learn from the arts about the practice of education'? given as the John Dewey lecture for 2002 at Stanford University, Elliot Eisner (2004, p. 10) offers this inspirational advice to teachers who see the development of creativity as a distinguishing mark of their teaching:

> a greater focus on becoming than on being, places more value on the imaginative than on the factual, assigns greater priority to valuing than to measuring, and regards the quality of the journey as more educationally significant than the speed at which the destination is reached. I am talking about a new vision of what education might become and what schools are for.

In this chapter I will discuss how both teachers and learners, individually and collectively, can see each other in a different light, and work together to lay foundations for building a school-wide culture of change, moving away from the use of 'ability' labels to create opportunities for learning from high-quality, open-ended authentic musical experiences from which to acquire confidence and competence. As they sing and play, listening carefully and talking about music making, they will build the dispositions that are characteristic of powerful musical learning as it occurs formally and informally, traditionally and otherwise. I will highlight particular features that show how forces affecting making music together are socially generated in classroom communities. I will also outline how the principles of learning music creatively together and the creative consensus around extending freedom to teach music creatively can best be provided. All of this implies approaches to fostering and shaping creatively oriented activities that allow room for children's, as well as teachers', creativity to be explored. The narrative that follows reviews the nature of teaching *creatively and for creativity* in music so that: (i) the core elements of children's creative music making can be developed; (ii) the children initiate, execute and 'control' a musical practice – whether as performers, composers, improvisers, notators, listeners or reflectors; and (iii) the music itself can be defined within the parameters of its community of practice as developed in the primary classroom (Barrett, 2006).

DEVELOPING YOUR OWN MUSIC PEDAGOGY AND PRINCIPLES

Whether taught by generalist or specialist primary teachers, teaching music creatively does not mean short-changing the teaching of the essential knowledge, skills and understanding of the subject; rather it involves teaching musical skills and developing knowledge about music in creative contexts that explicitly invite learners to engage imaginatively and stretch their generative and evaluative capacities. Creative teachers work as creativity generators. Creative teachers work with the tools and resources given to them for the process of extending children's music learning and music making as composers, song makers, notators, performers, improvisers, listeners and cultural makers/consumers. Creative teachers help children to express themselves effectively, and create music as well as critically evaluate their own work. Both UNESCO and the UN Convention on the Rights of the Child recognise the importance of creativity and highlight the role of teachers in fostering children's musical capacity to make connections, take risks and innovate.

But what do we mean by *teaching for creativity* and *teaching music creatively*? What can we (as teachers and as a society) learn by listening to children's voices, observing their experiences in creative actions, and creating with them? Teachers will gain immeasurably from listening to children's own initiatives, learning about teaching for creativity and teaching music creatively with them. But first, how should we view creativity? What should teachers make of the policy issues that say creativity is to be 'put' into all individuals (more softly conveyed as being 'fostered in' or 'taught to')? What are the gains for students and for teachers who make creativity blossom in reality when teaching music in the primary classroom? Children's musical and creative participation, in practice, means opening up opportunities for decision-making, with children and teachers engaging in music making together.

Gains for children

- Developing a practical, principled, positive sense of agency as musical learners.
- Developing inquiring minds and the capacity to generate and innovate with music.
- Developing musical skills and increasing learning capacity as musicians.
- Building the dispositions characteristic of powerful autonomous musical learners.
- Having the opportunity to create a shared language for engaging creatively with music.
- Ensuring the creative involvement of the teacher.

Gains for teachers

- Experiencing a way of learning and working together with children for change.
- Acting to build and expand opportunities for engagement with music.

- Increasing musical confidence and competence, commitment and creativity.
- Gaining insights that enhance and support professional development.
- Developing practices that are life-enhancing for everybody.

Gains for schools

- Creating a vision of an education based on children's and teachers' capacity to build a learning environment that is musical and creatively enabling for everybody through collective action.
- Creating a vision to guide school development.
- Improving and enhancing the capacity to learn as a learning community.
- Diversifying the curriculum, with distinctive views on music education that find expression in every aspect of school life.
- Developing a creative ethos and musical identity for the school community.
- Reshaping pedagogy and curricula to include shared values about teaching music creatively and the celebration of the classroom practices of teachers.

Harnessing the musicality and creativity and the curiosity and enthusiasm of children and teachers in collective action can prove very powerful in bringing about change in school communities. The assumption that continues to have currency, and that we challenge throughout this book, is that 'being musical' and 'creative' is confined to particular teachers and children rather than a human potential possessed by all and one that is open to development. The next section examines these areas. Whatever the context of education, both music's value (whether represented as a cultural practice, a way of knowing, a way of thinking, a way of feeling, a cognitive process or a symbolic form) and creativity are exercised in all aspects of life and learning and, by definition, increase the life- and learning-force, empower the life- and learning-drive, and release all our instincts to savour life and learning as the manifestations of essential feeling, the senses and the imagination.

THE PEDAGOGICAL PRINCIPLES OF PRACTICE

It is crucial for teachers to clarify their own and children's views of music (for some, in essence, a form of discourse, cultural practice, a way of knowing, the life of feeling, etc.) and creativity (for some, in essence, the generation of novel ideas), and what this means to them in terms of teaching and learning, both for the school community and across the curriculum. Considerable debate revolves around issues concerning the personal significance of music and creativity, the symbolic form of musical experiences, the role of process versus product, the influence of individual components such as learner personality, disposition and learning style, the role of skills, knowledge and environmental factors, and the importance given to various layers of musical activity such as materials, expression, form and value. These issues will surface later on. However, as argued by Barrett (2006, p. 205), a key factor 'in any discussion of children's creativity is whether children's culture is viewed as distinctive, moderated and developed through children's agency, or as an adult-regulated precursor to adult culture'. When teachers engage as learners (and as musicians) alongside children they get to view children's active engagement with their worlds. Teachers learn to trust their own and the children's creativity, and recognise opportunities where children's music making is seen working as an active agent, internalising the structures of adult worlds and reproducing these in novel, context-dependent ways, rather than the children being passive consumers of adult-generated culture.

Creativity as a concept covers a lot of ground and its meaning shifts in response to changing cultural contexts and conditions. A widely endorsed definition of creativity includes the creation of domain-relevant skills (themes particular to music making and children's creative endeavours and learning) and creativity-relevant processes (threads particular to teaching and teachers). Creativity includes the creation of an original (novel, unexpected) and useful (appropriate) product, including ideas as well as concrete objects. Creative people are those who create new and useful products, and creative processes occur when a new and useful product is created. Person-centred and environment-centred considerations are essential for understanding human creativity. The social environment is fundamental in Csikszentmihályi's (1997) systems view of creativity. He argues that in order to be creative an individual has to put personal effort into the creation of a product that is then valued as creative by other experts within the particular field and that the creative process or the creation itself brings some change to the domain it enters. Creativity is then jointly constituted by the interaction between and across the domain, field and person; therefore, the practices of both personal and social creativities are important.

Creativity emerges as children become actively engaged in exploring ideas, initiating their own learning, making choices and controlling decisions about how to express themselves using different sounds and practices (such as invented song making and other ways in which children make original music). Creativity, in essence the ability to respond creatively, arises when children produce imaginative activity which leads to creative products that are judged to be novel variations, original and unexpected.

Looking at creativity from the perspective of Csikszentmihályi's system view (1997, p. 330, as discussed in Burnard, 2006), creativity can be remarkably increased and enhanced by changing the field (i.e. the classroom) to make it more sensitive and supportive of new ideas, and by making sure that society (i.e. in the educational context, being the class) provides opportunities to participate more widely (seeing the field as a part of a broader social system). Creativity also emerges from the interaction between individuals working together through handling, making and elaborating in a *domain* (e.g. children's music making). The experts in the *field* (values) that support and inform that domain, in the primary classroom context (practices), are usually teachers who judge the products of children or other students. Resources (e.g. time, space, goals and group sizes) are a way of showing investment made in the creative production process and its valuation.

Drawing on the work of Malloch and Trevarthen (2009), the study of spontaneity in the musicality and music learning of childhood and children's creative and musical endeavours stems from views of creativity that acknowledge children's agency and their musical culture as practices which can be high in quality and meaning (Robinson and Azzam, 2009). In lessons that involve little or no creativity, ideas or tasks are presented that are already worked out or follow some generically prescribed method. It is, however, the teacher's creativity that makes an impact on the child's creative engagement and endeavours. A key aspect of creative teaching is the teachers' self-belief – their belief that they too are creative and are creativity generators. Creativity may, or may not, happen in all musical situations; every situation may be addressed creatively, but may not in itself be creative. Creativity in music, however, is often connected with composing and improvising. But in order to promote musical growth, teachers must constantly endeavour to encourage and help children to respond creatively in their dealings with music. The creative response is not a separate thing that only happens on some occasions and not on others; rather, the creative response must go on all the time. Only then are we making musical connections of the quality that is necessary for children's musical growth, which is, as we see it, the primary aim of musical education. The essential core of this is the role of the teacher. The promotion of musical creativity requires creative teaching. To map the way forward, to encourage, to guide and engage creative responses in children is itself a creative act.

Like musical ability, creativity is something we all have. We know it is not simply a gift given to the Mozarts or Michael Jacksons of the world. As teachers, we might not be as in touch with music and creativity as we once were as children, but take a moment to consider just how creative and musical we all are. When you teach, if you enjoy singing, sing. If you don't enjoy singing, then you owe it to your students to provide a highly musical environment and encourage intense interest in expressive musical performances. If you enjoy listening to and playing music, which all of us do, then playing and listening to music should be a central part of your teaching. Every day we tap into natural creativity and engage creatively with music. As infants, we develop a wide range of skills that can be described as musical. These skills do not necessitate extensive knowledge of the musical conventions of a particular culture, but rather an awareness of the aspects of music that are perceptible, memorable and pleasurable for children. Many of these skills are learned before birth, as the foetus becomes familiar with the internal sound patterns of its mother's body and associates these patterns with her physical and emotional state.

It is a skill that we have already learned both during very early formal music instruction or informally and spontaneously through our experiences of the familiar music of our culture. The best way to promote a child's musical ability is to acknowledge that all of us (and particularly children) possess a musical brain. We all respond to the intimacy of mother–infant vocal interaction and the reciprocity in the improvisatory musical performance of sound patterns that stimulate hearing, pattern recognition and the emotional connotations of sound patterns that underlie music. Our musicality grows through continuously evolving interactions in 'hearing' and 'performing' music in multiple settings – from the habit of singing lullabies after birth (which is musically, cognitively, emotionally and socially beneficial) to playing skipping games in the playground. Social factors, such as parental support, teachers' personalities and peer interactions, are central to how the musical brain develops. It grows inside the developing individual, who lives in a particular home environment, possesses internal proclivities, experiences external motivations and so on. As teachers, it is our responsibility to support an inquisitive and exploratory approach to children's learning through musical play and experimentation (see McPherson, 2006, chapter by Trehub on 'Infants as musical connoisseurs').

CORE FEATURES OF A CREATIVE APPROACH TO TEACHING MUSIC

A creative approach to teaching music encompasses several core features or dimensions of creative practice that enable teachers to make informed decisions, both at the level of

THREADS (teaching music creatively)	THEMES (for creativity in music)
Developing a culture of creative opportunities and ensuring the creative involvement of the teacher	Creating a community of musical practice (encouraging ownership, collaboration, autonomy)
Watching and listening to children	Making connections and working with the unexpected and the familiar
Building learning environments of enquiry, possibility and trust	Valuing openness to unusual ideas, curiosity and questions
Fostering learning through imaginative play, exploration and experimentation	Profiling agency (musical decision making/ musical interests)

▨ **Figure 1.1** Themes (for teaching creativity in music) and threads (for generic teaching creatively).

planning and in moment-to-moment interactions in the classroom. Woven throughout this book are the threads and themes shown in Figure 1.1.

This, then, is the vision of music permeating and expanding the practice of primary teachers at every level.

First principle: threads

Threads seek to foster *teaching music creatively*, thus engaging teachers to make music learning interesting and effective and use imaginative approaches in the classroom.

1 **Developing a culture of creative opportunities and ensuring the creative involvement of the teacher.** Significant research into effective teaching shows that creative teachers are creative role models themselves; professionals who continue to be self-motivated learners value the creative dimensions of their own lives and make connections between their personal responses to experience and teaching. This can involve collaboration between children and teachers, and reflection has priority over time. These interactions emphasise the importance of creating a 'holding environment' for learners, leading them to a shared understanding of how best to participate and learn.

2 **Watching and listening to children.** The commitment to extending choice is intimately bound up with another equally important focus of teachers' practice and development work: listening to children and taking on board their ideas, thoughts and feelings.

3 **Building learning environments of enquiry, possibility and trust.** Giving specific choices is one very practical way of encouraging children to express their preferences and act on them. Children need to be given opportunities not just to make their own selection from a range of activities offered by the teacher but also to contribute to the process of planning the tasks and activities to be undertaken by the class. Barrett (2006), in a valuable study of how young children create meaning through

creative musical participation in their early years, notes the importance of distinguishing different kinds of involvement in terms of children's participation. This participation should not be limited simply to activities and structures that have already been decided upon but should enable them to actually influence the overall organisation and learning possibilities by mapping moments of reflection and contemplation and encouraging children to incubate and contribute their ideas about the relevance of the activity set by the teacher. By standing back and letting children take the lead, teachers set up open-ended contexts where control is devolved, at least in part, to children, who are then more likely to adapt and extend activities in unexpected ways. The learning relationship needs to develop in ways that sustain and foster an increased freedom to learn and nurture creativity by risk-taking, communicating acceptance and building a shared understanding between the teacher and the children, and between the children themselves, as a common theme discerned among the class community as a whole.

4   **Fostering learning through imaginative play, exploration and experimentation.** For the teacher to find ways of being and learning together with children, which are personally and collectively satisfying, the learning journey needs to be characterised by practices such as teamwork, sharing one's thinking with a learning partner, learning through play and the teachers' empathy for children's feelings (a corollary being a child-centred approach, including listening to children as a vital tool for teachers and teachers' values). It needs to provide a route to creative thinking and problem solving across all aspects of children's learning through a steadfastness of purpose in exploring and experimenting. The teacher should trust the child, believing that the child has the desire and the potential to explore and experiment with music. The teacher should show care and respect for the individuality of each child.

Second principle: themes

Themes that seek to foster *teaching for creativity in music*, by contrast, focus on the development of children's creativity in music and their capacity to experiment with musical ideas and information, alone and with others.

1   **Creating a community of musical practice (encouraging ownership, collaboration, autonomy).** Teachers and children need to share responsibility for creative activities along with an understanding that the learning journey may be uncomfortable at times but that the shared experiences and supportive learning community ethos will enable everyone to flourish as musical learners.

2   **Making connections and working with the unexpected and the familiar.** Children are constantly growing and changing, seeking new challenges and new learning. This is also true of creative teachers. By seeing creativity as a set of dimensions and behaviours which focus on making connections – exploring the unexpected as well as pushing boundaries on the familiar – practices developed in the classroom and brought to the classroom by external creative and cultural partners can then challenge and stretch both children and teachers. Exploration of these dimensions can be ongoing within the curriculum programme.

3   **Valuing openness to unusual ideas, curiosity and questions.** Childhood is characterised within a wide variety of contexts, and children's musical creativity may

involve spontaneous song making, singing and dancing through the process of enculturation, in their home environment. Teachers need to be open to the creative experiences of children making music, exploring sounds, using expressive vocabulary and developing manipulative skills in response to specific cultural environments. Children's cultural competencies as consumers and users of digital multimedia technology in the context of leisure and the ever-widening range of music technologies increasingly enables them to draw on their own musical experiences and access any number of highly desirable sound worlds that support creative music making. Being open and curious about their creative ideas and cultural practices are the building blocks of musical communities in the primary classroom.

4 **Profiling agency (musical decision-making/choice/musical interests).** Importantly, this dimension recognises that what may be a creative endeavour and achievement in a child's musical world may not necessarily be viewed, judged or defined as 'creative' within the adult musical world in which the child finds her/himself. What constitutes creative choice, and the freedom to make decisions where cultural dynamics interact within the social worlds of the child in which musical creativity grows, is important. This is about creative inclusion, creative choice and how children construct and enable repertoires from the interactive possibilities, experiences and expressions of 'peer worlds'.

CREATIVE TEACHERS AND CREATIVE TEACHING IN MUSIC

Music is indispensable to the creative teacher. It is a subject that constitutes a body of knowledge, skills and understanding that has intellectual depth and critical rigour as challenging as any school subject area. Like any subject, it needs to be taught by committed and creative teachers and given the necessary time and resources. There is clear evidence that creative teachers produce creative learning and positive learning outcomes. Creative participation in music helps children to learn more effectively, thus developing their musical skills and inspiring new ways of thinking about, experiencing and doing music. Creative participation in music helps children to do better right across the whole curriculum. By embedding music in the primary school curriculum on a daily basis, teachers have demonstrated that they are able to improve literacy and numeracy. They are also able to harness children's passion for culture and create environments where they feel valued, empowered and motivated – attendance, attitude and well-being are all improved by engagement with music.

The creative teacher:

■ is not an instructor but a co-creator, supporting children as they develop their own music learning;
■ constantly looks for ways of engaging children's imagination and invention;
■ supports children in taking risks – to ask themselves 'what if' and go ahead and try a new approach; and
■ encourages children to evaluate and assess their own and each other's work.

SOME CHALLENGES INVOLVED IN TEACHING MUSIC CREATIVELY

Why does a vision of what teaching music creatively is so often get lost in what music teaching turns out to be? Perhaps it is that music is particularly hard to manage in the relentless schedules of primary schools. It is difficult for teachers to hold on to its nature and value. There are also issues of status, resources and commitment to extending choice, which are intimately bound up with teachers' practice and development work. As with the other arts, music suffers relegation to the corners of the curriculum and is elevated to the top of the lists of spending cuts. Even in the best circumstances, however, something less than musical transactions may often be taking place. I have seen music taught uncreatively in conditions where time and resources were more than sufficient and I have seen music taught creatively in unpromising circumstances. This, of course, is not an argument for starving music education of resources but a recognition that resources alone are not sufficient. As well as understanding the essential qualities of music there also has to be a sense of what it is to engage in lively and authentic music education. To this end I welcome readers to read on through the chapters of this book, engaging with the principles of practice and research that inform the key points that are made. These principles have their roots in the basic premise that musicality and creativity are possessed by all and can be developed in a learning environment where each individual knows that it is safe to take musical risks – an environment in which confidence is nurtured and where everybody can become caught up in the excitement of learning music creatively.

FURTHER READING

Alexander, R. J. (ed.) (2010) *Children, Their World, Their Education: Final Report and Recommendations of the Cambridge Primary Review*. London: Routledge (especially pp. 239–45, 471–4, 496–500).

Barrett, M. (2006) Inventing songs, inventing worlds: The 'genesis' of creative thought and activity in young children's lives. *International Journal of Early Years Education*, 14(3), 201–20.

Burnard, P. and Kuo, H. (2015) The individual and social worlds of children's musical creativities. In G. McPherson (ed.) *The Child as Musician: A Handbook of Musical Development* (2nd edition). Oxford: Oxford University Press, pp. 486–99.

Campbell, P. S. (2002) The musical cultures of children. In L. Bresler and C. Thompson (eds.) *The Arts in Children's Lives: Context, Culture and Curriculum*. Netherlands: Kluwer, pp. 57–69.

SOUNDING CHILDREN'S (INTER-)CULTURAL PRACTICES THROUGH MUSICAL PLAY

Kathryn Marsh

For many teachers, the planning of musical experiences for children in the classroom may have connections with the outside world, particularly in terms of inclusion of children's musical preferences. However, such musical experiences tend to exist, quite understandably, within the confines of the classroom and so may not take children's own music making into account. Outside the classroom, even within other areas of the school such as the playground, children are engaging in richly challenging musical activities of their own devising, often drawing on a range of cultural practices. In this chapter, some of the characteristics of children's musical play will be explored with the purpose of enabling teachers to incorporate some of these characteristics into class activities.

In particular, the chapter will explore:

- Children's ownership and curation of repertoire.
- Creativity as an integral component of musical play.
- Mediated learning in musical play.
- Communities of practice in the playground.
- Holistic and multimodal learning at varying levels of difficulty.
- Development of intercultural exchange, engagement and social connection.

Each of these characteristics will be outlined with reference to examples of children's musical play, followed by a section suggesting ways in which teachers can incorporate this play-based focus into classroom musical practice. Intercultural practices will be explored throughout the chapter.

CHARACTERISTICS OF PLAY AND LEARNING

The musical play of children of primary school age occurs in multiple settings and includes a great variety of activities. Campbell (2010) has outlined the many ways that children engage in 'musicking' by playing with musical toys, tapping out a rhythm, singing along with others on the school bus, listening to music at home or with friends or joining in with family musical activities that may involve the passing on of familial or cultural traditions. Increasingly, individual children or small groups of children may also participate in improvisatory play interactions with electronic devices such as Xbox, PlayStation or Wii at home.

In this chapter I will focus particularly on playground games; those found in the gaps between formal school activities, in playgrounds and waiting spaces, and especially those within the boundaries of the school, though I will also allude to other forms of musical play. Musical playground games involve the singing or chanting of words, accompanied by movements. Their major purpose is social, with interaction between children being very important. The games also involve considerable challenge, self-imposed by the children, with equal amounts of inherent collaboration and competition in order to enable them to function effectively. Children delight in word play in their games, with assonance, alliteration, repetition and 'nonsense' words featuring prominently.

In the playground, teachers may notice varied characteristics of these games as they are played by different groups of children from different cultures. For example, many singing games in pair, circle or line formation may demonstrate miming movements that reinforce the meaning of the words, or role enactment, as demonstrated by the international variants of 'When Susie was a baby'. Such role enactment often also includes an element of improvisation, demonstrated in the following clapping game verses from a Los Angeles school, where 'Susie's' exploits were improvised by successive players occupying this role as either 'Miss Sue' or 'Mr. Sue', depending on the gender of the central player.

Activity 2.1 Clapping game excerpt from a Los Angeles primary school

Players: Penny, Kiana, Pablo, Kevin Improviser: Penny	Players: Penny, Kiana, Pablo Improviser: Pablo
When Mr Sue was a baby a baby a baby	When Mr Sue was a baby a baby a baby
When Mr Sue was a baby	When Mr Sue was a baby
He went [Penny corrects: She] like this:	He went like this:
Penny: Ahaah hah!	Pablo: Whah! I want to change my diaper!
[Puts up head and cries]	[Flaps fists backwards and forwards]
When Miss Sue was a toddler a toddler a toddler	When Miss Sue was a toddler a toddler a toddler
When Miss Sue was a toddler	When Miss Sue was a toddler
She went like this:	He went like this:
Penny: Mummy I can see up your nose	Pablo: I want a toy!
[Points to Kiana's nose]	[Shrugs arms emphatically]
When Miss Sue was a teenager a teenager a teenager	When Miss Sue was a teenager a teenager a teenager
When Miss Sue was a teenager	When Miss Sue was a teenager
She went like this:	He went like this:
Penny: Oh I left my bra in my boyfriend's car.	Pablo: Where's my portrait? I can't find it!
[Crosses hands over chest]	[Flings arms around and stamps]
. . . .	. . . .

As found in the culmination of this game, where 'Miss Sue' becomes a devil and chases the other players, games may be exuberant and highly physical. For example, in the Punjabi game 'Zig Zag Zoo' (observed in West Yorkshire schools), the clapping pattern that accompanies the text ends with a punch to the opposing player (Marsh, 2008). Some games, such as 'Lobo' ('Wolf'), (which is played in a number of South American countries) may combine, at different stages of the game, singing and dancing in a circle, rhythmic chanting to the child who is 'in' and vigorous chasing (Marsh, 2016). However, many movements in children's games are more sedate, though often challenging in themselves. For example, some clapping patterns have multiple components of up to sixteen different movements (observed in multiple contexts in the USA, UK, Australia and Korea) or may be cumulative, with new movements added (and memorised) as the game unfolds (Marsh, 2008).

In recent decades, the ways children perform, learn and teach within their musical play have been an increasing focus of scholarly study. Researchers have investigated children's modes of learning, social relationships, engagement with the media, ethnicity and gender identities, contributions to children's well-being and the musical characteristics of different play traditions. A number of characteristics pertaining to children's musical learning, such as acquisition and transmission of play repertoire and skills, have emerged from these studies.

CHILDREN'S OWNERSHIP AND CURATION OF REPERTOIRE

In the classroom the teacher is responsible for the planning and programming of musical activities. Therefore, the teacher usually determines what music will be sung, played, listened to or created and therefore displays ownership of the repertoire. In contrast, with music in the playground or in self-regulated small-group play in the home, the children determine what will be played and therefore exercise both ownership of the music and choice regarding its selection and performance. Choice of repertoire is linked to identity and children may generate games that are expressive of both ownership and identity. One very clear example of this is the clapping game 'That's the way I like it', played by children in many English schools. Although the song originated in an American popular song from the 1970s, the many examples collected in several English locations contain personalised identity markers, as in this Bedfordshire version played by two 8-year-old girls:

> ABC hit it
> That's the way uh huh uh huh I like it uh huh uh huh
> That's the way uh huh uh huh I like it uh huh uh huh
> My name is Daisy and the game is netball
> Boys are never on my mind so|
> That's the way uh huh uh huh I like it uh huh uh huh
> That's the way uh huh uh huh I like it uh huh uh huh

More recently, this game has also been observed played by children in Australia, including two South Sudanese Australian sisters in Sydney, who personalised it with a range of extra movements. For children who are negotiating intercultural practices this game enables them to articulate or restate their identity within a new context, utilising the framework of a game that might have been learnt in this school or may have had familiar elements from known play.

As with the previous example of 'When Miss Sue was a baby' the personalised identity markers improvised by the children ensure that the ownership of the song is embedded in its newly created text or movements, so that the new version of the game implicitly belongs to the players.

INCORPORATING CHILDREN'S OWNERSHIP OF REPERTOIRE

This aspect of play-based learning can easily be adopted and adapted in a classroom setting by collaborating with child learners to choose repertoire. Some suggestions to foster student agency and ownership with regard to repertoire choice include the following:

- Provide learners with control over some classroom repertoire. Children could be invited to bring their favourite music into the classroom. They could contribute regularly to a shared source of musical examples, sung or recorded or downloaded onto mobile phones, iPads or classroom computers. This material could be stored in a digital repository on the class or music computer, tablet devices or karaoke player.
- The digital repository could be complemented by a book of favourite songs or game lyrics (with some documentation of movements if appropriate) in order to facilitate peer teaching.
- Teachers could contribute to this repository, providing songs that they enjoy and would like to teach. Teachers could also select songs and other musical examples from the repository that have attributes on which they would like to focus musically, thereby extending on children's musical knowledge using repertoire that has been initially chosen by children.
- Children's engagement could be fostered by small group or individual choice projects. This would enable children to work with friends in order to develop musical understandings or performance capabilities with repertoire that they enjoy and find challenging. Such an approach has been adopted widely in the UK as a result of the Musical Futures project, based on the informal learning research of Lucy Green (2008). This approach has largely been implemented with young adolescents in middle school and therefore focuses on popular music as the basis of student choice. However, it has been found in an Australian primary school classroom that when 10- and 11-year-old children are given the freedom to choose repertoire for small group performance development, they select music from a range of styles (Benson, 2012). Bishop (2014), Campbell (2010), Lill (2015) and Marsh (2008, 2013) provide examples of children's varied musical preferences stemming from many different sources.
- Teachers can observe children at play in the playground and invite them to share playground games with other children in the class. This provides the opportunity for children to share and engage with culturally diverse games and to compare games that contain familiar elements but have some variability, for example, texts in different languages. With permission of the children, such games could be recorded and used as the basis of music learning activities. As the owners of the games, children with game expertise could lead aspects of lessons in which the games are taught.
- Children can be encouraged to create their own arrangements of repertoire that they have contributed, either from game or other sources.

CREATIVITY AS INTEGRAL TO MUSICAL PLAY

Although there are playground traditions, from the previous examples it can be seen that when children play together they constantly engage in creative reworking of musical, movement and textual material, rather than focussing on reproducing a fixed product. In the classroom, teachers have been encouraged to provide opportunities for improvisation and composition, but these have often been conducted within preconceived and sometimes limited frameworks explicitly devised by teachers. Teachers may also have fixed ideas of the predicted outcomes of children's creative endeavour. While set frameworks and expectations are also found within children's musical play, the aesthetic decisions are ongoing and their own, allowing fluid and steadily developing outcomes that are more personally satisfying to the players, often exceeding classroom expectations, as demonstrated in the following vignette.

Case study 2.1: In a rural English primary school

In a small primary school in the Midlands, a 5-year-old girl, dressed in a furry cat costume sits on a chair in the karaoke corner, holding the end of a skipping rope like a microphone. As it is nearing Christmas, a recording of 'We Three Kings' can be heard in the background. With her two friends sitting at her feet as an attentive audience, she proceeds to improvise a song in the persona of a cat, as part of what appears to be a game of cats and dogs (the other two players are chewing toys as they listen). The entire text consists of repeated 'meows'; however, the song is quite musically sophisticated, incorporating the specific lilting rhythm, repetition of pitches and some harmonic characteristics of the carol in the background. While diverging experimentally from the carol's structure, the cat song demonstrates the 5-year-old singer's implicit understanding of standard formal structures, developed through her extensive experiences of listening to recordings and performances of Western classical music at home.

Reproduced in modified form from Lill (2015), with permission.

Children regularly juxtapose new text, music or movement with known elements in their musical games to create constant challenge and interest, as discussed by two 9-year-old girls in West Yorkshire:

Ajeet: Miss, we usually copied it a bit from the Punjabi version and then we took it from all these [demonstrates other movements] . . .
Kathy: Why do you do that? Why do you make up new ones?
Fateh: Because all the others are boring.
Ajeet: If you've known them for such a long time you're always doing them and you get to half of them and you're like 'oh you don't want to do this now' and then you decide to make your own up.

Children may work with given 'formulae' that are fragments or building blocks of text, music or movement that are derived from a tradition. However, novelty is an important part of playground game practice, allowing children to respond to new and different sonic and kinaesthetic stimuli, by transforming these into something that meets with both individual and communal player approval (Marsh, 2008). Reporting on a recent English study of children's playground play, Bishop (2014) terms this process 'revoicing' (p. 55) and Willett (2014), referencing terminology associated with popular music, 'remixing' (p. 133). Regardless of the term that is used, what is important about this process is that children throughout the world draw on whatever is in their musical, social, pedagogical, linguistic and cultural environment to create something that in some form is unique to them in their social group and can be used for interactive social purposes, thus bridging linguistic and cultural divides. In discussing children's play on the Caribbean coast of Nicaragua, Minks (2013) notes that the 'singing game performance is an example of interculturalism in practice, because it shows how diverse resources for communication are integrated in the context of interaction' (p. 228).

INCORPORATING CREATIVE MUSICAL PLAY IN THE CLASSROOM

A number of strategies to build on children's natural creative proclivities in play can be utilised by classroom teachers.

- Allow children to creatively manipulate and change repertoire over time as they do in the playground. The creation of multiple versions of songs, games and instrumental pieces fosters ownership and the development of compositional and performance skills. Teachers can collaborate with children in providing opportunities for these variations within whole class activities or as small groups. For example, children can be invited to change text or movements within a performance of a game or action song, as in the development of new verses with corresponding actions. Or the teacher can work as a facilitator of longer-term individual or small group projects (see, for example, Wiggins, 2011).
- Such creative reworkings necessitate the provision of time to revisit revised material, new arrangements and new compositions. Rather than requiring that children create a finished 'product' by the end of a lesson, teachers can initiate longer-term creative projects with children, whereby children determine both the length of time for completion of the project and what constitutes the 'product'. Chapters 3 and 4 further explore the ways in which teachers can work with children collaboratively to improvise and compose.
- Provide a wide range of challenging musical stimuli for improvisatory and compositional activity.

MEDIATED LEARNING IN MUSICAL PLAY

For many children, such stimuli are delivered by the media as an ever-changing source of repertoire to learn, as in the playground, by repeated listening, watching and emulation of performances disseminated by audiovisual media. The Internet now provides an extremely accessible source of highly diversified musical performances for children to observe and learn alone or with friends, and to share with peers at home, in the school playground or in other informal settings. Such activities are multimodal, involving aural and visual stimuli and sonic and kinaesthetic responses from children (Willett, 2014; Young, 2007).

However, children also appropriate material from the media that may be intended for an adult or teenage market, thereby developing or reinforcing musical preferences and performance skills within this process. As they do this, children are learning in a self-directed way from virtual teachers, and are therefore able to reach a level of performance achievement that is well beyond what might be expected. The following examples are drawn from very different geographical contexts but both aptly demonstrate this phenomenon.

Case study 2.2: In a West Yorkshire primary school

In a West Yorkshire school two 11-year-old girls, one Bengali and one Punjabi, shelter at lunchtime in a classroom from the November rain. As they discuss musical preferences, they demonstrate their favourite songs, beginning with a Madonna song, 'Like a Prayer', performed as a clapping game. They then go on to reproduce a Bollywood movie song and dance sequence learnt from videos at home with exceptional stylistic accuracy. The Bengali girl who leads the singing changes her vocal style to effortlessly emulate first Madonna and then the performance characteristics of the Bollywood song, 'Bole Chudyan', and the two girls exactly recreate the movements that accompany the dance in the film sequence (Marsh, 2008).

Case study 2.3: In an Australian community setting

A suburban shopping street is lined with a number of restaurants that have outdoor seating, which spills over into an adjoining small plaza. Several small children, aged from approximately 3 to 5 years, are playing on the steps of the plaza as their parents sit at the nearby outdoor tables. The oldest of the children holds a mobile phone, which is playing a video clip of a popular song. With the music playing audibly, she faces the younger children and models dance movements to the song which she can see on the phone. The other children arrange themselves in a dance formation that makes ideal use of the steps and imitate these movements, occasionally suggesting additional movements of their own and thus gradually developing a relatively complicated dance routine as the song is played multiple times. They happily work on this routine for at least 20 minutes, their enjoyment never flagging, despite the concentrated effort involved.

In both altering 'traditional' playground games and creating new singing games and other forms of musical play, children's appropriation of material derived from the media involves not only reproduction but also creative manipulation. The previously mentioned Bollywood song performed in the West Yorkshire playground was also transformed into a clapping game that incorporated movements from the movie's dance sequence (Marsh, 2008). Many comparable examples of creation and recreation have been found in a recent British project called *Children's Playground Games and Songs in the New Media Age* (Burn and Richards, 2014).

While global media can provide children with a constant source of new musical, kinaesthetic and textual stimuli that encourage new multimodal practices, they may also enable children to maintain traditions in novel ways, as seen in the following vignette.

Case study 2.4: In an Australian primary school

In an Australian primary school, two refugee girls, one Iranian, the other Iraqi, speak at length about their ways of learning popular songs from both Western singers and singers from their homelands and surrounding countries, using YouTube clips as their primary source. As avid consumers of the *Australian Idol* television franchise, they re-enact performances of these songs for each other (in a range of languages, including English, Arabic, Persian and Turkish), taking turns to be performer and judge, the latter providing supportive performance tips. More remarkably, they outline a range of strategies that they use for making new songs. These include a compositional activity derived from a birthday party game, where different languages and dance movements are selected from slips of paper put into a hat. From the chosen characteristics, the girls devise new songs and dances in completely new languages that are known only to them, creating a musical world for which they have complete ownership and in which they entirely belong (Marsh, 2013).

Many children in migrant communities use the Internet and satellite TV to maintain connection with and learn current popular hits in their first language. This enables children to maintain varying forms of identity and inhabit global as well as local communities of practice despite geographical distance. Moreover, many games are now learnt by children through YouTube examples or tutorials (Bishop, 2014; Lill, 2015). This allows games to proliferate internationally, so that games originating in one place may become familiar to children in many cultures. One example of this is the Cup Game, which has become a global phenomenon through a combination of dissemination through movies, YouTube and playground transmission (Lill, 2015).

INCORPORATING MEDIATED LEARNING INTO THE CLASSROOM

There is a very broad range of repertoire on which both teachers and students can draw. Again, child choice is important here and teachers can provide access to YouTube for performance clips that children can watch and emulate, in addition to downloadable lyrics for songs. Increasingly there are opportunities for online uploading of children's creative work. Other forms of media, such as CDs and DVDs, can be employed to diversify choice.

- As stated previously, teachers can provide popular music and a wide range of musical repertoire in the classroom, including that requested by students. Both repertoire and the associated learning activities should be musically and cognitively challenging.
- Online sources provide opportunities to extend children's learning beyond that which they might initially choose, but their selections can provide a starting point for musical activity. When children in a classroom come from diverse cultures, their online

selections can be shared and used collectively to initiate singing, movement and other performance activities. The musical attributes of music from representative cultures can be explored and used as the basis for improvisation and composition and contextual details can be investigated in conjunction with members of the community.

■ Children can be given access to class computers or tablets for downloading music of choice, which can be listened to individually or shared with others. Computers can be set up as learning centres that children can access at varying times of the day. A bank of learning activities could be provided either on the computer or in close proximity to it so that children could be prompted to think analytically and critically about the music that has been accessed and to collaborate with others in their assessments.

COMMUNITIES OF PRACTICE IN THE PLAYGROUND

It is evident from the foregoing descriptions of collaborative play that children's musical play operates within communities of practice, both in relation to 'traditional' playground play repertoire and through shared knowledge of particular popular music repertoire (Harwood, 1998a; Young, 2007). Drawing on the work of Wenger (1998), Barrett (2005) describes children's communities of musical practice as 'communities in which children are the active agents in the determination of the location, the participants, and the nature and range of the activities involved' (p. 261). Communities of practice are typified by the dimensions of 'mutual engagement, joint enterprise and shared repertoire' (Barrett, p. 267). In play situations, knowledge of play repertoire and performance practices may be acquired by individual children but is then more widely shared with others in social situations that include or exclude participants from the 'community'. For example, Young (2007) reports that, in southwestern England, young children's engagement with karaoke in the home frequently involves friends and family members in extended forms of sociality. In the playground, children work with each other to create and perform their games, and express a preference for collaboratively developing play material with others, as can be seen in the following discussion by two girls in West Yorkshire (Marsh, 2008):

Jana: Yeah, well it's easier if someone's helping you 'cause if you make it up on your own it's really difficult . . . You don't usually make it up on your own. You usually make it up with a group so they know it.

Helen: 'Cause then all of the people can have like ideas to put in it and then you get more things to use in it.

Jana: It's really hard if you make it up on your own.

Helen: 'Cause you can't really think for yourself as much as in a group.

Within the playground community of practice, children may take on differing roles, which allow them to participate at differing levels commensurate with their varying abilities. Typically, children have the opportunity to watch on the side of the game; practise clapping patterns with another novice player on the sidelines; join in a circle game, watching carefully and emulating movements while internalising the song; or perform some or all of the singing and movements in a game within a circle or pair of performers as competence and confidence develops. Harwood (1998a) has described African American girls' play as an example of what Lave and Wenger (1991) term 'situated cognition': legitimate peripheral participation in a community of practice. Marsh (2008) has also described how, in multiple cultural contexts, different children's contributions to a game are accepted by members of a group or pair as legitimate forms of participation, even though some players are very adept and others are novices.

Because of the miming movements, repetition and the preponderance of 'nonsense' words which do not require full comprehension for participation, games are easily learnt by children either across language barriers or within minority languages, with game repertoire being replenished by children who have left or visited home countries recently, as shown in the following example.

Case study 2.5: In an Australian primary school with a large population of refugee children

Two Assyrian girls from Iraq have become firm friends, despite one of them having arrived in Australia six years previously and the other arriving within the last year. They share many recess and lunch times singing Arabic popular songs, practising dances learnt at weddings and other social occasions and playing numerous singing games. The newly arrived player has brought a wealth of games from their mutual homeland, some of which are known by her friend but others which are less familiar. One of these is 'Fatimah', a game about a woman who has seven children. The children in the game demonstrate various attributes of ideal behaviour: sleeping, being good, singing, brushing teeth, washing hands and dancing, all of which are portrayed by mimed actions. Although the newly arrived player is much more confident in her rendition, over multiple repetitions, her friend learns the song at her own pace, as she is able to initially join in by watching and imitating the miming actions and gradually the words. At the same time, the newly arrived player, who is often reluctant to participate in classroom activities, is empowered and given a feeling of self-efficacy by her superior knowledge of the game.

Differing ways of playing games may be simultaneously accepted as legitimate forms of performance practice, and may be incorporated into revised versions of games. This can result in multiple variants which add to playground repertoire (and therefore provide the novelty that children enjoy in their games) while accommodating difference.

In the same Australian primary school, a game with seemingly endless variants, known for example as 'Sarmakadora', 'Sormakadora' and 'Simaca Dora', is one of the most popular in the playground and also one played by children from a range of linguistic and cultural backgrounds, including South Sudanese (Dinka), Sudanese (Arabic speaking), Bosnian, Indian (Marathi), Vietnamese, Serbian and Iraqi. The nonsense words in this game mean that English language proficiency is not required for full participation, and that offerings of new versions are easily accepted and incorporated. Both words and movements are repetitive and so easily imitated and learnt, even by novices in the playground, allowing newly migrated children to join in with the game across linguistic borders. Not surprisingly, the games that encourage the greatest amount of intercultural engagement are those that have virtually no text, beginning only with an opening verbal formula with no semantic meaning such as 'Slam Yak Yak' or 'Sisilala' to introduce the rest of the game that is entirely comprised of challenging clapping patterns which all children can attempt, regardless of cultural affiliations.

Another aspect of playground singing games that enables intercultural exchange and inclusion in playground communities of practice is the recognition of similarities between formulae used in games from host and home countries. For example, the familiar vertical clapping movements, inclusion of numerals and 'scissors, paper, rock' words and movements allow easy adoption of the game 'Tic Tac Toe' by newly arrived Sierra Leonean migrant girls in another Australian playground (Marsh, 2016). This characteristic, in addition to those discussed above, means that playground musical play can create an intercultural space where newly arrived migrant and refugee children can belong (Marsh and Dieckmann, 2016), contributing to the shared goals of the playground community of practice.

INCORPORATING PLAY-LIKE COMMUNITIES OF PRACTICE

Inclusive participation in musical activities is key to ensuring that classrooms can flourish as musical communities of practice. Enjoyable and engaging musical activities that allow for differing kinds of participation are an important part of establishing such communities.

▨ Rather than asking children to identically participate, for example in whole-class performance activities, create a range of roles for children, or ask children to identify and take up such roles themselves. For example, a child who has high musical competency (having perhaps learnt an instrument within a school extracurricular program or externally) can lead the class group or perform a pivotal melodic part of a performance. Another group can devise a dance sequence to accompany a musical performance. Children can perform more or less complex parts of a piece depending on competence and confidence, but a rotation of roles can enable children to rise to greater musical challenges as their confidence and competence increases.

▨ Provide regular opportunities for small groups and individuals to work independently from the teacher and allow students to choose friendship groups for small-group projects.

▨ Provide opportunities for children to coach their peers. They may do this to the side of a large group, using aural, visual or tactile modelling to assist less able peers.

▨ YouTube versions of games on class computers or tablets can provide examples of game variants from varying cultures. Children can see similarities and differences and note that there are multiple variants, all equally engaging. These can be used to encourage creative variation of games within and outside the classroom.

HOLISTIC AND MULTIMODAL LEARNING AT VARYING LEVELS OF DIFFICULTY

Just as game participation may be seen as a whole entity to which its members contribute in varying but equally acceptable ways, children's approaches to learning a game are also holistic. In the classroom, teachers typically break down components of a musical activity into parts that are seen to be more manageable for children to learn. Line-by-line teaching of songs is frequently employed, or songs are segmented into verses and choruses for teaching, with difficult phrases being given particular attention and practice. In contrast, children in both the playground and when learning at home from electronic sources learn songs (and accompanying movements if these are part of a performance) as a whole, playing a game or recorded song repeatedly in its entirety many times in order to learn it. If children make a mistake they return to the beginning of the song and sing it through completely or until a point where they experience too much difficulty to continue. Children rarely break a song or game into component parts for learning. This appears to be the case in many cultures, and has been observed with children in English, Bengali, Punjabi, Australian, Eritrean, Korean, North American, Norwegian and Iraqi play traditions (Marsh, 2008, 2013).

Another difference relates to children's organisation of their learning. Unlike teachers carefully planning for graduated musical activity within a classroom, children who are engaged in self-directed musical learning in the playground do not necessarily consider the level of difficulty of a game or song in the same way as an adult. Children are aware of forms of difficulty, particularly in relation to movement patterns, and at times they may use this knowledge to scaffold the learning of a younger or less adept peer. In many cases, however, children will decide upon repertoire and learn it effectively because it interests them, regardless of the level of difficulty.

Case study 2.6: Children in a South Korean elementary school

In an elementary school in Busan, South Korea, a group of 11-year-old girls are playing a complicated game involving sixteen different movements of fingers, hands and arms inside a spare room during one of the multiple breaks in the school day, which are often too short to enable children to go outside to play. Several boys watch the game for a while then ask to join in. They are accommodated into the circle and the girls demonstrate the game right through at a slightly slower tempo. The boys are familiar with the song, which is the theme song of a children's television programme and some of them have seen the game played a few times before but one is a complete novice. The whole group starts to play the game, with the novice watching intently and joining in with most of the movements. At the end of the game he asks for clarification and the girls demonstrate the complete clapping pattern through with the song before the group performs the game again. In less than 10 minutes of watching and joining in, all of the boys can perform this very complex game with its lengthy song and movement sequence adeptly (Marsh, 2008).

As can also be seen in this example, children learn new repertoire by aural, oral, kinaesthetic and tactile modelling and imitation; that is, by closely listening to and observing aural and visual models provided by other children and by actively joining in the play in various ways so that they have tactile reinforcement of their movements as they are learning (Harwood, 1998a, 1998b; Marsh, 2008). The same forms of multimodal learning occur when children engage with mediated models (for example, karaoke or YouTube) at home (Bishop, 2014; Lum, 2008; Young, 2007), though Bishop notes that the didactic nature of some YouTube videos, where children consciously give directions on how to play clapping or other musical games, has meant that the holistic learning characteristic of the playground is not always maintained.

INCORPORATING HOLISTIC AND MULTIMODAL LEARNING AT VARYING LEVELS OF DIFFICULTY

The musical and kinaesthetic complexity of children's play is frequently very high, and much more difficult than it is assumed to be by adults. To compensate for this mismatch of assumptions and reality, children can be given some say in how things are structured for learning. Teachers can also plan for children's holistic approach to learning in addition to the opportunities for peer teaching in the classroom discussed earlier (Marsh, 2008).

Most importantly, children need to be given the chance to work with much more complex material in the classroom, not simple activities that are deemed to be age-appropriate but in reality undersell the creative and performative capabilities of children. The kinds of strategies suggested for teachers to ensure the creative involvement of themselves and their children include:

▓ Sometimes the repertoire and activities used in a classroom are limited by a focus on developing particular notational skills rather than developing the aural/oral, kinaesthetic and improvisatory skills through which children most naturally demonstrate their learning. Although developing the ability to read standard notation has its place in the curriculum, limiting repertoire and musical activities for this purpose fails to take account of children's musical preferences and the highly developed multimodal skills that they can bring to learning.

▓ Some of the rhythmically complex aspects of children's playground games can be used as a starting point for musical activity. For example, clapping games frequently have a different metre in the clapping pattern from that of the song or chant that it accompanies (a pattern of a three beat clap against a four beat song), or may have clapping cycles of up to sixteen beats, as previously described, or even more complex rhythmic features. Children can be asked to improvise or compose a piece that transfers these rhythmic complexities to voices and instruments.

▓ Using whole musical models, teachers can provide opportunities for children to learn aurally through many repetitions. Such repetitions of repertoire can occur over months. There can be many levels and forms of initial participation and teachers can vary the different ways in which the repertoire is presented and in which children can participate, for example through listening, movement and improvisatory experiences.

▓ Musical learning should encompass learning stylistic elements, drawing on the resources of multimedia technologies and multimodal (aural-visual-kinaesthetic) forms of acquisition for individual, small group or whole-group learning.

CONCLUSION

Children engage in musical play as a joyful activity, one that constantly demonstrates their innate creativity and ability to negotiate cognitive and musical complexity. It can only be to the benefit of children's musical learning to include features of their musical play within a classroom curriculum. Teachers can actively work with children as partners in curating repertoire, devising challenging musical learning activities, facilitating rather than directing learning, acknowledging connections with the media and providing opportunities for creative endeavour and intercultural engagement to flourish.

FURTHER READING

Burn, A. N. and Richards, C. O. (2014) *Children's Games in the New Media Age: Childlore, Media and the Playground*. Farnham, UK: Ashgate.

Campbell, P. S. (2010) *Songs in Their Heads: Music and Its Meaning in Children's Lives* (2nd edition). New York: Oxford University Press.

Harwood, E. (1998) Music learning in context: A playground tale. *Research Studies in Music Education*, 11, 52–60.

Marsh, K. (2008) *The Musical Playground: Global Tradition and Change in Children's Songs and Games*. New York: Oxford University Press.

Marsh, K. (2013) Music in the lives of refugee and newly arrived immigrant children in Sydney, Australia. In P. Campbell and T. Wiggins (eds.) *Oxford Handbook of Children's Musical Cultures*. New York, NY: Oxford University Press, pp. 491–509.

Marsh, K. (2016) Creating bridges: Music, play and well-being in the lives of refugee and immigrant children and young people. *Music Education Research*, 1–14. doi:10.1080/14 613808.2016.1189525

Marsh, K. and Dieckmann, S. (2016) Interculturality in the playground and playgroup: Music as shared space for young immigrant children and their mothers. In P. Burnard, E. Mackinlay and K. Powell (eds.) *The Routledge International Handbook of Intercultural Arts Research*. Abingdon, UK: Routledge, pp. 358–68.

Marsh, K. and Young, S. (2016) Musical play. In G. McPherson (ed.) *The Child as Musician: A Handbook of Musical Development* (2nd edition). Oxford, UK: Oxford University Press, pp. 462–84.

CHAPTER 3

ENGAGING INTERACTIVELY WITH CHILDREN'S GROUP IMPROVISATIONS

Pamela Burnard and Jenny Boyack

INTRODUCTION

Teaching is inherently improvisational. Teaching creatively is an improvisational performance where interaction and relational engagement are necessary to the performance. The name that we give an activity or process (such as 'teaching') acts as a 'frame' for how we put it into practice. As with 'unscripted theatre' and 'jazz music', where there is a body of accumulated knowledge built up around the terms, so too with 'teaching' do teachers make a conscious effort to develop improvisational expertise. Research on teacher expertise[1] has found that expert teachers have mastered a large repertoire of scripts, plans and routines, while at the same time have become experts at appropriate and disciplined improvisation. Educational practices of improvising and improvisational repertoires suggest that improvisation involves learners and teachers as performers (acting out who they are and who they are becoming) where they use forms of understanding such as mathematical, dramatic or musical, that are improvisational and collective, unscripted and disciplined (Sawyer, 2004). In the immediacy of performance, teachers and children go beyond who they are and what they know to create new ways of relating to each other and to the learning content.

A really useful way of looking at the potential value of creative group improvisation is to consider it as an interaction between teachers and children engaged in the performance of creative processes with everyone participating – because everyone *really can do* group musical improvisations. Musical improvisation is a process that can – and should – be nurtured in and across all school phases. It offers a set of experiences to inspire creative musical expression in any context. The book *Free to be Musical: Group Improvisation in Music* (Higgins and Campbell, 2010) suggests that we do not think about group improvisation as the archetypal portrayals of expert or genius jazz musicians (such as Miles Davis) but rather that the dominant image of improvisers can be everyone (including, in particular, teachers) who can 'embark on significant journeys of musical discovery that not only increase musical knowledge and know-how, but also connect the experience to their wider world' (p. 3). In so doing it encourages teachers to express their individuality and the differences between themselves and their students to produce outcomes that are both original and valued in relation to a peer group and community of learners, whatever the phase of education.

The premise of this chapter is that teaching music interactively, where the dynamic relationship between teacher and children celebrating and engaging simultaneously in group improvisation is powerful and performative, can provide building blocks for children as they *develop a culture of creative opportunities* through their contribution to and interaction with every individual in the classroom community.

BUILDING LEARNING ENVIRONMENTS OF IMPROVISED POSSIBILITY

Whether the wider role that teachers play in both being creative themselves and encouraging creativity in others involves them as a novice, a seasoned generalist or specialist teacher, teaching is an improvisational activity that requires interactive relationships (Sawyer, 2011). The key thread in these relationships is that *developing a culture of creative opportunities and ensuring the creative involvement of the teacher* is central to the creative development of children (Cremin, 2009a). It is surprising, perhaps, that this is a spectre that some primary teachers want to keep at arm's length. Teachers who are *not* identified as being 'good at music' or those who position themselves negatively in relation to dichotomies (and unhelpful binaries) such as 'musicians/non-musicians' or 'creatives/non-creatives', find it difficult to take up a position which suggests that they are 'good at music'. For many teachers, having to do so will require the development of new musical attitudes and approaches.

For teachers in all stages of their professional lives, from initial teacher education to continuing professional development and postgraduate study, this will need the development of a music maker's disposition; it will need them to make time and space to think about music and creativity in their own lives, as well as in their teaching. They will need to recognise music as an aural time-based expression and *adopt a performance-based stance towards teaching*. This means that teaching must be taken very, very seriously and they must acknowledge that although the approach is playful it has a serious intent. What is offered is an invitation for teachers to serve the interests of pupils. Teachers need to decide how best the children's interests can be fostered or promoted by developing their practical knowledge by personal reflection and interaction with others. Placing group improvisational play and music performances in the primary curriculum, in its broadest sense, and in ways which are not being constrained by the planned learning programme, as illustrated in examples given later on in this chapter, can embrace the development of the individual teacher, the children and the school's creative potential.

BEING IMPROVISERS TOGETHER

Music, like drama, is a performance-based activity which lends itself to improvisational approaches. Improvising can be as simple as an individual child doodling with a musical idea and trying it in lots of different forms to find musical statements that satisfy or lead to ongoing exploration. It may involve the teacher joining *with* children to craft group improvisations that are both personally and collectively fulfilling. However it may also be a genuinely collective creative process for the class and teacher, perhaps incorporating an intentional performance outcome of a collaboratively made piece.

Improvising music together means that music is made and created in the course of a performance in real or immediate time; the making and creating processes operate in the moment. Improvised music represents knowledge made in real time, where the vocabulary and grammar of music is played out and the act connects the mind and body.

Improvising music plays a key role in the development of learners' capacities to negotiate between multiple spheres – between the self and the world. This role is a genuine synergy between received knowledge and original inquiry, between social consensus and individual expression, between the learner and the community and between the child's world and the adult world (Custodero, 2007).

Improvising offers children and teachers the chance to engage in different working processes, which lead into investigations of different kinds of musical constructions. A number of strategies to build on children's natural proclivities in improvisation can be utilised by educators in the primary classroom (Burnard, 2002).

▨ **Creating wider music improvisation and creating culture** in the school through offering children out-of-class opportunities to explore musical sound. An example of this would be making classroom percussion instruments available in the way that sports equipment or library facilities are accessible for children in break times. These informal opportunities for children to engage together with sound ideas build confidence, generate novel ideas, allow for sharing and learning from others and pave the way for more focussed exploration during in-class improvisational times.

▨ **Working towards a pedagogy of repertoire rather than recipe** where children can converse, create and draw on their musical experience, knowledge and understanding, to engage creatively in the immediate here-and-now worlds of music making. Such activity can include developing a single idea in order to build a section or a whole piece of improvising, thus making and shaping sound play and musical possibilities in playful and instructive ways.

▨ **Experimenting with different ways of singing and playing in turns and turn-by-turn structures** using known call-and-response songs, or songs between a lead singer or player who 'calls' and another singer/player, or group of singers/players who respond. The response may be very short, little more than a shout or two in reply, may be an exact echo of the leaders' part or it may be a short phrase which complements, reflects or elaborates using on-the-spot sound explorations, or on-the-spot inventions of variations, or the invention of new rhythmic events as a warm-up to the performance of other music. Improvising can also offer rich opportunities for the purposeful and co-creative use of existing musical ideas and understanding.

▨ **Fostering a stance as close listeners**, following the surface of the music and tracking the thinking as it unfolds, will often indicate how the patterning of the music arises, how ideas evolve and are repeated, transformed or left behind and how the impact of the music itself feeds back into the making process as the child hears the music unfolding. The development of the skills associated with the processes of evolving music, of spontaneous and planned improvising, is central in learning creative music making.

▨ **Using improvisational tasks to develop interactive rules of engagement**. This has the potential to create learning environments, which are motivating contexts where children learn to observe by ear and by eye and to practice repeatedly what they have observed; this leads them to imagine unknown territory in real time and enrich the ideas and possibilities on which learning relationships, and playing out different roles in groups, can draw. Roles can include being a leader, a follower, a matcher, a disruptor, a blender and an inverter. Hocketing, which derives from the French *hoquet* (hiccup), where single notes or a few notes are sung or played in turns, can be fun to improvise. Passages in hocket are frequently found in thirteenth- and fourteenth-century vocal or instrumental music. They are always fast and the effect of hocketing is to give life to the texture. Children can alternate playing sounds with their voices, taking a song and half-singing, half-playing with recorders, ocarinas or whistles.

■ **Experimenting with form and freedom to use genre-specific and genre-free improvisations across the curriculum** such as with drama and writing, which can be used as a prompt to secure knowledge of what is to be taught and learned. For example, a genre-specific approach based on predesigned motif and other musical materials has parallels with ways of listening to poetry and stories and has a particular parallel in the patterns, rhythms and evocative power of memorable language. When drama is used as a prompt in shared writing – to support the writing of a specific genre, for example – then musical improvisations in all forms can harness children's curiosity and agency in using their own personal voice to break from the models of culture or improvisatory styles of music. These might be steeped in the aural traditions of certain musical styles, performers and genres, such as jazz; children might be prompted to use the sound for their own personal expressions. Improvised scenarios can be set up in sound-based improvisations, and acted out as a kind of dress rehearsal for writing or as an oral writing frame. This kind of 'genre-specific' approach might be used to combine music and drama, music and writing or music, drama and writing.

In the contexts of teachers' confidence to explore group improvisations in daily classroom routines, a very clear example is given in the case study below. Here the context is framed as a professional development session with generalist primary teachers and teacher educator Jenny Boyack from New Zealand. What follows is an activity which actively fosters trust, courage and confidence to experiment with different contexts of group improvisation.

Case study 3.1: Developing trust, courage and confidence to lead group improvisations

At a professional development session for generalist primary teachers, I shared a favourite music activity that I call the 'Improvisation Circle'. This involves placing six classroom percussion instruments (e.g. hand drum, tambourine, triangle, claves, two-tone woodblock, guiro, sleigh bells) in a circle on the floor and calling for a volunteer to sit behind each instrument.

The players are instructed that they can play their instrument in any way they like provided that they do not damage the instrument or anybody else! I suggest that players can explore different sounds on their instruments or listen to what others are playing and fit in with/complement that or play something that cuts across what others are playing. I remind them that they are free to change how they play at any time.

Six teacher volunteers came and sat behind the instruments and the other teachers closed their eyes. They were asked to listen and remember as much about the music as they could so that they could describe it to someone who wasn't present.

My role was to be a conductor/composer moving quietly around the circle and touching the six instrumentalists on the shoulder when I wanted them to begin playing and touching their shoulders again when I wanted them to stop. I reminded them that although I decided *when* they would play, they were free to choose *how* they would play.

I don't remember that particular piece of music except that when it finished the assembled teachers broke into spontaneous applause and the improvisers glowed with satisfaction at what they had created. There was a discussion about what the listeners and the players had experienced and it gave me an opportunity as leader to weave in the language of the musical elements, to question and encourage deeper thinking about the music that had been created.

What I do remember is one teacher saying emphatically 'I can *do* that! I can put six instruments in a circle on the floor and tap children on the shoulder'!

There is a postscript to this case and story. The generalist teachers were enthusiastic about offering an activity like this and many of them went on to use it in their classrooms. However, it's important to remember that the actual improvisation time is only the beginning of the activity. The discussion that follows is critical for musical learning.

Leading the discussion requires teachers to have good questioning skills and to work on developing their own musical perception and knowledge. There is a range of questions that could be asked of children. Here are some:

■ What kind of things do you learn when you're an improviser, a conductor/composer or a listener?
■ What changes did you notice in the music?
■ What were some of the things that caused the music to change?
■ What did you think about when you were tapped on the shoulder to play?
■ What did you think about when you were deciding whom to tap?

Teaching children to improvise in groups should be an artistic event. Teachers do not need to turn these experiences into a technical event, into something without fun and emotions, without creativity. They should rather work artistically, offering sustained opportunities for improvising together as a class, engaging themselves as well as their class as a community of improvisers, playing together, performing playfully with positive feelings and creative dispositions and learning through group improvisations.

REFLECTING AND TALKING ABOUT IMPROVISED ELEMENTS

The demands made on the listening teacher by improvised group work can be considerable. As well as taking in the overall effect of the improvised piece and the combined processes through which it is being evolved, particularly in group performances, the teacher has to track the musical roles of the individuals in the group. Teachers can gain considerable insight into children's musical work by *tuning in to, listening carefully to and observing improvised music-making in progress*: hearing and seeing how individual players come up with an idea, how individual ideas evolve and how group ideas evolve and are fleshed out, developed and responded to by the rest of the group. But also important is *listening to children talk* about their experience of improvisation, of having made their own piece in the moment and interacted musically with others.

Improvising music is children thinking aloud in sound. For some of the youngest children, the stream of music made as sung, or made as played, is, indeed, all there is. The music they make is transient and, although it may be quite clearly structured, it is often, very naturally, improvisational and evolved in the moment. *Close listening*, following the surface of the music and tracking the thinking as it unfolds, will often indicate how the patternings of the music arise, how ideas are repeated, transformed or left behind and how the impact of the music itself feeds back into the making process as the child hears the musical drama unfolding. *Close listening* without intervening can be an invaluable learning experience for the teacher. *Close listening* to children's working processes (such as the ability to come up with new and musically interesting ideas, ways of exploring, developing and repeating ideas and the use of silence) while bearing these processes in mind as they improvise enables the teacher not only to relate more easily to what children make, but also helps the teacher to learn from children and to become a more confident improviser.

A teacher may *tune in to children's musical language* by listening as an observer and fostering discussion and reflection during the review and feedback process. The opportunities to be actively creative within a medium such as music; to share, evaluate, analyse and discuss the possibilities with children in circumstances in which they have control and are able to play; and to take risks and exercise critical judgement should be embedded in primary education. Open-ended questions are important – questions such as 'How did you contribute to the improvisation?' 'Tell us about some of the ways you worked together in this improvisation?' 'What do you think the audience will make of this improvised piece?' 'What were the surprises?' and 'What does it feel like to perform in this way?' The teacher should invite the children to share their feelings about improvising when someone else is guiding or acting as a facilitating conductor, leading them in particular directions.

It is important for teachers and children to *reflect* on how the players interactively improvised musical ideas and how these ideas were harnessed, repeated, developed, captured, reshaped and manipulated. In these discussions the meanings behind the improvisation – emotionally, socially, creatively and musically – come to the fore. Such knowledge and understanding will inform teachers' planning of subsequent improvisational events by alerting them to areas that are underdeveloped and might benefit from focussed instruction, to individual or group strengths and to opportunities for moving in new and unexplored directions. Another dimension, and possibly deeper insights, can be gained through talking with the child or, even better, interacting musically with the child. A teacher can join in with children's improvisatory work by both listening and contributing. Doing so provides another 'viewpoint', which is creative and essential to give children ownership of their learning. It is important to recognise that teachers, like children, are talented, inventive and capable as music makers.

Setting the creative task is a skill that is central to teaching music creatively. Engagement is often what teachers describe as 'on-task'. However, creative behaviour does not always conform to on-task codified behaviours. Those children who are creatively engaged seem to challenge, ask more questions, disagree and take risks. This is true of musical settings too. For many teachers, setting creative musical tasks which call for improvised responses can be daunting. To nurture a deeper level of creative engagement in music it is essential to dispel the idea that a response is wrong. Instead, suggest to children that responses that don't appear to work so well can also be played with and modified so that they sound more satisfying.

Teachers need to allow themselves to set tasks which develop the child through emotional, cognitive, physical and musical expression. All children who engage work within the boundaries of the task, but those who find creative engagement absorb the task and create meaningful musical responses. Teachers will see evidence of learning through children's improvisational approach to teamwork, their ability to make independent decisions and their confidence to improvise alone and in groups in a focussed way.

In the literature on creativities in education, Craft (2015) highlights the importance of the creative potential of all individuals and the role of possibility thinking in a creative approach to life for everybody. Many different writers and researchers have recognised and described the personal qualities and dispositions we need to develop as creative teachers and learners. Craft, Cremin, Burnard and Chappell (2007) look at children's creative *decision-making processes* and identify what being actively creative within a medium – in which they have control – means, and examine how they are able to play, take risks and exercise critical judgement together. The children show:

▨   openness to experience the creating task – for music, developing spontaneous or planned improvisations;

▨   enjoyment of experimentation and musical journeying in the search for musical form – illustrated in the degree to which they allow the musical events to determine the form of the emerging piece;

▨   playfulness, personal courage and pursuit of musical possibilities and purpose – the application of imagination to produce purposeful group improvised performances in which they develop and shape musical events, making musical conversations in pairs and engaging in group storytelling with musical roles; and

▨   active and deliberate focus of attention and skills and a high degree of personal investment that can be seen in the level of absorption and intensity with which they become engaged in order to shape, refine and manage ideas in the process of creating.

Case study 3.2: Reflecting on establishing improvisation circle routines

Once children are familiar with how the Improvisation Circle activity works (it usually only takes one 'round' with the teacher as conductor/composer), this becomes an activity that can be the basis for an endless number of creative experiences.

Restrict the conductor/composer to starting and stopping each player *twice* unless they have a *particular musical reason* for doing more. This maintains the interest and keeps each round to a reasonable time. 'Eyes closed' for the listeners is part of the routine and frees the improvisers to focus on their task rather than on what their classmates might be thinking. Enforce a 'no talking' rule and be firm about it. Acknowledge that it's hard not to speak, especially when the music is wonderful, and remind the children that there will be time to talk at the end.

Sometimes it's tempting to say 'there's time for one more round before the bell' and skip the discussion of the previous round. Avoid the temptation! It's in the discussion that much of the satisfaction and learning comes to the fore for both the children and the teacher.

Researchers have studied the concept of 'possibility' thinking or 'what if' and 'as if' thinking as manifest in the learning engagement of children aged 3 to 11. Research reveals that children working with ideas collaboratively recognise one another's ideas and build these into personal and collective responses to tasks. Recognising the possibilities inherent in children's group improvisations and posing questions as the driving process for making sense of their own improvisations as well as exploring the nature and dynamic of group improvisations with others is crucial in developing a creative learning culture. Asking questions can facilitate learning:

- What if we improvise the piece again but swap instruments?
- What if we improvise a piece making imaginative use of our voices?
- What do we notice and enjoy as listeners?
- How did we respond to the improvisation challenge?
- How is our confidence to make music and talk about it changed?
- Which elements of music (pitch, rhythm, dynamics, texture, tempo, timbre or tone colour) did we focus on? How can we weave new dynamics into the music?
- What kinds of technical language in music are we developing?
- Which tone colours work well together?
- Which tone colours and instrumental qualities provide interesting contrast?
- What techniques for playing different instruments can we vary?
- What are some of the different ways to create musical sounds on the same instrument?
- How can we vary the rhythm but keep the pitch the same?
- How are different musical moods built?
- What are the different musical choices we make as improvisers?
- What if/how can we make subtle changes and shift the musical interest in a piece?

Applying the use of questions to an Improvisation Circle activity, the first questions need to be for listeners *before* the improvisation begins. Providing something for the children to listen for doesn't mean that this is what all of them will hear. Sometimes the music just takes over and the focus becomes that child's individual experience and enjoyment of it. The important thing is for listening to be an active experience and for the children to share their thoughts afterwards. Be excited when you hear a child say 'I don't want to play, I just want to listen this time'. One thing that can help teachers with improvised activity is to build a bank of focussing questions or statements. Here are some suggestions:

- Listen for all the things you hear in the music.
- Try and remember the order of the instruments.
- Remember how the music changes from beginning to end.
- Listen for a time when the music seems exciting (tense, comfortable, empty, easy, energetic, heavy, smooth, etc.) and think about exactly what's happening to make it like this.
- Find adjectives to describe some parts of the music.
- Imagine yourself playing along with one of the improvisers.

Sometimes it's good, when the round finishes, to let the children share their initial impressions with their friends. You may even get them to write some of their ideas down before they talk as a class. Here are some discussion starters to try:

- What do you remember about what happened?
- Were there any surprises in the music?
- In what different ways were the instruments related to each other?

Try and steer children away from evaluative comments about the different instruments (e.g. 'I liked the drum'), and get them to focus on how the instruments were working. Remember to ask the improvisers about their experience (e.g. 'What did you think about when you were tapped on the shoulder?'); likewise, question the conductor/composer (e.g. 'Did you have a plan as you worked?').

'TEACHER IN ROLE' AS IMPROVISER

In creating a community of practice, the children learn to monitor their behaviour but also to reflect on the commitment and engagement of their teacher. Rather than always standing at the front of the class adopting a teacher-directed stance, teachers can experiment with a variety of roles, both purposeful and playful. One of the most significant conventions in classroom drama is *teacher in role* (TIR). This has a parallel in classroom music where teachers can imagine themselves as someone else, taking on the role of improviser and participating with the children from this perspective. Such an approach allows teachers to model the commitment and belief involved as they participate in different ways in the improvised task and musical setting. By assuming the role of improviser themselves, teachers tend to unite and engage the class in the collaborative music making and musical play. It requires teachers to model the commitment and belief involved participating in different ways in the improvised task and musical setting. In musical contexts, when teachers assume the role of improviser they unite the class and engage them in collaborative music making and musical play.

Teacher in role as improviser is central to successful creative engagement in music. Seeing the teacher as a fellow musician in a shared endeavour is the key to developing relationships in the music classroom. Teachers can help to shape and direct the musical experience, negotiating with the children and supporting, extending and challenging their musical thinking from inside the music through improvisation. Improvisations might also focus on a particular element, e.g. dynamics, duration or timbre. Interactions can explore combinations of matching, continuing, contrasting or complementing.

There are many ways teachers can take part as improvisers. These include:

■ Conducting whole-class improvisations and sharing musical ideas they've heard or played at home.
■ Playing with a partner: two players on one keyboard can try contrasting a smooth, joined up line with very short, detached notes. Another idea is for the teacher to model exploring and experimenting with the playing of spontaneous ideas together with the children. Using generative improvisational playing with a response partner – having a 'conversation' where sometimes both 'talk at once' and at other times use a call and response, responding to each other's musical ideas.
■ Negotiating with the class (rather than unilaterally deciding on) a 'rule' or sets of rules and then following them, e.g. only using certain notes, always going on from where the other player leaves off or starting one at a time, with different pitches and timbres, and then adding doubled notes into the basic rhythm – similar but different.
■ Role-playing the improvised discovery of how the timbres of different instruments sound when they play at different pitches or how the volume of the two balances up. Teacher and child can face each other and, working with a xylophone and glockenspiel, can find considerable amusement in 'copying' the playing action, sounding 'opposite' and using different mixtures of copying the sound and turning patterns

upside down and backwards. They can try improvising different ways of using instruments or using several different types of beaters.

■ When teachers participate in an improvised musical conversation with very young children, they discover how intrinsic improvisation is to young children as part of play, movement or the ordinary round of daily life. Children improvise songs spontaneously as early as they acquire language. Left to play with instruments, they meticulously investigate the sound world offered and go on to pattern and order sounds into musical shapes. One or two can improvise while another group, or the class, listens. As they listen, teachers can invite children to notice, remember and then describe to the players and singers what they hear. For example the audience may notice when two players or singers keep in time but play different things or copy each other or either match, or try out, complementary or different ideas.

In profiling group improvisation as daily planned activities included in the primary classroom there are a number of available options (Table 3.1).

■ **Table 3.1** Strategies for learning journeys in group improvisation

Story structure	Group improvisation with the characters role tracking events as a sounded storyboard in which the tale has a beginning, middle and end; mapping out the dramatic structure of the scene in terms of mood and pace, then using this outline as a framework for improvising (or composing) music to match; creating a poster with ground rules for improvising in groups; highlighting particular elements in different group tasks and parts of the story structure. Significant phrases and phases of the story can use particular musical motifs in order to aid recall.
Conversations/ dialogues, roles of group members	Role-play in pairs (player A and B) or three-way Skype conversations or interviews in role; groups decide on roles such as leader, reporter and scribe and review these during the extended activity; groups can improvise on particular scales, e.g. C, D, E, F sharp, G sharp, A sharp; discuss the music which results in relation to the character given by the pitch set; take turns and focus on improving their telling.
Sound (play and story) scripts	Music improvised for a story or dramatic music from a story in small groups; very often the starting point for creating a piece of music theatre is a story which already has its own shape, characters and setting. The music can set the scenes and atmospheres, accompany dance or mime, be used to tell the whole story with characters singing spontaneously all or some of the time or be used between scenes of a play or to add improvised sound effects.
Diary	Thought-tracking in sound/an interior monologue using repeated patterns (ostinati) which use different tempi, rhythm and pitch patterns and which use one timbre or combine two or three. Collect these and record. Listen and discuss the mood set by these patterns each day.
Characters	Using improvised rhythm patterning to convey aggression, calm, authority, reminiscing; using improvised sounds of words to support character – hard or soft consonants etc.; using improvised voice quality and pitch range to support character; using improvised dynamic variety in different ways – contrasts, levels, accent.
Scenes	Write a short scene for a character onstage, introducing him or herself or reminiscing about some past deed or event. Set their state of mind (calm, angry, tense, afraid, etc.) to improvised music.

Teachers may choose to focus on particular forms of improvisation which can be sung or performed as sounded dramatisations, pantomimes, sounded role-plays, sounded play scripts, sounded stories or specific soundscapes performed to illuminate events of history in a history lesson or excite interest in a poem or geographical region. Alternatively, teachers might choose to focus on one or two significant activities so as to recreate or re-envision learning narratives across a range of units using improvisation as an immersion and exploration tool for initiating, developing and reflecting on learning, depending on the children's emerging needs and interests. Letting the children lead during the learning journey will ensure that they take a degree of ownership and control of their learning, fostering their possibility thinking and engagement in music creativity.

Group improvisations can be particularly accessible to children because of the immediacy of context that positions them in significant musical roles (Burnard, 2002). When children improvise music with the group, with every group member knowing that they are welcome to contribute, the group's product results from realising democracy within the educational process, where the contribution of every individual counts (Craft, 2015) (Figures 3.1 and 3.2 offer examples of group improvisation settings).

■ **Figure 3.1** As players move in and out of the musical space there are observable changes in demeanour and musical offerings; the result of a complex interweaving of personal and collective ideas and attributes. These teacher education students are involved in a group improvisation task. At this particular moment, there are two pairs of musical conversations occurring with players looking across the group and responding to each other's contributions.

(Photography by John O'Sullivan.)

■ **Figure 3.2** Esther and Isaiah are engaged in a musical dialogue with an older child on a drum. Although playing together on the cymbal was their choice, there was initial negotiation between them in terms of 'territory' and acceptable dynamics. Isaiah wanted to hit the cymbal as loudly as possible and Esther, a year older, was at pains to moderate his playing, sometimes directly and at other times leading by example. Although Isaiah learned a little about conventional playing techniques from Esther, she also learned from him that there is a joyful freedom in pushing the boundaries!

(Photography by John O'Sullivan.)

CONCLUSION

When children are given space, time, trust and freedom to be creative, they will engage playfully and imaginatively in both individual and group improvisation in music. Whether they are listening, watching or performing as an individual or as part of a group improvisation, all have the opportunity to respond to the musical setting as the music unfolds.

NOTES

1 Research on teacher expertise has been summarised in Sawyer's (2011) introductory chapter entitled 'What makes good teachers great? The artful balance of structure and improvisation'.

2 See the chapter 'Developing drama creatively' in *Teaching English Creatively* by Teresa Cremin (2009), who posits the idea that 'drama, the art form of social encounters, offers children the chance to engage creatively in fictional world making play' (p. 26). A very wide selection of classroom drama conventions makes use of improvising.

FURTHER READING

Burnard, P. (2002) Investigating children's meaning-making and the emergence of musical interaction in group improvisation. *British Journal of Music Education*, 19(2), 157–72.

Craft, A. (2015) *Creativity, Education and Society: Writings of Anna Craft*. Selected by K. Chappell, T. Cremin and B. Jeffrey. Stoke-on-Trent: Trentham Books.

Custodero, L. A. (2007) Origins and expertise in the musical improvisations of adults and children: A phenomenological study of content and process. *British Journal of Music Education*, 24(1), 77–98.

Sawyer, K. (2004) Creative teaching: Collaborative discussion as disciplined improvisation. *Educational Researcher*, 33(2), 12–20.

Sawyer, K. (2011) *Structure and Improvisation in Creative Teaching*. New York: Cambridge University Press.

CHAPTER 4	# CHILDREN COMPOSING

CHILDREN COMPOSING
Creating communities of musical practice

Pamela Burnard, Jenny Boyack and Gillian Howell

INTRODUCTION

Music composition has traditionally been regarded as a sophisticated skill or ability that requires many years of formal academic training, possibly beginning in a secondary school context and continuing into conservatoires or academies of higher learning. However, there is evidence of sophisticated levels of compositional skill in children aged 5 to 12 years and of qualitatively different ways of approaching composition tasks. For example, Joanna Glover (2000) in her seminal book *Children Composing 4–14* suggests that children view musical creativity as the product of values, risks and courage, rather than as a technical endeavour. Teachers conducting research from within the learning environment emphasise the importance of providing time and freedom for children to compose.

This chapter will reflect on ways of supporting children's composing pathways, processes and products in diverse communities. Central to this is the need to recognise the primary classroom:

▪ as a dynamic learning community. Such a view is underpinned by the assumption that creativity is a social and cultural construction in which teachers' and children's compositional engagement with music is discernible within and across their individual and social worlds. Important questions and considerations support the development of such a community. What do teachers value about children's compositions? What kinds of conversations occur about these compositions? What criteria do children and teachers apply when both are consumers (as listeners, downloaders) and producers (as music makers and creators/composers and performers)?

▪ as a dynamic practice where the role of the teacher is one of creative leadership. This fosters questioning, challenging and exploring ideas, keeping options open, reflecting critically on ideas, making connections and supporting *what* children 'do' as composers and *how* children develop as composers. A key challenge is for teachers to demonstrate sensitivity around their own preferences, positioning between high and low cultural fields, and the production of aesthetic judgements.[1]

In addition, the chapter will consider two approaches by which teachers can enable creativity and suggest some methods for supporting these approaches. Firstly, teachers need to shift from a focus on *managing* children's composition in primary classrooms (thereby placing themselves in a central role where the expert adult offers induction to the novice child). Instead, there can be a blurring of the lines between teacher and learner with teachers taking on the role of facilitator and guide, and participating in composing alongside children. The message here is not for teachers to work without plans but rather to:

■ provide tools for exploration and encourage children to immerse themselves in compositional tasks;
■ seek opportunities to stimulate and unlock children's learning, and cultivate and shape children's individual and collective identity and autonomy as composers;
■ empathise with children as composers;
■ exercise children's musical imaginations; and
■ generate and communicate new ways of composing together, empowered by the act of self and social expression.

Secondly, at times, it is appropriate for teachers to stand back and create space for children to step into and take ownership of their discoveries. At such times, the teachers' role remains active as they observe aspects of children's composing activity and develop the capacity to celebrate the wholeness, the complexity and the newness of children composing.

WHY MUSIC COMPOSITION IN PRIMARY EDUCATION?

There is clear evidence that the processes of children composing provide positive educational and social outcomes. Composing helps children to learn, thus developing their cognitive skills and inspiring new ways of thinking. Composing also helps them to achieve more; participation in music making and creating helps children to do better right across the whole curriculum. As is the case for writing, painting and dancing, composing music encourages children to develop their imaginations. By embedding composing and the creative process in their learning, teachers have demonstrated that children develop a sense of being self-confident and complete musicians. This is shown along the lines of 'I can sing and play and listen and move and talk about music, and I can also work with the raw materials of music in a way that shows I'm creative too!'

It is in this spirit that Higgins and Campbell (2010), in an inspiring and accessible resource *Free to Be Musical*, argue that teachers need to take, on the one hand, responsibility for music leadership in their classroom, whilst, on the other, and at the same time, relinquish control, being mindful of the principle that small changes can result in dramatic, large-scale effects.

However, a major role of the teacher is to help children gain an ongoing sense of themselves as developing composers. In this chapter some of the characteristics of children composing will be explored with the purpose of enabling teachers to incorporate some of these practices into class activities. This means:

■ establishing a classroom climate conducive to quality and progression in composing;
■ fostering expectations of each child as an individual to develop her or his own composing pathway;

■ helping children to find a musical 'voice' that they can recognise as their own; and
■ creating communities of practice in composing.

For music composition to be valued as an important method of learning in primary education the teacher needs to develop a culture of creative opportunities for children to work on self-devised composing projects, based on their own skills and interests as well as teacher-led and group-devised composing projects. The other opportunity lies in establishing the class as a community of composers, working alongside each other and together, generating interest, curiosity and a supportive context in which individuals feel able to take the risks inherent in any creative work. It also means ensuring the creative involvement of the teacher in developing the children's own composing pathway, building on their own personal musical skills, interests and imagination by creating and composing music *alongside* them. If the teacher's principle mode of understanding children's creating music or musical creating is imaginative participation in their creative process, this tends to confirm the view, frequently expressed, that an essential aspect of a teacher's own education must be a broad base of real participation in creating music. The perspective that everybody is capable of being creative and that school-based creativity fosters children as writers and composers in primary education, given the right learning environment, is now commonplace.

PREPARING THE CLASSROOM FOR COMPOSING AS A WAY OF LEARNING

Teachers need to perform, present, save and listen to their own music alongside their children's in order to share a vigorous dynamic of practice – integrating the 'composing, performing, listening' trichotomy into the daily lives and living being of children's music making and teachers' ways of thinking, skills, understanding and vocabulary – that will support primary school children's composing development. It may seem that teachers will only be in a good position to develop new ways of thinking about children's creativity by direct experience of *children's* music making and creating. However, we argue that teachers' own active creative involvement is a critical factor in enriching, interesting and challenging children in pursuing their own creative work.

There are numerous studies that examine in detail the musical content of a teacher's interaction with a group of pupils across a period of time. These studies tell us that creative teachers set up learning environments in which musical insight, response and creation thrive anew, because musical decision-making is nourished as an everyday, unconstrained way of thinking. Teachers can support fruitful and creative ways of interacting with children making their own composed music. Activities can arise from a mixture of improvisation, in which familiar finger patterns lead the way, and aural experimentation with what the instrument can do. There can also be activities or a performance occasion where children take on different roles, transforming the original piece by creating new ways to perform it.

It makes good sense for teachers to encourage children to bring music composed for their own instruments into school. A *class composing forum* provides the opportunity to hear some of this music, or it can be made available for individual listening through MP3 or a *listening centre* via intranet platforms or computers. Sharing composed music for different instruments can become a central aspect of the primary curriculum where music composed by children can easily be adopted in learning programmes. Some suggestions for teachers to encourage the development of a learning culture that offers plentiful creative opportunities include the development of classroom practices which emphasise the following:

- Listening to children's compositions as a window for them to reflect on their actions, thoughts and feelings in the communicative process.
- Joining with children to make songs and pieces together and inviting professional composers and community musicians from outside the school to contribute to the development of compositional classroom practices as composer-teachers. They may offer new ideas, materials and ways of generating different compositional ideas, through which teachers and children can tune in to new ways of extending, adding, responding to and initiating ideas through regular engagement in creative music workshops.
- Promoting compositional opportunities which may arise to meet certain curriculum purposes but also as an opportunity for composed music to be collected, collated and curated as an anthology of children's expressions of their learning, identity and community over time.

In working towards creating a learning environment in which children feel entitled to articulate their views as composers, and where composing activity and the composing pathways taken by each child are celebrated, the realities of children's experiences of composing need to be tracked by enabling work to be collected on a tape, disc, MP3 player, iPad or laptop. Composing notebooks, together with audio recordings, contribute evidence for teacher assessment and provide a record of progress that can go with the child into the next class. A majority of children can manage these effectively and simplified recording sheets can be used to help those who find it hard.

GAINING CONFIDENCE TO BE A 'COMPOSER': MAKING IT A REALITY

The rich diversity of today's participatory musics, from jazz to pop to 'world', from iPhone/iPad apps to downloading MP3s, allows for a teaching approach that balances individual and class work. Children's compositions can be listened to, sung or played by others, captured and kept and revisited at any time. Their composed music can arise from improvisations, from music rooted in instrumental technique or familiar styles or can be reinventions of traditional tunes or new arrangements of accompaniments to their song making and known vocal pieces. The interplay between individual and group work enables primary children to blossom, developing work according to their own imagination, skills and experience, and being stretched beyond these through the group interactions and travelling beyond the limits of just musical 'pieces'.

At the heart of children's collective and connected compositional experiences lies the role and nature of participation. Hands-on involvement in the creative and compositional process makes children active agents in the work, able to infuse it with unique experiences of sounds and the world. The following illustrative case of progression in children's compositional tasks and teaching strategies is contributed by Jenny Boyack, a primary school music specialist in Palmerston North, New Zealand.

Case study 4.1: Composing 'soundwalks' in the early years

When we consider the kind of work we might expect from older children in the senior years of primary school, it's useful to think about experiences in the early years that will contribute to these later outcomes. The use of soundscapes, a popular creative music activity for older primary school age children, is a case in point.

My version of soundscapes in the early years of primary school is what I call a 'soundwalk'. It involves working with a whole class of children and thinking/talking about the variety of sounds associated with a particular place or experience. This is a wonderful activity as a follow-up to a class trip.

Let's imagine you've been to the beach for a trip, maybe as part of a language experience unit, or to explore the natural environment as part of the science curriculum. Bring the children onto the mat and together list the many different sounds heard at the beach. Use simple techniques like getting the children to close their eyes, picturing the scene in their heads, imagining walking on the beach and recalling the sounds that accompany their picture. The list could include the sound of the waves on the shore, the whistle of the wind, the cry of gulls, the squelchy sound of wet sand, the clack and crunch of shells, the whish of the grasses on the sand dunes, children's laughter, etc.

When your list is complete, the teacher and children together choose four or five favourite sounds and start thinking about the order in which they'd like to play/hear them. For each chosen sound, work with the children to find a way to represent it musically. Don't stop with the sound itself but discuss *how* you will use the sound to create a 'mini-music' stop on your soundwalk. For example, the children may suggest using tambourines and maracas to represent the sound of the waves. Ask them about whether the sea sound changes, and let different children experiment with playing these changes on the instruments. In all the discussions, use the word 'music' frequently. Refer to 'our music', 'the musical sound of the waves', 'using our instruments in a musical way', or 'making our walk as musical as we can'.

Now take a large sheet of paper and beginning at any point on the page draw a graphic representation of your first sound. This may involve diagrams, instrument sketches, onomatopoeic syllables, words or any other symbols that will be a reminder to the children. Do this for each of the chosen sounds until your large sheet of paper has four or five sound pictures in their own space. This is your musical score.

Discuss different ways of moving from one sound to another – running, walking, creeping, jumping, splashing, hopping, swimming, sliding – and then use graphic symbols to connect the sound pictures in the order in which you'd like them played. Let the chosen symbols represent the different character of the movements. Once again, work with the children to find musical ways of realising/representing the movement symbols in sound, and let them experiment and demonstrate using body percussion, found sounds and instruments.

It's now time to play the graphic score of the soundwalk, as musically as possible. Choose groups of children to play the different parts and support them as they practice. Rehearse the piece and discuss how it could be made or played more musically. Record yourselves playing and listen to the result, taking time to think about any changes and additions that will add to the musicality of the piece. When it comes to performing, use a pointer and move it sensitively over the sound pictures and the movement sections. For example, your pointer might swirl around one of the sound pictures to show how the sounds connect smoothly and without silences. If you are representing the intermittent calls of the gulls or the more accented sounds of the crunchy shells the movement of your beater might mirror this. Some of the movement between sound sections may involve everyone matching a sound to a symbol and moving in time with a steady beat. There are no recipes for the outcome. Rather the collaborative process allows the teacher to highlight and reinforce the provisional and evaluative nature of musical composition.

Over time, build a class collection of soundwalk scores and have them available for children to play in their own time. Listen for what happens when a small group settle themselves down and perform one of their class compositions. Are some children taking a music leadership role as they remember how the piece 'goes'? Are they evaluating how well they are doing and suggesting ways of improving? Is the previously composed piece becoming a springboard for extended or new musical ideas? Are the children delighting in the results of their playing? Watch, listen and enjoy these magical moments!

The significance of using a multimodal approach to facilitate children's collaborative compositions is central to creative classroom practice. The activities include playing by ear and from notations, improvising and composing, as well as promoting access for everyone. This kind of celebration of creativity is important as it affords teachers the opportunity of bringing many classes of young children together to find songs of their own and then to own them, giving children more than just a glimpse of that wider context of meaning that participation in performances has in life, and the opportunity to express and share the experience of music making together. Research emphasises the musical, personal and social benefits to children that arise when all can be involved in musical performances of their own and others' compositions, arrangements and improvisations.

Case study 4.2: Composing 'soundscapes' in the later years

Soundscapes are a wonderful way for small groups of children to create their own music in response to a theme, experience, poem, special place – the possibilities are only limited by teachers' and children's imaginations. If older children have had a range of classroom instrument experiences in their early years, they will have a repertoire of musical ideas and structural frameworks to draw on when they're given a soundscape task. For example, they may demonstrate:

- confidence achieving a range of sounds from the same instrument;
- ability to control the dynamics (louds and softs) of different instruments;
- understanding of different rhythmic frameworks;
- a range of composition strategies such as the development of short musical ideas that can be extended, combined or repeated;

- imaginative combining of tone colours; and
- awareness of the need to structure musical ideas into a cohesive whole.

Good preparation for a soundscape task is likely to pay off in terms of the end result. Consider how you will communicate the initial task to children so that they are clear about what is expected. When first working on group music compositions with a new class, a few parameters regarding things like length, structural devices or maximum number of instruments can give the children confidence to make a start. Think about:

- the number of children in each group – six is about right because it allows for a range of sounds and ensures that every child is important;
- how you will form the groups – self-selection, teacher selection, numbering off, gender balance;
- a process for distributing instruments – you might want the groups to do some planning and make some preliminary decisions about their composition before they start grabbing all the good instruments!;
- a separate composition space for each group – verandas, storerooms, withdrawal rooms, teacher's office; and
- providing sufficient time for the children to complete the task – a number of shorter sessions is usually preferable to a single longer session because the time between allows ideas to develop and grow.

Be ready to provide support for groups who are struggling with the task. This could include:

- encouraging groups to make decisions quickly and live with them;
- recognising the overuse of sound effects rather than musical representations of objects/events, e.g. stamping feet on the ground to represent footsteps is a sound effect; playing a steady beat on a hand drum and getting louder or softer is a musical representation;
- listening to what has been created so far and helping the children to recognise 'musical' patterns or ideas that can be built on;
- spotting when the musical ideas are too complex to be performed and helping them to simplify the soundscape;
- identifying a lack of cohesion in the soundscape – in this situation, encourage the children to use repetition and layering/sequencing of ideas to build unity as well as variety; and
- being conscious of dissatisfaction because the music sounds boring. This is the opposite of the above issue. In this instance, encourage the children to separate some of their musical ideas/sections with contrasting music and to look for simple ways to introduce tension, e.g. the addition of a different tone colour or upsetting an established rhythm.

Finally, think about the context in which the groups will perform their compositions. Ensure that good audience behaviour is reinforced and provide a focus for the other groups as they listen. Record and play back performances. Ask the audience for appreciative comments (these can relate to such different aspects as the commitment of the musicians, the effectiveness of the group process, the creativity of musical ideas or the unexpected or unconventional use of instrumental/voice/environmental sounds) and the performing group for things they might do differently next time. A performance process that works well is to have a classroom-based performance as a 'dress rehearsal', thus allowing time to refine aspects of the soundscape that can be strengthened or improved, then a second performance to parents, another class or even the school assembly.

Networked environments can provide support and inspiration to teachers and children alike. They enable children to collaborate and work creatively across a cluster of schools. Teachers can share ways of consulting and feeding back to children on composing, building a toolbox of strategies which can then be used in different school contexts with children of different ages. Children's views can be fed back, collaborations can occur within a local area network and, as Internet access becomes more available and reliable, there is scope for national and international collaboration.

DEVELOPING CONFIDENCE TO TEACH COMPOSING

Teachers often set tasks without taking time to savour the uniqueness of children's responses, focussing instead on the end products. Finding confidence to look for stimulating and exciting ideas as starting points for composing, and subjecting these ideas to critical examination, means that teachers can and should be obliged to evaluate most critically those same ideas that they are actively using in developing their creative practices. When teachers undertake their own individual learning journey to see how to relate to the individuality of their children it is important that their experiences of creative practice are rooted in their own and their students' experiencing, playing, making, moving, listening, dialogue, guided reflection, innovative contemporary arts experience and stimulated critical reflection. The aim should be to make everyone feel that they are composers and that they *can* do it well, and that composing music can enhance the learning experience (Hennessy, 2000). Some suggestions to develop the process of children composing include the following processes:

- **Exploring**: particularly common for starting a piece in open-ended tasks.
- **Experimenting**: a good starting point when helping to create new and novel elements and developing ideas.
- **Discovering**: can be a particularly useful and surprising action when organising and merging different ideas or renewing or modifying old ideas.
- **Constructing**: the constructing process and children's compositional models are well documented in the literature (for examples of various models see Burnard, 2006; Burnard and Younker, 2002; Odena, 2012). This is important in the construction of a new piece of music and its performance.
- **Revising**: this is an important process for composing, and is particularly important for reaching the final result but also for the group revision process where children challenge each other's musical ideas and offer new solutions and end points and reach agreement on final outcomes (for examples, see Webster's chapter, 'Towards pedagogies of revision: guiding a student's music composition' in Odena, 2012).

- **Playing**: this is important during composing activities so as to try out, evaluate and verify which ideas work better than others.
- **Practising and rehearsing the piece**: this is also important because the goal is not only to compose but to learn and memorise the piece so that it can be confidently performed.
- **Collaborating and cooperating** in group activities involves communication between players and the defining of roles, rules and relationships. There may be a leader assigned who conducts or proposes the primary ideas, while the material may be developed by other members who are assigned various leadership roles. Individual ideas need to be tried out, received, modified, adapted and revised. This requires a democratic process involving all of the players.

All of these dimensions are important elements of the creative processes which emerge in individual and group compositional settings. Doing things as a community in this way means teachers will find that the children's learning is so much stronger, that they remember things better and that they are learning things that the teacher had not planned for.

CREATING COMMUNITIES OF COMPOSITIONAL PRACTICE

What follows are ideas developed by Melbourne-based primary music educator and community musician Gillian Howell, whose work has evolved in intercultural environments in Australia and beyond, and in particular with recently arrived refugee and immigrant children. Gillian's workshops explore creativity through collaborative composition activities and utilise visual and other modes of expression to generate musical material and develop it into large-scale compositions. Students and teachers together form a collaborative community and this encourages teachers to further examine their own understanding of creativity. For Gillian, being imaginative (using imaginative play to move children beyond established patterns of thought and from the known to the unknown towards the generation of new fields of ideas) and exploring for the purpose of discovery (experimenting and taking risks, openness to new ideas and experiences) is how she typically engages in the process of teaching for creativity and how she approaches teaching music creatively. She does not go for simple activities that are deemed to be age-appropriate but rather works from simple starting points involving *exploratory* and *discovery* play processes from which larger creative projects are developed along with more complex material that trusts in the creative capabilities of the children as collaborating composers. She asks 'How can children reveal what they can hear and imagine?' and 'What are the qualities of compositional voice you [the teacher] want to hear? What are the compositional voices the children want to share?'

Most importantly, creative activities take place in an encouraging and accepting space, where all ideas are welcome and no one has all the answers. Gillian feels strongly that every idea that gets blocked or dismissed (whether overtly or implicitly) can discourage everyone in the group. Some children will offer their ideas in jest, or to make their friends laugh, but there are often gems contained in these casually tossed offerings! Similarly, less verbal children may reveal preferences through unconscious twiddling or 'noodling' – Gillian pays attention to all of these. Indeed, these moments of cautious or unconscious musical offering are where children may first share rhythms, melodies or other musical elements from their own musical worlds and cultural backgrounds. The alert teacher remains highly attuned to these offers (even if they happen informally or at a time when the children's focus should be elsewhere), ready to respond, encourage and perhaps incorporate them into the classroom composing. Not only does this make for more diverse compositions, it validates and encourages the unique cultural contributions each individual in the class can make. This can be incredibly empowering for those coming from minority backgrounds, or who are recent arrivals in the country or the school. Ideas will flow when everyone feels safe to share their thoughts – however unformed or approximate – and take creative risks with the group.

What follows is an activity that utilises the Flexible Score (see Activity 4.3) and invites children to represent the complexity of a sound – its shape, texture, colour and duration – through visual means. The focus on visual rather than verbal depictions creates important intercultural possibilities. It opens up space for those less comfortable articulating their ideas to describe their experience of sounds in richly expressive ways. In Gillian's music workshops with recently arrived immigrant children, visual elements play an important scaffolding role in communicating musical ideas (Howell, 2009, 2011).

Activity 4.1 'Sound into image' – a composition-based music workshop using visual and aural modelling for Early Years children

Step	Activity	Teacher role
1. Discussing, negotiating and agreeing on a specific vocabulary	As a group, discuss sound properties, labelling sounds as 'wet' (very resonant, long-ringing), 'dry' (sounds with little or no resonance and/or fast decay) or 'sticky' (any sounds that are in between the two extremes).	Establish the definitions with the group. I find the metaphor of a stone being dropped into a pool of water (and creating long-lasting ripples), contrasted with the same stone dropped on sand (and creating a small indentation) as a useful visual representation of the concept of wet and dry sounds.
2. Exploring and experimenting	Explore a range of instruments by playing sounds one at a time and deciding if they are wet, dry or sticky.	Depending on the class size and age of the children, this can be done in small groups, spread around the room or in a circle, each child with an instrument.
3. Deciding, listening, evaluating and cooperating	Children select an instrument and decide on a way to play it. They listen carefully to its sound.	This task requires an instrument for each child. Nontraditional sound sources can be used alongside conventional percussion instruments. Encourage the children to listen carefully to their instrument's sound, noting its wetness, dryness or stickiness. They may need space from each other to do this. Avoid 'problem-solving' for the children – this is about their considered response, rather than a 'right' or desired answer.

Step	Activity	Teacher role
4. Mapping, drawing, representing and visualising sound ideas	Each child draws a visual representation of their sound on a piece of A4.	The teacher will need to prompt children's thinking with questions, in order to help them translate their sound into visual information. I find the following questions useful: *Is it a big or small sound? Is it a bright or dark colour? Is it a smooth or jagged sound (considering the way the child has chosen to play it)? Is it constant, or broken up?*
5. Trying out and finalising ideas, rehearsing, honing and critiquing outcomes	Put all the images on a wall with blue tack, with the children assembled in front of it with their instruments. It can be just a random, arbitrary order at this stage. The teacher points to each image in turn and the child plays the appropriate sound. The group then decides how they would like to order the images, to create a class composition. Move the pages around the wall until you find an order that everyone is happy with. Play it through as you experiment and test out the new ideas.	The questions help children begin to imagine their sound as an image and will encourage them to commit an idea to paper. Again, the teacher will need to encourage thoughtful responses from the group with careful questions and some suggestions of their own. Try these questions: *What combinations did you think sounded particularly effective or interesting? Which sounds flowed smoothly into each other? Did you like that? Which sound would make a good beginning/ending?* You may wish to group wet sounds together and dry sounds together. Initially, it is often helpful for the teacher to model the score's flexibility and the decision-making process: 'I liked the sound of these two together. Shall we put them at the beginning/middle/end?' while actively moving the pages. You may also find you need some sounds to be repeated several times. If possible, ask that child to make multiple copies of their drawing.
6. Performing and recording	Perform the piece from start to finish. Record it on video, or in audio format for later reflection.	Create some formality around the performance; make sure everyone is ready and in place. Explain that the bit of wall right before the first image is silence, as is the bit of wall after the last image. Point to these to start and end the piece and maintain the group's focus.

Step	Activity	Teacher role
7. Reflecting on the journey	Upload the recording to Soundcloud or similar so that it can be shared more widely. Listen to the recording as a group and discuss individual contributions and ideas, as well as the group achievement.	You can use the timed comments feature of Soundcloud for individual students to label their own sound where they hear it, encouraging their ownership and sense of connection to the group work.
8. Revising in the light of feedback and reviewing whether any aspects of the piece need improving	Group discussion of whether any ideas need revising. Shared views on editing and new idea formation or whether there are further improvements to make in the piece and/or performance aspects. This may be the time that peer-assessment of stated criteria (collaboratively developed) is discussed.	At this point of the evaluative process the teacher's role as facilitator becomes critical. Use of a shared and inclusive language to describe, communicate and evaluate ideas and their implementation is important, as is the use of questions to guide children's critical evaluation and thinking. This means consultation and listening of the highest order rather than ready-made assumptions about what constitutes 'good' and 'bad'. Remind the students that this is *their* work. They can add or change anything that they want. An awareness of context is important. Was there an overarching intention for the piece? As a group, consider how effectively this has been realised or communicated, revisiting earlier metaphors (e.g. of a stone being dropped into a pool of water and creating long-lasting ripples). The evaluation process can also place the group composition into a broader context. What parallel compositional techniques and music conventions have been used in this piece? Encourage them to consider some of the musical decisions they chose *not* to make (e.g. instruments chosen, playing techniques utilised). How might the music sound if other choices were made? Lastly, invite the children to consider their revision process. Were they revising the work as they went, or at the end? Ask thoughtful questions necessary for children to discover what might be profitable for revision. Let them be the decision-makers and exercise independence as change seekers.

■ **Figure 4.1** Students create graphic symbols for a flexible score. (Image courtesy of Gillian Howell. Photography by Tarrant Kwok.)

Flexible scoring, as used in Activity 4.1 and shown in Figure 4.1, where the individual elements in a piece of music are identified and isolated on separate pieces of paper and reordered as desired, encourages students to experiment with and consider the many ways that their invented musical sounds, textures, motifs and sections can be combined and organised to make a substantial piece of music. Indeed, it is this iterative process of inventing, trying, adapting, changing and changing again that really emphasizes to the students the creative power they have. The following quote from a teacher in a Melbourne English Language School for primary-aged recently arrived immigrant/refugee children (for whom teacher-talk about 'composing' or 'songwriting' or 'improvising' would simply not be understood yet), describes the way the students become more aware of their ownership of the music being developed:

> Maybe they don't understand at the beginning, but I think it clicks that it is their music because of the way it's changed. 'Oh yeah, this suits us better, so forget about that, now we're doing this!' [. . .] It is actually changing all the time until we get to the one that suits us. Especially the older ones, I think they know they've got the input [. . .] I think they're very proud when they've put it together, done a concert [. . .] proud of their ability, and of the fact that they're playing music that no-one has ever played.
> – Alice, class teacher at MELS
>
> (Howell, 2011, p. 53)

The next critical step in the composing process is making decisions about the desired way to order and organise the sounds into a (more) fixed composition. Children will quickly become adept at inventing and creating sounds, textures and patterns; however, the structural decisions about order and form can be more complex to develop. Consideration of frequently heard music conventions is a helpful way to focus the group's thinking about form and structure. Music from around the world and across eras is likely to share some structural conventions (i.e. ways of combining and organising sounds to create interest and effect), forms or ways of organising the musical material. Structural conventions are particularly useful, because they are familiar (we have all heard them, even if we haven't labelled them before), they work across all genres and they provide the framework that helps us to organise our musical ideas.

Gillian Howell uses the following structural conventions to guide the students in organising their musical ideas and creating contrast and interest:

- The fade-in (starting quietly, getting louder).
- The fade-out (going from loud to quiet).
- Layering in the instruments/parts one by one.
- Dropping out one by one.
- The surprise (something unexpected that takes the music in a new direction or gets the audience's attention; surprises can involve a new/unfamiliar musical idea and may also act to spotlight the return of more familiar material).
- The chorus or refrain (a section of music that returns several times through the structure – its familiarity creates a sense of order for the listener, and anchoring points for the ensemble).
- The big–small–big overall structure.
- The small–big–small overall structure.
- Moments of total silence.
- The big finish (where there is consistent build-up to a mighty, emphatic musical ending).
- Beginning–middle–ending (as with a story, where something needs to happen in the middle of the piece in order to create the need for an ending).
- A storyline or narrative (using the beginning–middle–ending structure and getting children to create a simple three-sentence story to use as a frame).
- Ternary form, a piece of music with three distinct sections but only two contrasting sections of music. One section is played twice in the structure – first and last – and the other is played once only, in the middle.
- Intensifying the musical parameters (sudden as opposed to gradual change in all parameters; for example, from slow to fast notes or from large to small intervals, from dramatic contrasts in pitch or rhythm or increasing in tempo at the same time as getting lower and slowing down).

There are many others. Drawing attention to the use of these and other conventions during classroom listening sessions is a useful strategy for helping children to recognise these as real compositional devices and to understand their overall musical effect.

Aim to include conventions that can be heard in multiple musical styles and genres. Refer to the conventions when making decisions about how to organise your invented musical material. Note that these conventions are primarily *structural*, and useful for *ordering* musical ideas. Other compositional decisions involve choices about expressive and narrative qualities, such as levels of intensity, or deliberate efforts to invoke a particular emotion or feeling. These can be explored concurrently with structural decisions or as a separate step.

Listen to any songs or pieces of music that you like and see if, together as a class, you can hear any of the above conventions or if you can identify and create labels for some others. Don't neglect to include music of different cultures – this is an opportunity to enrich the students' listening experiences as well as provide opportunities to note the different and like ways that music is organised in different cultures and genres. Significantly, this is a listening task that does not require the teacher to be more confident or experienced than students as it is a journey of shared discovery and discussion where the goal is to discern structural patterns a composer has employed that could be replicated in the classroom. However, as part of their lesson preparation, the teacher may choose to let them do some focussed music listening on their own or with friends, prior to undertaking it with a class, in order to practice identifying and labelling different compositional conventions. Listening to music with friends is a pleasurable way to prepare a lesson!

One of the main goals of this preparatory process is to create a shared vocabulary for ideas and discussion. This makes it possible for students to play an active role in deciding how to organise their chosen sounds, and to experiment with placing their sounds into different structures. Some will work better than others, but all can be tried. The vocabulary enables broad participation, because it is created in situ and evolves collaboratively. This brings the added benefit of enabling rather than alienating participation, particularly for those who have little previous experience of music making, for there are no right or wrong answers, only musical ideas to try out and select. Activity 4.2 illustrates the open-ended nature of this process.

Activity 4.2 Gillian's creative workshop for exploring music conventions to structure a collaborative composition

Step	Activity	Teacher role
1.	As a group, discuss the above list of conventions.	Describe each convention or invite descriptions from the class. Help the group to differentiate between similar conventions, e.g. the fade-in and the layering in of parts one by one. Try some out using body percussion in order to give each student a tangible experience of their expressive impact.
2.	Listen to three contrasting pieces of music. Discuss which of the above conventions you can hear in use. Add any others that are identified during the listening and discussion.	Select musical examples to play that you feel offer clear use of a particular convention (or several). You can also invite children to select a song to listen to. Using a playback platform that shows the waveform of the music gives a useful visual reference for pointing out where particular conventions appear. Encourage active, critical, focussed listening. You may wish to play only short excerpts. Listening in this way is intense, and hard work.

Step	Activity	Teacher role
3.	On a piece of A3 paper draw a simple graphic symbol for each convention, using black markers on white paper or a similarly strong contrast (these pages will need to be seen from a distance).	Have the students work in groups of two or three to plan their design. Alternatively, if time is short, you can create these symbols yourself. These pages can be used in multiple composition and improvisation projects, so you may wish to laminate them.

The music convention symbols created through this task can also be Blu Tacked to the wall in later composition projects that utilise Flexible Scores. For example, if the class decides to follow a big–small–big structure for their composition, they can consider which of the individual sounds/textures/motifs they have best suits a 'big' or 'small' section of music and group these sounds under the 'big' or 'small' symbol as appropriate. If the group decides they want to include a musical 'surprise', they can place this symbol on the wall above the score and decide which of their bank of possible sounds will most effectively create this 'surprise'.

Learning to recognise the structural conventions in familiar pieces of music takes practice as it requires a very active, focussed approach to listening. Musical memory also plays an important part. These are skills that can be developed by the whole class – teacher and students – together. Practice gives experience, and experience leads to confidence. Confidence in music, the most abstract of all the art forms, gives the community of learners a sense of their own success and motivates them to continue to grow and progress. Encouraging a team approach to music making, and instilling a sense of ownership and responsibility both in the process and in the final product, is integral to developing the learning culture and community of composers that will forge new pathways together.

Children's musical creativity does not follow a linear path (see Figure 4.2). Be prepared to explore each idea as it arises and worry later about where it might be used, expanded, reduced, fixed or finalised. This is characteristic of children's approaches. The key message here, and a theme threaded throughout this book, is, as Abbs (2003, p. 17) expressed so cogently:

Education exists to set up a conversation down the ages and across the cultures, across both time and space, so that students are challenged by other ways of understanding and, at the same time, acquiring ever new materials – metaphors, models, ideas, images, narratives, facts – for shaping and reshaping and testing again that never finished process, their own intellectual and spiritual lives.

Abbs (2003, p. 17)

Intro / build-up

■ **Figure 4.2** A graphic symbol for an 'intro: build-up' convention. (Image courtesy of Gillian Howell.)

Gillian's exemplary activity of the Flexible Score project resonates with the emphasis on shaping and reshaping, and integrating new ideas into children's work as they arise. This is collaborative and creative work, foregrounding skills that prepare children not only to cope with a quickly evolving, globalised world, but also to develop creative dispositions and creative skills that will sustain and advance culture. The outline below of the Flexible Score approach can be adapted to suit all sorts of composition projects that generate music in discrete sections, by small groups or individuals. It demonstrates the way a Flexible Score supports students' thoughtful and considered decision-making about musical structure and composition. The flexible format of individual pages makes it simple to reorder the sounds in order to experiment with different combinations, and the visual representation removes the need for children with ideas to be able to explain these verbally. Rather, they can *show* what they would like to hear, and this makes for a more inclusive and accessible creative process (see Figure 4.3).

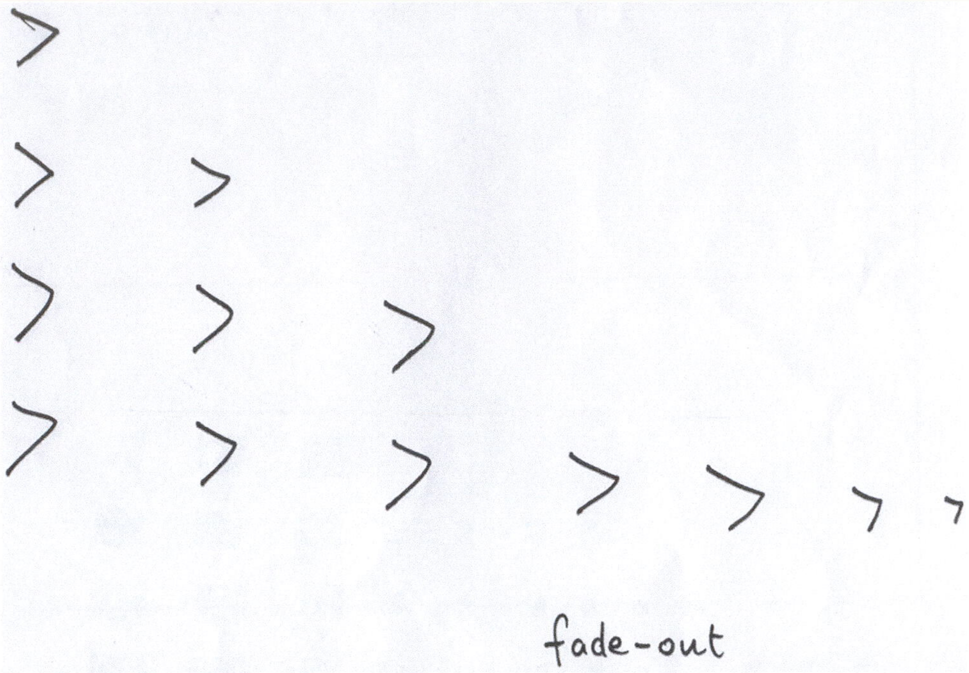

Figure 4.3 Graphic symbol for a 'fade-out'. (Image courtesy of Gillian Howell.)

Activity 4.3 Musical meanings, symbol use and compositional pathways

Step	Activity	Teacher role
1.	Create sections of music, using the earlier 'Sound Into Image' explorations or other methods of sound generation.	Children can do this in small groups or alone.
2.	Give the section of music a name (e.g. 'the footsteps section', 'the twinkly bit') and write it on a page (or create a graphic symbol to represent it). There should be one separate page of A4/A3 for each short section of music, sound or musical idea.	The names are useful markers and descriptors (e.g. 'let's start again from the footsteps section') so they should bear some relationship to the music! It's also helpful if images are recognisable for the whole group, not just the creator – but this is not essential.

Step	Activity	Teacher role
3.	Spread all the pages on the floor or Blu Tack them to a long empty wall where the whole group can see them. Start with an arbitrary order, but proceed to move the pages (names or graphic images) around as desired, in order to explore possible structures and the ultimate order of the piece.	Blu Tack is important – if you use glue or tape, you lock the order of the music in place. Being able to move the pages in order to try out different combinations helps the group to decide what they like best and how to structure the piece. Remember you can experiment with vertical (concurrent) combinations as well as horizontal (consecutive). Teachers may also choose to utilise music convention symbols at this stage to help guide the structural decision-making. If someone has a new structural idea – try it! Playing things through (rather than just imagining them) is incredibly important at this stage, as it validates the contributions of individuals and demonstrates that all ideas are possible and have merit. It also engages and develops the children's critical listening skills. In time, the group will become skilled at audiating (hearing in the mind) the sounds represented by the images, recognising the qualities of each sound or music section and hearing different possible combinations in their heads.
4.	Decide an order and play it through in order to assess it. Discuss any changes you might like to make and the reasons for these.	Encourage the students to critique their work and make thoughtful changes. Ask questions to trigger their thinking: *What did you like in the order we just played? Did the sections flow well? Did the music have a sense of shape and logic to it? What sections didn't work as well as others? How could we further enhance the most dramatic/peaceful/quiet/powerful moments? Does our piece communicate what we want it to?*
5.	Move the pages around and play it through again, repeating this step as many times as you like. It may take several iterations until you find the one that suits the whole group.	The decision-making the students engage in with the Flexible Score is painstaking and can feel frustrating, but it is important. It takes creative work beyond the invention of sounds into structuring, ordering and combining. The Flexible Score makes this process visible for the students.

As teachers, we need to help children do more than simply experience composing; rather, we should help them to develop a composition-orientated vocabulary for talking about composing and reflecting on their learning as composers. Children get great satisfaction out of talking about diverse creativities in relation to their own composing processes and authorship of compositions. They need to feel that it is legitimate for them to contribute actively to discussions about composing and make sense of their own engagement and meaning making as composers. The language needs to be culturally inclusive (e.g. 'cycle' applies to African and Indian music, not 'bar', which is a Western term and relates more to notation than to aural experience. Similarly, 'cluster' not 'chord', and 'keynotes' not 'Tonic and Dominant'). Equally, the musical palette needs to be inclusive in terms of both children's interests and experience *and* teachers'. Sounds and rhythms that reflect the diversity of children's backgrounds and interests can only enhance the music and generate strong feelings of ownership and agency among the young composers. It is crucial that teachers truly access and connect with every child's culture. We do not suggest that this is easy but recognise that it requires commitment, patience, taking chances and collaborating with each other as a learning community.

CONCLUSIONS

Children and teachers learn best from each other in a partnership environment where the learning community is informed by exploration in practice and where risk-taking is encouraged. As teachers realign priorities to the learning community landscape, encourage the exchange of ideas and approaches and explore the potential that everyone has to compose and create in a focussed environment where children have a voice, teacher confidence should prevail and their own identity as composers can begin to be redefined (see Figure 4.4). When

■ **Figure 4.4** Labels for a flexible score. (Image courtesy of Gillian Howell. Photography by Tarrant Kwok.)

teachers give themselves permission to act as facilitators of compositional activities (rather than being the ones with all the answers), they will become part of an enabling community of musical practice in which children and teachers share the joy of creating music together.

NOTES

1 Musical creativity need not just involve teacher and student but also visitors to the learning community such as local cultural and community artists or experts from the digital music world community. Engaging in partnerships with others involved in real world practices and settings makes learning more relevant, useful and transferable. Dynamic communities of practice are seen as critical elements of situated creativity. See Burnard (2012) for considering composition practices in a number of contexts. Also see Odena and Welch (2012) and how teachers' perceptions of creativity and the influence of their backgrounds on their perceptions develop and influence their practice as teachers. (Both chapters are published in an edited book *Musical Creativity: Insights from Music Education Research*, Farnham, Surrey: Ashgate.)

FURTHER READING

Campbell, P. and Higgins, L. (2010) *Free to Be Musical.* New York: Rowman & Littlefield.
Glover, J. (2000) *Children Composing 4–14.* London: Routledge.
Howell, G. (2009) From imitation to invention: Issues and strategies for the ESL music classroom. *Musicworks: Journal of the Australia Council of Orff Schulwerk*, 14(1), 61–66.
Howell, G. (2011) Do they know they're composing?: Music making and understanding among newly arrived immigrant and refugee children. *International Journal of Community Music*, 4(1), 47–58.

CHAPTER 5

BECOMING PERFORMERS
Creating participatory spaces collaboratively

Pamela Burnard with Emily Okuno, Jenny Boyack, Gillian Howell, Deborah Blair and Marcelo Giglio

INTRODUCTION

At the heart of collective and connected learning experiences, particularly in the performing arts, lies the role and nature of *participation.* As with the processes of group improvisation and composition, the principles of leadership for facilitating participatory practices in the primary classroom involve teachers working as coaches for musical performance and as collaborative participators in specific performance organisation, orientation and activity. Reflecting on what makes for creative teaching distinguishes the *creative workshop*, *educational culture* or *learning environment* from the practice of 'painting by numbers' where product, rather than process, dominates. Working as a learning community, in a creative environment which supports live music making and personal development, the primary classroom needs to address a wide range of interests and experiences. Engaging children collaboratively in participatory practices means all parties should be open to the other's views, regardless of whether or not they are expressing an opinion in the other's area of expertise or interest (Cooper and McIntyre, 1993). The key characteristics of enacting a facilitative leadership role in this context and way of thinking are described by Eisner (2004, p. 10), who talks about a vision of what schools are for and of what values creative practice should have:

> a greater focus on becoming than on being, places more value on the imaginative than on the factual, assigns greater priority to valuing than to measuring, and regards the quality of the journey as more educationally significant than the speed at which the destination is reached.

The message here, and it is essential to be clear from the outset about what is meant by *participation in music*, is that the teacher needs to take on a facilitatory rather than an instructive role. Participation is usually understood to mean hands-on involvement in a process. But engagement with music – whether as listeners, creators, makers, players or performers – is an *active* act. The interrelatedness of these roles or expressive modes of behaviour or communication is what makes participation in music such a creative and collective pursuit. Whether the performance is improvisational, based on notated compositions, or a mix of both, whether the performer is a 'specialist' singer, violinist, dancer, actor, composer or an 'all round' performer who can (from memory) sing, dance, tell stories, compose and improvise, music performance is a vehicle for artistic communication, collaborative decision-making and engaging creatively with one's environment, which encourages a team approach to music making, and instils a sense of ownership and responsibility both in the process and in the final product. Exchange of ideas and skills among the participants becomes an integral part of the process, thus deepening one's understanding of, and connection with, music. In particular, the chapter will explore:

- Creating collaborative spaces for performance communities.
- Inclusive spaces for engaging all children as creative performers.
- Spaces for celebrating collaborative performances.
- Moving from rehearsal through to performance spaces.

Children and their teachers can be empowered participants as performers, arrangers, improvisers, composers, conductors and listeners if they engage democratically in participation practices. Final performances from creative workshop processes *do not have to* have rhythms, melodies, harmonies, structure and notation, and they *do not have to* involve instruments, professional musicians and special venues. They do, however, usually contain three elements:

- Music collaboratively derived in the workshop.
- Repertoire considered and materials collaboratively prepared outside the workshops.
- Improvisation, collaboratively informed by the nature of the previous two elements.

But how can teachers establish an exploratory, questioning, risk-taking, reflective, inquisitive and consensual space into which they can introduce children to working collaboratively? Does this mean operating at the edge of chaos? Resisting the temptation to impose too much order? Classroom rules of engagement and strategies give value to new ideas, even if an idea appears at odds with the prevailing stasis, and give children more control in exchange for positive learning commitment on the grounds that it can be challenging. So what do teachers and children bring into the space for learning that will support developing a sense of community? What are the conditions for emergence and fostering (and sustaining) such a learning culture?

Even performing small and personal (rather than collective) performances provides an interactive and participatory means for children to claim ownership of learning and knowledge creation through active involvement in its presentation, whereby they are enabled by everyone to share and collaborate. The ultimate success of participatory and performance-based learning journeys may be uncomfortable and risky at times, but these shared experiences and a supportive class ethos will enable everyone to flourish in what they bring into the space and what they take away (see Figure 5.1). Each of these characteristics will be outlined with reference to examples of children as musicians and performers and of the development of children's musical performances, followed by a section suggesting ways in which teachers can incorporate this performance-based focus into classroom musical practice.

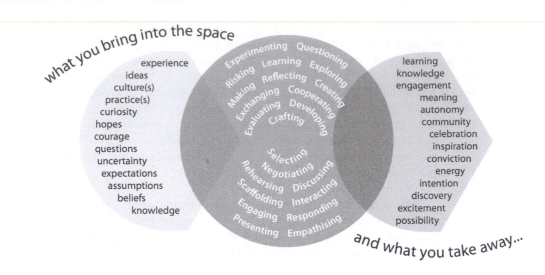

what you bring into the space

experience
ideas
culture(s)
practice(s)
curiosity
hopes
courage
questions
uncertainty
expectations
assumptions
beliefs
knowledge

Experimenting Questioning
Risking Learning Exploring
Making Reflecting Creating
Exchanging Cooperating
Evaluating Developing
Crafting

Selecting
Negotiating
Rehearsing Discussing
Scaffolding Interacting
Engaging Responding
Presenting Empathising

learning
knowledge
engagement
meaning
autonomy
community
celebration
inspiration
conviction
energy
intention
discovery
excitement
possibility

and what you take away...

■ **Figure 5.1** The space of collaborative performance practice.

CREATING PARTICIPATORY SPACES IN COLLABORATIVE COMMUNITIES

Music is a conversation in which no one partner has exclusive control. The construal of music making as being about the production and reproduction of songs is only part of the story. Composing involves improvising and performing involves improvisatory dimensions; the lines between composition and performance are hardly neat. Playing and singing 'in time' or 'in tune', and what Laurence (in Harrison, 2007) refers to when making music with children as 'the empathic relationship' (pp. 10–11), is where working cooperatively on a performance involves:

> empathising [where] we enter actively and imaginatively into others' inner states to understand how they experience their world and how they are feeling, reaching out to what we perceive as similar while accepting differences, within a context in which we care about their well being and our shared humanity. We need, and can learn, both cognitive and affective capacities for empathising . . . In an empathic relationship we are more interested in sharing power rather than exercising it over others – so this tends towards being non-hierarchical. There is also a willingness to really strive to understand another person, and also to enhance that person's possibilities rather than to limit them.
>
> (Laurence, 2007)

Thus, participatory practices constantly strive to celebrate living culture, where the physical and human resources, the ideas to be presented, the experiential background of the participants, the range of instruments and expertise available and the performance context (classroom, hospital ward, concert hall, competition, etc.) involve educationally shared values achieved within a collaborative enabling and inclusive forum. One such cooperative context shows empathic relationships, where each child's voice is encouraged and where all others listen well to those voices which arise (multi-voicedness) from joint activity. This is where creating and communicating music are readily defined by children as the force within their own particular pathways of learning in a real collaborative space. The potential of making use of resources beyond the school gates leads to children working alongside community musicians and connecting with the wider community of ideas and practices.

Case study 5.1: Narrative of children preparing for performance activities in West Kenya

1. Children creating music

It is a few minutes before noon, on a sunny, fresh day in Sagam Primary School, a coeducational day school set among the rolling hills of Yala Division in Gem, Siaya county of Western Kenya. On a day like this, learners engage in a variety of performance-creative activities, whose final destination is the performance stage for the school prize-giving festivities.

The class teacher of this Standard 6[1] group of learners, Miss Achieng, had earlier announced to the class her wish that they prepare music for the occasion. She had then taught a four-line short song, with words that pronounced a welcome message to the invited guests. The learners were in the middle of a rehearsal when visited by Eric, an intern from Germany attached to Professor Akuno of Maseno University, who recorded what he observed.

Pupil 1 [speaking in Kiswahili, the national language]:	We are pupils from Standard 6. We are going to sing a song in praise of the guest of honour.
Pupil 2:	[sings the opening line, as a cue for pitch and tempo]
Pupil 2 [spoken]:	Three, sing.
All:	[Sing the song as taught]
Pupil 2:	[Interjects a call at the end of the 'official song']
All:	[Respond with the last line of the song]

At this juncture, several pupils interject, at which point the final line of the song becomes the response. After a few 'calls' the original short song, now transformed into a kind of refrain, is sung by all. A number of pupils then take turns calling out short phrases, to which the chorus (class) respond. This call–response and chorus design is repeated one more time. The song ends eventually with the original four-line song.

In this narrative, the short song that was initiated by the teacher becomes the theme around which learners create a complete song. The four lines, typically a double period, make a tune that lends itself to subdivision. This allows for extension through the addition of clauses that act as calls to which a line of the original short song becomes the response.

Learners deliberately and systematically take turns adding their own individual texts with matching tunes. Having known the cultural occasion for song preparation, learners generate lyrics that are appropriate to the songs becoming appropriate to their function. It is this performance occasion that allows learners to transform the original song through their personal, innovative input.

2. Performance

The Kenya Music Festival takes place annually during the second term of the three-term academic year. Competitions begin in May and finish during the second week of August, with participants moving upwards from a local to regional and eventually a national performance stage.

One of the categories of competition at these festivals is called 'Singing Games' and is further organised in two classes: African and Western Style. For these classes, 6- to 8-year-old children transfer playground songs and activities to a stage in a performance hall. In so doing, the role of the music transforms from the edutainment of the performers to serve the function of entertaining observing guests. With this knowledge, some pupils retain the spontaneity that characterises childhood music making, while others appear to know how to pause and wait for the applause/laughter to die.

In these games, mockery songs, for example, are acted out, with the object of the song's ridicule taking on that role and playing out the appropriate response to criticism, i.e. crying or moodily walking off. Participation in these games presents learners in multiple roles:

1   Musician: the learners actually perform the music, demonstrating a level of mastery of the music, lyrics and accompanying movement.
2   Educator: one of the roles of childhood songs is the education of the participants. The words of these songs demonstrate learners' awareness of several issues in society, as children's songs are also a reflection of societal experiences.
3   Entertainment: this is the third dimension that concert-stage performance of singing games adds to these songs. This is purely for the delight of a watching audience. It is far and separate from the salient entertainment of the participating pupils, who benefit from this on a different level. These three are aspects of communication, which in turn is an element that is learnt through participation in music making. Through performance, the young children take on the serious roles of performers, which, in this context, is also the role of an educator. When performance is located on the concert stage, the additional role of entertainer is realised.

It is therefore clear that even children, age being no limitation, actively engage in serious music making activities. (Emily Okuno, West Kenya)

STRATEGIES FOR ENGAGING ALL CHILDREN AS CREATIVE PERFORMERS

Another way of exploring not only into the collaborative performance of music but into becoming more empathic in making music with children is to conceptualise the 'doing' of music as it is essentially concerned with human interrelationships, which is an idea explored by Christopher Small, who coined the term *musicking* to express it (Small, 1998). Small argued that in musicking we make and uphold our own 'ideal' relationships, so that the power of musical sounds acts together with the feelings and responses we experience while making, playing, singing, listening to – or even dancing to – these sounds, in order to enable us to form and 'celebrate' these relationships. We see this celebration enabled in the following activity, which is contributed by Jenny Boyack, teacher educator, Massey University, New Zealand.

Activity 5.1 Let your instrument tell a story

Human beings are creative with language every day of their lives. By the age of five or six children have mastered an impressive array of language skills and conventions, can utilise a wide range of expressive techniques to engage an audience, communicate increasingly complex ideas and respond confidently to others' contributions.

We can encourage young children to make music in ways that are similar to their making of stories. It helps if a class set (plus a few more!) of percussion instruments is one of your regular classroom resources. Teachers don't need to play an instrument or read music to try the following mat-time activity.

Choose an instrument from the box and tell the children that it wants to 'speak' to them. They will listen intently as you improvise a short story on your drum or tambourine or claves. Bring a child forward to choose an instrument that has a conversation with your instrument. Perhaps ask another child to join you for a three-way conversation. I wouldn't interpret my story in words and neither would I ask the children to translate their own or anyone else's musical stories. Let them focus on exploring what their instrument can communicate in its own voice.

This simple way of opening up improvisation can be the start of an infinite number of musical storytelling possibilities. In the process of exploring classroom percussion instruments in this way, and as a result of listening to their classmates' offerings, children develop a repertoire of musical ideas similar to the linguistic ideas they develop through daily language interactions. Here are some ideas:

- The children work in pairs with their instruments to have musical conversations. After a time they find a different partner for a different conversation.
- Ask the children to use ideas from their musical conversations to develop a short musical story with a beginning, middle and end. Remind them that in their story the instruments can speak on their own and together. As they get

more confident with this activity, increase the size of the groups, provide a 'topic' for the story or some other motivational starter, set parameters for the story just as you might for a written language exercise, experiment with different performance formats, get them to illustrate their stories and so on.

▨ Tell the children that their chosen instrument has a sad or happy story to tell them, or a secret to share, or an exciting adventure to relate. They should find a space on their own in the classroom and listen while their instrument talks to them.

▨ Have a musical 'news' time. One child chooses an instrument and tells that instrument's 'news' to the class. You can use the 'any questions' routine with musical news just as you do with spoken news. Two or three children choose an instrument to ask a question with and the child at the front responds.

For all these activities, teachers need to be ready to model, provide guidance and set boundaries – this is usually to do with the length of the musical stories! And they need to listen to how the children's expressiveness, confidence, inventiveness and enjoyment grow through engagement in these composition and improvisation activities/performances.

Children enjoy playing and performing together. Performance briefs can include performing music for neighbouring primary school assemblies or for parents. Playing something original, reworking other people's music, or showcasing a term's whole-class improvised and composed pieces, along with the performance of some group improvised pieces and solo performance items from members of the class, can entail the development of all sorts of dynamic skills which articulate the relationships within the group. Who leads and who follows? What influences the musical outcomes? How are social outcomes related to the musical design and organisation of the performance? How does the performance mirror the relationships between the learning communities?

Musical performance, as an activity, provides a paradigm for most of the rest of our lives. Having a conversation with someone involves rules of engagement and conventions of grammar, during which time we manage to keep an idea alive, develop themes, make jokes or solve problems. Most of all, in conversation we are supporting and enhancing the relationship with the person we are talking with. Interaction in music places the same emphasis on interpersonal and emotional dimensions. Building a collaborative space (as shown earlier in Figure 5.1) provides a platform for team building – creative choice – whereby enabling and communicating empathic relationships come from what you bring into the collaborative performance space and what you take away from coming together to collaboratively perform music (Mills, 1993).

BECOMING COLLABORATIVE PERFORMERS

Gillian Howell is a creative director and community musician who works with groups of people, including those in primary school communities, to develop artistic practices and perform original music. As an artist-in-residence and workshop facilitator in diverse cultural and creative contexts, Gillian has worked across Australia, in remote aboriginal communities, in East Timor and several other post-conflict and developing countries with primary school age children, collaborating together on songwriting projects, workshops and music-making events. The Alphabet Dance project was first developed with recently arrived immigrant and refugee children in transitional English Language Schools in Melbourne, Australia and links literacy goals with creative dance, ensemble work and performance.

The Alphabet Dance (upper primary)

This is a collaborative music, dance and literacy project that takes place over a series of consecutive teaching occasions. If the goal is to complete a full 'alphabet' of dance moves and use these to choreograph short routines, working in weekly or bi-weekly increments across a school term is an effective timeframe. Consider developing the Alphabet Dance (Figure 5.2) as part of the class's daily physical activity and to enhance literacy work and spelling. It's an engaging and creative way to get students moving and utilising other knowledge (cultural knowledge, literacy, spelling, etc.) in a collaborative performance project. The Alphabet Dance was designed to build confidence and engagement with spelling for English language learners, but the model can be applied successfully to other languages as well and is a dynamic vehicle for multimodal intercultural classroom learning and sharing.

Activity 5.2 The Alphabet Dance

	Step	Activity	Teacher role
1.	Exploring and developing material	As a group, assign a dance move to each letter of the alphabet, then practise and memorise it. This can be done as a whole-class or small-group activity.	Students can suggest dance moves from any style or genre – it's ideal if the moves reflect their interests and cultures. The moves don't need to flow at this stage – the focus is on creating twenty-six different moves, rather than sequences. The teacher will need to invite or elicit suggestions for moves from a range of students and encourage the group to go over the letter-moves they have created, in order to refine and memorise them. Ideally the teacher is dancing and learning alongside the students.
2.	Sequencing	Once the alphabet is complete, students work in small groups to develop dance sequences that spell out words, phrases or full sentences.	This task requires teamwork and patience. Allow the work to develop incrementally over a series of consecutive teaching occasions. The teacher is encouraging and reassuring students, becoming familiar with each of the sequences and reminding groups to work slowly at first, to maintain focus and to work as a team.

	Step	Activity	Teacher role
3.	Creating a 'unison'	The whole class develops a short sequence of moves to use as a 'unison' chorus, in their eventual choreography.	This task is teacher-facilitated, but with their small-group work behind them students will be able to offer forward suggestions and put them into action to create this unison sequence.
4.	Selecting form and structure	Watch each group's sequence. Decide an order in which they will be performed.	Ask open-ended questions and prompts to facilitate the students' decision-making in structuring their dance. *Is one of these sequences a strong finish? Which is a good opening? Should they flow from one to the next or should we intersperse them with the unison sequence? What are the other groups doing when one is performing? Can any of the sequences be performed simultaneously? How many times will we perform the unison sequence in the whole piece?*
5.	Trying and critiquing	Run through the suggested order and see if all are happy with it. Change the order of segments (though not of sequences) until you have a structure that everyone is happy with.	Encourage students to consider their choices critically, and to try out more than one possible structure. The teacher is a fellow collaborator here and should make their own observations of strengths and weaknesses, leaving space for the students to propose solutions and alternatives.
6.	Rehearse and perform	Take time to rehearse slowly and frequently, as the Alphabet Dance needs to be memorised. Performances could be formal, in-school performances, but could also be planned as playground flash mobs, busking performances at the local shops and so on. Film the students' work and share with the local community via the Internet.	Explore different ways to support students to memorise their work for performance. In addition to regular, slow repetition, consider filming rehearsals and getting groups to watch and critique themselves; ask students to draw stick-figure diagrams of each of the letter-moves in their sequence or to sit in silence, mentally going through their sequence. As a teacher, you need to manage the pace of the rehearsal process to ensure students don't peak too soon before the performance date, or are not sufficiently prepared to give a satisfying showing of their creative work. Processing time is important for memory work – work regularly in short bursts rather than spending an extended single block of time on rehearsing and preparing.

■ **Figure 5.2** Photo of the Alphabet Dance. This image shows a large-scale Alphabet Dance
led by Gillian Howell at Federation Square, Melbourne, Australia, May 2012.
(Image courtesy of *The Song Room*. To see a full video of the Alphabet Dance,
please visit http://www. youtube.com/j51ER8Faqsc.)

FOSTERING COMMUNITIES OF PERFORMANCE PRACTICE

Allowing children to work creatively with their voices in whole-class, small-group and
individual activities not only provides for self-expression and the exploration of identity
but also fosters learner agency and ownership. There are many ways in which to make
vocal engagement a holistic experience. This can make vocal work accessible to all pupils
where the voice can be used as an instrument through which to experiment with creative
music performances such as songwriting, soundscapes, tone clusters and creating and performing graphic scores. Asking the class to bring a song which means something to them
can mark the start of creating a class songbook. This might include songs from their own
culture or specific songs which are sung at home or that are specific to playgrounds, out-
of-school clubs or social and cultural activities, all of which can be used to support the
fostering of a class community songbook. The following narrative provides one such
example drawn from a New Zealand primary school where Dave, a non-specialist primary
school teacher, adopted an approach to teaching music in his classroom that is shared by
Jenny Boyack, a Massey University music educator.

Case study 5.2: Incorporating children's collaborative creativity in a whole-class setting

Sometimes everyday classroom experiences provide a pathway into creative performance ventures. Dave is a primary teacher with a class of 6- and 7-year-olds. He plays the guitar and sings with the children most days. One afternoon the children were on the mat reading through a set of poems on large posters. You can probably imagine the scenario – 25+ children sitting cross-legged with their eyes fixed on the words and pictures, chanting rhythmically and expressively and repeating each poem two or three times before the teacher turned over to the next one.

Because they were going to be moving from poetry into a singing session, Dave absent-mindedly picked up his guitar and began to strum along using very simple chord progressions – maybe a D chord strummed a few times, then moving to a G, maybe an E minor thrown in for contrast, or an A and back to D. Nothing fancy or complicated. As the children chanted away above the gentle strumming, Dave noticed that they appeared to be listening to the chords and introducing a little melody into their chanting. He nodded encouragement and the children collectively began to pay attention to the tune that seemed to be emerging from the already stable rhythm. Each time the poem ended he took them back to the beginning without a break until a simple little tune had replaced the spoken chant. At this point Dave stopped and said 'we've made a song'. The children were amazed and delighted and eagerly repeated their song again and again, softly, slowly, smoothly, brightly, until it was firmly memorised – and Dave sensibly recorded it onto his laptop.

'Can we do another one?' Dave then flicked through the charts with them and together they chose a different poem to work with. They chanted it through a couple of times to ensure that the rhythm was steady and, once again, Dave strummed softly underneath the chanting. Once more, fragments of melody emerged from the children and he noted that there were everyday song conventions present in their tune – repeated patterns, playful use of syllables and words, rising and falling melodic shapes to fit with the length of the word phrases and sensitivity to the expressive features of the poem. And before they knew it, they had a second song.

When I visited Dave's class a few weeks later to observe a student teacher, at the end of the visit Dave asked, 'Would you like to hear our new songs?' By now their repertoire of original poem-songs had expanded considerably and the children were enthusiastic about performing them. The songs were simple and effective, beautifully matched to the content and mood of the different poems and clearly 'owned' by everyone.

This is something that could be tried using two or three chords (D, G and A on the guitar, or C, F and G on a ukulele) and a simple four-line poem. The secret is for the teacher to settle on a chord pattern and encourage the children to create a tune that works with it. Strum away and wait for a song to be born!

What is key here is the expectation and understanding on the part of the primary school teacher that his classroom should celebrate singing and song making as an ordinary part of learning. Teachers are song users, and by collaborating with child learners to choose

repertoire for singing but also to collaboratively create songs in a classroom setting, improvised singing can become an educational practice.

Case study 5.3: Deborah Blair's interdisciplinary starting points for facilitating performance opportunities

When teachers seek to include music in the classroom but are not sure where to start, I encourage them to begin with their own strengths so that they can approach the activity with confidence. These ideas are for teachers whose strengths may be in literature or language arts. Teachers might start with a scene from a book the children are reading and know well. A short brainstorming session prior to and/or after the project would serve to scaffold students' creative and reflective process. Using classroom instruments, voices, or iPad apps, students would create or improvise music that would serve as a soundscape for the text. When studying poetry, students could create sound effects while the poem is read. For stories with specific characters, students could create a motive or melody for each character as the story excerpt is read or acted out. Students may also enjoy creating unusual soundscapes: woods, zoo, factory, moon, seashore, shopping mall, etc. The idea is to create a soundscape but for each student to leave 'space' in their own part of the improvisation for others to enter, for each 'voice' to have a role, to figure which timbres to use, when to start and how to finish. These open-ended musical experiences provide multiple entry points for musical expression, musical processes and multiple levels of learner participation within a holistic setting.

These improvisational experiences, when students are free to work together, are especially suited to be child-directed. Teachers new to the process may give up if first attempts do not meet expectations. Like all things, the students' musical ideas and collaborations tend to improve with each new attempt. If the teacher has facilitated this activity with the whole class, this can soon shift to smaller groups where musical decisions can be more intentional and the improvisation can move into a planned composition.

Teachers might also consider projects where students improvise or compose music with a focus on creating texture – layers in sound using two-part poems (like a duet) or four-part poems as the language arts connection. These poems are intended to be read with multiple voices and are good metaphors for multiple layers or voices in music. With appropriately paired literature and musical models (invention, fugue or band with similar number of layers), students can enter the musical process with a deeper understanding of texture – a musical structure that may have been tacitly known but now has been intentionally named and explored.

FOSTERING A PARTICULAR KIND OF COLLABORATIVE APPROACH: SCAFFOLDING

But what is the range of dispositions that teachers need to foster within the participatory practice of performance? How can teachers enable children to experience greater freedom and control over their learning collaboratively? This chapter has provided a selection of examples, rather than a comprehensive list, as is the case in all of the earlier and latter chapters. The goal is how to reconcile the strong agreement within the whole class while fostering the freedom for individual children to do their own thinking and find their own way. How do teachers facilitate creative performances that are both individual and autonomous *and* collective and interdependent? Openness combined with questioning, stability and inventiveness, for instance, makes for a dynamic mix. Children do not simply follow their teachers' lead or the lead provided by more dominant members of the group. Creative consensus and collaborative practice needs to be an inventive and participatory one; working around common themes and threads (as suggested in Figure 1.1, Chapter 1, and Figure 5.1, this chapter) means children learn from each other while still controlling and shaping the path of their own learning, for and with their particular class of children. Collaboration is especially creative, sparking ideas across the group, while leaving children free to develop their own distinctively individual practices. Each person's experiences, questions, new ideas, dilemmas and successful practices become resources for the whole group. The creative consensus gives the group a coherent framework for an ongoing shared enquiry to which everybody contributes (i.e. what you bring into the space) and from which everybody can learn (and what you take away).

Case study 5.4: Creating 'scaffolds' for creative teaching

At each start of a creative lesson, I tell the children that each group (three or four pupils) will make an 'original' piece of music. It is important that children know that this is new for the context of the class. My first aim is to ensure that children discuss the processes of play and the role of imagination. Then we discuss ideas about expression and the rules of engagement in generating communication styles. As the teacher, I have to adapt reflexively and creatively to the class.

That is why as a teacher researcher I have focussed on developing teaching sequences that put the creative activity of children in the centre. From the findings of my observations of teaching in different countries (Giglio, 2010), to enable collaboration among the children during the composition task and to avoid obstructing this interaction we need to introduce 'creative scaffolding' to our classes. This involves:

- Orienting the children's attention to the creative task at hand; their relationships with teacher – deliberately choosing to present themselves as real people – and children need to be non-threatening and accepting of each other.
- Negotiating and agreeing the time remaining to work on certain aspects of the activity.
- Observing, listening and empathising with the children, seeking to view the world and the process of learning through the child's eyes through discussion (without interrupting them).
- Indicating that the children have to come to an agreement together – a creative consensus – to discuss certain ideas and shared understandings of their endeavours and decisions so far.
- Confirming to the children, with each new situation, and finding ways to look for unique solutions that are congruent with their principles and community, then finding principled and constructive ways forward.

> ■ Providing and maintaining steadfastness of purpose and support for children by pulling together and supporting one another, finding the strength to hold onto their principles and taking steps needed to make room within their learning community for risk-taking. Finally, making the connection between the different kinds of work on relationships and the core purpose of extending freedom to create participatory performances collaboratively.
>
> This kind of 'creative scaffolding' is fundamental to the role of the creative teacher. (Marcelo Giglio, Switzerland)

CONCLUSION: KEY POINTS

Primary education is about the future. It facilitates acknowledgement of our environment, respects its heritage and invests in the new. Collaboration among learning communities, their musical practices and creativity is an essential ingredient for this process. Given place, time and resources (in the context of the extensive range of primary core curriculum priorities), children, in the act and process of performing music (whether using informal learning practices such as free experimentation with instruments and imitation of pop songs, the traditional music repertoire they share as a group or formal music making), can develop skills of collaborative shared working, musical empathy, expressive communication, independence of thought and curiosity. Most importantly, performances which feature music making and creating can provide opportunities for children to choose between following and flouting the rules and norms, pushing and breaking boundaries between the old and new and using music to express something unique (Mills, 1993). By providing these opportunities, teachers allow children to do what they tend to do naturally to be creative in music – and allow themselves to become creative teachers.

YOUTUBE EXAMPLES

Video footage of the Alphabet Dance is available online at http://www.youtube.com/j51ER8Faqsc

NOTE

1 Sixth year of primary (elementary) school, 11 to 12 years of age.

FURTHER READING

Fleishman, P. (2000) *Big Talk: Poems for Four Voices*. Somerville, MA: Candlewick Press. Illustrated by Beppe Giacobbe. This is a collection of poems to be read aloud by four people, with colour-coded text to indicate which lines are read by which readers. It is a toe-tapping, tongue-flapping inspiring resource with beautifully illustrated and orchestrated spirited poems. This innovative book weaves a tapestry of rhythm that will inspire primary children, particularly suitable for 8- to 12-year-olds.

CHAPTER 6

SINGING THE PRIMARY CURRICULUM

James Biddulph and Jane Wheeler

INTRODUCTION

Singing is a unique form of embodied knowing and a vital experience in all cultures. The experience of singing alone and together is natural and enjoyable for all people and offers opportunities to inspire creative musical expression. Coming together to sing is a form of peace-making, a spiritual journey and a powerful way to connect and release the musical imagination in ways that are personal and social, instructive and playful, and communal and collective. Moreover, in a globalised world of human activities and increasing interaction of cultural traditions, singing together has infinite possibilities for broadening relationships and musical associations and breaking down social and cultural barriers, leading to journeys that both teachers and children can take. Singing presents vital and powerful possibilities for intercultural learning, where musics from diverse traditions build new learning about diversity, culture and communities (Aróstegui and Ibarretxe, 2016, p. 70). Children begin their musical journeys with song, exercising their natural childhood penchant to invent songs and experiment with their voices, as evidenced in music research on children's creativity (Campbell, 1998). From their own cultural reference points, through song and music making in classrooms, children can step towards understanding 'the relationship between different cultures as a social space to be shared' – a venue where differences are valued and grounded in democratic values (Aróstegui and Ibarretxe, 2016, p. 71). We suggest that singing activity in primary school can result in healthier and happier school communities (Davies, 1992).[1]

In this chapter, we explore the possibilities of bringing children's singing into the primary curriculum, how singing can be related to other subject areas and knowledge contexts and then embedded in the life of primary schools and established as a powerful means for creating fulfilled and strong communities. We explore children's musical worlds from a child-orientated perspective, with a focus on their abilities and skills, balanced by a respect for, and interest in, what they hear and do as they observe the world in which they find themselves. We offer creative approaches to 'releasing the voice', which involve learning through imaginative play and building environments of trust where all diversity is celebrated and establishes democratic notions of education. These include *themes*, which focus on *developing children's musical creativity* and their capacity to experiment with musical ideas and information, alone and with others, and *threads*, which involve generic principles of creative pedagogical practice for teachers to *teach creatively*[2] using their own creativity as practitioners and singing leaders. These two processes are very closely related.

Historically, influenced predominantly by Western culture, singing and how it is judged have been related to bel canto traditions, which value impeccable tone, control of a large voice range, ability to show dexterity and complete mastery of breath. As Rao,[3] an inspirational choral teacher and master conductor, argues, there is a sense of singing linked with values of *uniformity* rather than diversity, *exclusivity* rather than inclusion and *perfection* over reflection (Rao with Pearson, 2005). Contemporary reality television programmes such as *Britain's Got Talent* and *The Voice* propagate these traditional 'exclusive' attitudes: the deeply held myths and assumptions about singing quality rooted in Western thought. Conversely, there is increased interest in communal singing, with the work of Gareth Malone (presenter and conductor) with choirs set up in army communities, disenfranchised communities and places, like inner city estates, where singing is assumed not to exist or be valued. Rao's *Circle of Sound* (2005), in which she advocates the transformation of singing education so as to find 'musical' and 'social' bridges across cultural 'gaps', is a valuable asset to any teacher's professional library and, indeed, has the potential to transform any teacher's pedagogic practice.

The first task for creative primary teachers in developing singing in the primary curriculum is to *find innovative and creative ways* to alter such beliefs and assumptions and address the following questions: how do we model and practice the belief that singing is a diverse, inclusive and reflective practice? How do we show that creative singing and song making is educationally relevant and socially/culturally/humanistically important – a way of connecting with children's musical worlds and cultural practices? How do we challenge the perceived hierarchies in music genre and quality so that all musics are 'world musics' rather than dividing the world into binary oppositions (e.g. classical music and world music)? How do we develop the confidence of teachers to share and value their own and their students' creative potential so that these become the driving force for learning in their classrooms?

REFLECTING ON TEACHER THINKING: MYTHS ABOUT SINGING

Singing is as natural to human behaviour as breathing (Rao with Pearson, 2005; Welch, 2003). And breathing is an essential part of singing. As a highly complex process, singing involves vocalisation in infanthood, linguistic codes of early speech, enculturation of language and the learning of conventions and symbols associated with this. Advances in technology reveal that singing is a 'whole brain activity [. . .] probably uniquely involv[ing] the integration of musical, speech, visual, motor and emotional systems of the brain' (Welch, 2003, p. 5). Moreover, experiencing singing together has wider benefits, including raised self-esteem, increased well-being and a more positive self-image. Not only is singing good for you and enjoyable, but there are numerous traditions which value singing as a spiritual activity: singing in church, chanting Hare Krishna mantras or singing in harmony in a South African township, to name but three.

One can trace the etymology of the word 'breath' to the Latin *spiritus* or *spirare*, which has three meanings: breathing, life and spirit. To breathe is to live. And so singing, as breathing, is about learning to live, with the potential to connect with oneself, as an individual, and with others, as a community. It involves learning about similarities and exploring differences through the sharing and learning of musics from a wide and diverse multicultural world.

Whilst educators have always acknowledged the importance of singing in schools, the increased bureaucratisation of education and top-down accountability agendas over the last two decades have reduced the amount of time dedicated to singing in the primary curriculum. Likewise, due to limited teaching and professional development opportunities, teachers have been unable to develop their confidence and skills in singing teaching sufficiently for them to embed singing creativity in the primary curriculum. The 2007 UK government's response was to dedicate £40 million over four years to Sing Up, a flagship strategy to reinstate singing in primary schools. With this came training, Internet and magazine resources, an award programme and a raised awareness of the value and benefits of singing in schools. Sing Up emphasises the following:

1   There is value in singing in primary education because of the significant positive impact on the lives and singing abilities of children.
2   Singing abilities and attitudes are socially and culturally embedded. Therefore, in increasingly ethnically diverse school and classroom contexts, there is significant value in developing the singing experiences of children so that pedagogies are sensitive to the complex multicultures within which children sing, dance and make songs.

Following *The Routledge International Handbook of Intercultural Arts Research* (Burnard, Mackinlay and Powell, 2016) that locates the importance of the arts and music in learning with/through/about diverse cultural practices, we advocate the need to develop open creative attitudes to understand the song-making potential of the primary classroom by placing children at the heart of their music making as *active agents* in their learning. This will give rise to higher levels of engagement, greater purpose and meaningful musical/social/cultural learning in school – learning which breaks down perceived and real barriers between school and home and between children and adults.

BUILDING ENVIRONMENTS FOR TEACHER CONFIDENCE

When teachers and learners embark on a learning journey to develop singing in the curriculum creatively, they need to demonstrate a curiosity and desire to learn about *their own* singing voices. There is much research (see Hennessy, 2000, which explores how teachers view themselves as musical or not) and thousands of anecdotes that express the damage that life experiences and formal education can do to people's self-perception of their singing abilities. Sometimes passionate yet unaware teachers/adults inadvertently comment on a child's voice, resulting in a deep-seated belief that the child cannot sing. Being told to mime or sing quietly, or being encouraged to join another club are stories which resonate in many staff rooms. As teachers reposition themselves as the learner, in order to adopt new and fulfilling roles for themselves as singers, they become the agents of their own change and try out ways of working with children's singing voices – in doing things differently, they learn to make space for the new, the other, the unanticipated and the unexpected.

FOSTERING CREATIVITY THROUGH SINGING IN A NEW PEDAGOGY: GOT LEGS? YOU CAN DANCE. GOT A VOICE? YOU CAN SING.

The challenge, first and foremost, is to champion the belief that everyone can sing with the mantra: if there is a voice, and it can speak, then it can sing. This inclusive belief is necessary to convince all children that they too are singers. It does not mean that everyone will go on to become a professional singer, but it does mean everyone will learn to develop their singing voice and feel confident to express their voice in a community of singers, whether in a choir, in the playground or with friends in a karaoke bar. Below are three creative activities to begin the process of developing teachers' confidence to 'release' their voice creatively.

Activity 6.1 Humming poetry

Humming is an effective warm-up technique that can be used to prepare the voice for singing; this activity helps to build confidence in using text, rhythm and simple sung voice.

1. Start with a simple text, a favourite poem or nursery rhyme, for example, 'To sing or not to sing, that is the question'.
2. Explore the rhythm of the text.
3. Chant it out loud and memorise it.
4. When the rhythm is secure, remove the words and hum the rhythm on one note.
5. Try a different note, exploring the range of your voice.

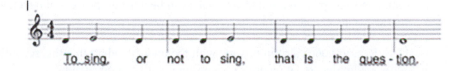

6. Add the text again, singing on one note; try changing the note on one or two words.
7. Teach this to your class.

MODELLING HUMILITY: SEEKING OUT THE CONFIDENT SINGERS IN YOUR CLASS

Children are natural singers and song makers (Campbell, 1998) but often their experience and expertise is not drawn into the classroom and they become a wasted resource. The positive effect of using music from children's own culture (e.g. their playground songs, music from their homes, songs from computer games and cartoons) cannot be overstated. Welcoming their playing, singing, dancing and chanting in classroom contexts makes a statement about the value of their music and is more likely to create an open and trusting environment.

The following activity may be a way of empowering children, leading to the development of a singing culture, which begins with their own experiences and enculturation and uses their own ways of teaching each other, drawn from other learning contexts.

Activity 6.2 Modelling humility

1. Invite children to lead a song in class.
2. Seek out the confident children and provide time and space for them to teach *their* music to other children. By altering your position from teacher to learner, there is modelling of risk and humility, a sense of a collaborative learning community and an 'official' valuation of their singing creativities. By singing along with your class as a member of the group rather than as a leader, there is an opportunity to rehearse your singing voice in a safer context, in preparation for the time when you lead with your own song.

Activity 6.3 Learning to love your voice: the process

The voice is a very intimate and personal aspect of being a human. With the realisation that no one else sounds like you comes the realisation that with a voice comes a brain, thoughts, language, expression of emotion – your vehicle to express who you are. At first, no one enjoys hearing their own voice, but learning to hear how you sound and accepting the sound you make can be a useful process in developing the confidence to sing at school.

1. Record your voice in private, with the understanding that this recording will not be shared. Or record a conversation with a good friend.
2. When you listen to the recording, try and listen deeply to the musical qualities in your voice. How deep is it? How high? Is there a nasal quality? What is the rhythm of the monologue or dialogue? When do you breathe? How deep or shallow is your breath? And how does this sound in context with the other sounds your voice creates?
3. If you make several recordings at different times in the day, what are the differences in your voice?
4. You could also record yourself making many different sounds, enjoying the creation of croaks, squeaks, grunts, rumbles, drones and yawns. The list is endless.

This activity emphasises the dynamic and fluid nature of the human voice, influenced by health, hydration and atmosphere, with physiological and psychological factors, at one specific time. It is an ever-changing instrument and one that needs a comprehensive care package together with regular exercise. At the start of each academic year, self-portraits, accompanied by targets for the year, are often made in primary schools. Why not record children, with an iPhone or digital video camera, so that they can hear their voices? The message is often more powerful and values the unique sound of each person as they speak of their targets and visions for the future.

CREATIVE STRATEGIES FOR PREPARING THE VOICE: BUILDING ENVIRONMENTS OF TRUST, LANGUAGE ENQUIRY AND IMAGINATIVE PLAY

As with athletes and sportspeople, the only way to improve your singing performance is through a healthy lifestyle, by taking regular exercise and stretching beyond the limits of your current abilities. We must develop an almost carefree confidence that there *are* ways to develop the voice and musicality.

Table 6.1 presents techniques borrowed, shared and adapted from the vast expertise offered on websites, through professional development, and through working with singing leaders. This collection, based on 'Four Bs' – balance, body, breath and begin – has been well received in primary contexts from East London, UK, to music projects in Namibia, Kenya and South Africa.

■ **Table 6.1** Strategies to focus on for facilitating good quality singing

Preparation Process	What You Do . . .	Key Words to Remind You
Balance	Create activities to place the body firmly under the shoulders with tall but relaxed neck, back and knees (imagine hanging like a puppet on a string, or stand as wide as you can, with feet tight together, then settle with feet exactly under hips and shoulders, with hands gently by your sides).	Feet position and balance
Breath	Imagine that you are holding a large beach ball in your curved arms in front of you. Use your arms to gather in the air, ready to blow up your imaginary beach ball, pulling your arms in to your belly or diaphragm as you do so (see Rao with Pearson, 2005, pp. 54–7). Then, as you blow the ball up, filling it with air and enlarging it using a slow out breath, let your arms show the ball filling as they flow away from the body to surround the ball.	Beach ball breathing
	Try panting like a little puppy dog, keeping your hands on your belly or diaphragm to feel the fast breath control that your body already knows. Then try slowing the panting down, rather more like an old dog after a walk on a warm day.	Puppy dog breathing

(Continued)

■ **Table 6.1** (Continued)

Preparation Process	What You Do . . .	Key Words to Remind You
	Increase the control of your breath by breathing in deeply for a count of four, then hissing out for a count of eight. Repeat exploring hissing out for longer each time, up to twenty-four! Take care to notice if there is any dizziness and take a break if so. If you are new to singing, your body may not be used to breathing this deeply, which is different compared to breathing for ordinary conversation.	Maths breathing – counting in and out
	Try pretending to be blowing up a balloon, allowing it to grow as big as you like. Then let it fizzle out, making a 'ffff', or 'ssss' sound as it does until all the air is expelled from your lungs.	Balloon breathing
Body	Draw a figure of eight with the tip of your nose to loosen and bring attention to the alignment in your neck. Pull your shoulders up to 'tickle' your ear lobes, and then drop them with a deep sigh out. Imagine you're watching a tennis match 'live' and loosely follow the ball in a rally from one end of the court to the other, left to right.	Drawing eight with your body
	You can make up any shake out routine. A favourite is the 'rubber chicken'. Shake left arm, right arm, then left and right leg vigorously (counting to eight on each, then four each, then two, then one). At this point, the most popular part is to jump up in the air shouting 'Rubber chicken!' and collapse down in a floppy, folded posture.	Rubber chicken
	Massage the face gently and repeatedly pat your shoulders and arms, moving down your body to your legs.	Body massage
	Scrunch up your face as though you've tasted a very sour lemon, then open up your face muscles as though you've received a great surprise.	Lemons and surprises
	Imagine a large, sticky toffee in your mouth and work it all round your teeth with your tongue, to the top, the back and to each corner, as if trying to release it from all the gaps in your teeth. It's helpful to vocalise as you do this, to begin to connect the sound of the voice with the articulators in the mouth and the mask of your face.	Toffee chew
	Experiment with tongue twisters, repeating them several times at a gradually faster pace, being meticulous about articulating every vowel and consonant clearly. Examples: unique New York, six thick thistle sticks, three free throws, red leather yellow leather.	Tongue twisters
Begin	You are now ready to begin singing. Just do a quick check through the steps: balanced, relaxed, upright body and breath flowing with ease.	Creating the space
	You can hum one note at a time, hum a scale or two or hum the first line of the song you intend to learn. Or you could sing some short warm-up games from the Sing Up website.	Humming

FOSTERING CREATIVE VOICE WORK IN THE PRIMARY CLASSROOM

In this section, three strategies are shared relating to developing the singing creativities of children. The first scaffolds creative song making by starting with a familiar melody and guiding the children to adapt and rearrange it so as to evolve it into their own new song. The second highlights the creative teacher's insight, finding creative starting points from real-life experiences and stimuli. The third shows the importance of language in song as intercultural learning and singing creativity. The ideas involve:

- Exploring and experimenting with sound and voice sound production.
- Collaboration with peers, teachers and experts in their field (e.g. further education students).
- Risk-taking.
- Improvising and composing through song making.
- Performing and evaluating.
- Sustained and deep listening skills.

FAMILIAR SONGS AS A START FOR SINGING CREATIVITY: 'TWINKLE TWINKLE LITTLE STAR'

For a really safe, secure process leading to the creation of a brand new song, show children how to start with a song they know really well, for example, 'Twinkle Twinkle Little Star'. Following this technique, with small, well-instructed steps, singers of all ages can begin to create a song.

- **Decide on the topic** of the song to be made. This could be chosen by the children or may well be a way of consolidating or celebrating their learning in any topic, for example, creating a song about the Tudor period of history.
- **Brainstorm** the subject and have some ideas about the key information the song might share. This is a well-known literacy activity to generate ideas and develop language.
- **Form creative groups** of no more than five in a group, so that everyone can contribute their ideas. Choose a scribe to write down the group's ideas.
- **Sing** 'Twinkle Twinkle Little Star' together to remind everyone and ensure that even children who have English as a second language know the melody and structure of the song.
- **Analyse** the structure of the song. For example, notice that the first line melody rises and the second line melody falls, and therefore the two are different. We could call these A and B:

A. Twinkle twinkle little star,

Twin - kle   twin - kle   lit - tle   star,

B. How I wonder what you are.

How | won - der   what   you   are.

The next two lines differ from the first two but are the same melody as each other, so they can be called C and C:

C. Up above the world so high
C. Like a diamond in the sky

Then the last two lines are the same as the first two lines, so can be called A and B. Therefore, the structure of the melody of 'Twinkle Twinkle Little Star' is A, B, C, C, A, B.

▪   **Find new words** that fit the song melody and tell the story, or give information to supplement what the pupils are writing about. For example, Line A, 'Twinkle twinkle little star', might become 'Keeping fit we run and play', or 'Sing together, make new songs'.

In   the   dead   of   night   we   run,

Moon - light   guides   us,   mid - night   sun.

▪   **A new melody** is the next step, once all the new text is in place, not forgetting that lines A and B can be repeated, so there is no need to find new text for all six lines. To make the new melody, notice how each line of 'Twinkle Twinkle Little Star' works. If it rises in pitch on a word, experiment with it falling in pitch and vice versa. If there is a little step between notes, try a larger step. For example:

In   the   dead   of   night   we   run,

Moon - light   guides   us,   mid - night   sun.

■ **The rhythm** can now be explored to see if it can communicate the new text more clearly and with greater musical interest. Where the even beats of the 'Twinkle Twinkle' rhythm have worked before, some syllables of the new text might 'tell the story' better if they had a swing rhythm or if they were held for longer. For example:

In   the   dead   of   night   we   run,

Moon - light   guides   us,   mid - night   sun.

■ Finally, the new song is ready for a **new arrangement**. Depending on how much creative musical play the pupils have experienced, they may have skills in body beats[4] or in building ostinato patterns.[5] Ask them questions like: How will your song performance start? Will it be a solo line? Will everyone in your group sing together? Is anyone singing or playing a backing rhythm? What happens in the middle? Are there any movements to help communicate the text? How many times do you sing the song? How does it vary each time? How does the piece end?

Providing an opportunity to perform a rough draft of each group's work will help the children to see other possibilities and experiment with their ideas before deciding on the final arrangement of their song. Making a recording of each performance for the pupils to listen to offers them an opportunity to develop deep listening skills, as well as the sheer enjoyment of hearing their work. It is always a surprise to discover the diversity of interpretation and response to the creative task, even though they all started with the same beginning: 'Twinkle Twinkle Little Star'. This same process can be followed with other simple, short songs from around the world, like 'Frere Jacques' from France or 'A keelie' from Ghana, both to be found on the Sing Up website (www.singup.org).

'ON YER BIKE': DEEP LISTENING FOR SINGING CREATIVITY

Once a teacher opens up to the possibilities of creative play with the voice, the sky's the limit. The world is full of stimulus and wonder, from the sounds around us to new ideas being explored in the media. One such stimulus is a Honda car advertisement with music created by the composer Stephen Sidwell.[6] The composer's composition process involved deep listening, which was necessary to explore not only the car sounds but also to show how the human voice could replicate the sounds of the car's journey. It is a potentially powerful contemporary stimulus for creative voice work with primary children.

Inspired by this advert, Solid Harmony, an East London mixed-age youth choir set about creating an 'alternative', environmentally friendly version, called 'On Yer Bike'. Having agreed to develop this creative voice composition, 'homework' was given to encourage *deep listening* (to local traffic, sounds in the park, noises on the streets) and *explore creatively how to recreate these sounds vocally*, as Sidwell had done in the advert. The teacher's role is as facilitator, guide and believer in the possibilities, as Sue's reflection shows.

Case study 6.1: Sue's role as facilitator, chief guide and believer

The first thing is . . . I arrive at the rehearsal and I say have you seen that amazing Honda ad with the choir and some of them have and others don't know what I am talking about . . . I said 'Wouldn't it be amazing if we did something like that' . . . environmentally friendly like a bike ride . . . and they all started talking at once and I heard this boy Jackson saying 'Yeah I could ride my bike' and I tried to get some ideas together but failed miserably and they talked over each other for about 45 minutes – but loads of ideas were coming so I stood back. Then we started exploring ideas; some of them were a bit extreme, and some of them laughed at each other and their imaginations went a bit wild like trying to make aeroplane sounds and they were asking and exploring 'How do you make the sounds of the city?' And then we agreed to talk to the media department and ask if there were any students who wanted to help and Jackson said again that he was the cyclist or rather insisted that he was . . . we talked about the routes down by the park and about sounds and how we might make them. I agreed to get a copy of the Sidwell music for them and then they had to think about how they would make the sounds with their bodies.

Key messages for teachers:

- *Engage in humour* – not becoming one of them but *allowing* their enjoyment of connecting in their own social-cultural context.
- It's about *trusting* them while keeping an awareness of their safety in the environment.
- *Awareness of youth culture* – the appearance of all talking together is actually excitement and engagement. Trust that they monitor themselves and arrive at a consensus.
- The teacher's role is to *facilitate the discussion* between the young musicians, to observe if voices are not heard and interject to ensure space is allowed for those voices and to discuss the ideas that can be included.
- The teacher is the *collector of agreed ideas* and the mirror or synthesiser (you repeat and mirror back the ideas that they have created).

■ The teacher has the *authority* to make a final group decision taking into account all the boundaries and limitations related to the task, drawing from personal, professional and creative experience.

This relaxed, humorous learning culture, where giggling was allowed, was necessary to encourage the maximum amount of creativity from the singers. And laughing relaxes the muscles and voice, thus producing better sounding singing groups! The contemporary stimulus engaged the singers and they observed a great deal, including people talking on their phones, shop music spilling into the streets, puddles splashing, aeroplanes taking off at a city airport, traffic, wheels spinning, birds singing, the wind in the trees and much more.

The familiar technique of a visual score[7] (see Figure 6.1) could be created to bring together the sounds suggested, with singers given the responsibility of creating the bicycle journey. As suggested above, pupils were given agency to teach one another and practice each sound, during which complex whole-mind activity is evident as they assess, reject, accept, revise and review the sounds that they make. The teacher's role is to manage any tensions in the relationships within groups, focus groups by giving time limits and ask questions that develop what they do with occasional suggestions of how they could improve. The project was uploaded onto YouTube.[8]

■ **Figure 6.1** A visual score.

LANGUAGE PLAY

The increased opportunities for intercultural contact in our daily lives requires a response from educators to develop opportunities for intercultural learning in our school class-rooms (Jackson, 2014, p. 1); this is essential for music learning, we suggest. Our rich language classrooms provide a great resource for developing music learning that values diverse musics as equal and vital opportunities to connect. When we invite children to investigate and explore sound through really listening to unfamiliar languages that require them to 'get their tongues around', we encourage a curiosity about people, ways to express themselves and different cultures. This offers a subliminal message of respect for one another.

Exploring songs in languages not spoken in the classroom can put all pupils on a 'level playing field' in spite of the number of children who might have English as a second language. Furthermore, singing songs in languages spoken by only a few children in the class can give them a considerable confidence boost and help first language English speak-ers develop an awareness about how it must feel to be struggling in a new language or how wonderful it is that their peers are fluent in more than one language.

So, to really explore a language through song has much further-reaching conse-quences than experiencing the sheer joy of singing.

Sounds in language

Each and every language is placed in its own way in the mouth. For example, Eastern European languages have a rich sound with lots of 'sh' and soft 'g's, requiring a very active and skilful tongue against the hard palette and forward, dark vowel sounds. Whereas, in general, African dialects require mostly hard consonance and are very short on diphthongs. American dialects require far more 'twang' and horizontal, smiling vowel shapes to sound authentic, more of an 'a' than an 'ah'.

Take 'Bebe Yo' for example. This is a modern song from Senegal on the World Voice website, written by Mezzo Jutta (https://schoolsonline.britishcouncil.org/classroom-resources/world-voice/bebo-yo). In English, we might pronounce the title 'Be be Yo', with the 'Yo' including the diphthong 'oh' and 'w', as in 'show'. This immediately sounds English, and not African at all. To sound authentic we need to work at stopping short at the 'Yo', almost nearer a short 'your', as in 'more'. When you speak this out loud, notice how much more authentic the language sounds. Simply exploring this with children can open up a whole world of attention to detail and respect for others.

PERFORMING SONGS CREATIVELY

The more positive opportunities primary children have to experience their voice as their own unique, kinaesthetic, tactile instrument and as a mental and physical manifestation of self, the greater the chance that continued positive attitudes to singing will be found in secondary school and, beyond that, into their adult lives. Performance itself has a particular cultural tradition and there are diverse ways of performing songs.

Knowing when and what to perform is an important skill. Performing a challenging song too early can result in negative self-assessment, an uncomfortable performance experience and embarrassment for both performers and audience. The first task is to choose an appropriate repertoire. Sing Up has assembled a good collection, which they have catalogued in categories that ease programming and make explicit the links with subject areas and the age or needs of pupils. Knowing that younger primary children sing most comfortably in a higher register than feels natural to adults is helpful. For example, commonly children aged 5 to 7 will sing comfortably from middle D up to the D above. Once singing confidently in this range, their vocal chords will become stronger and more flexible, and will gradually elongate as they grow, allowing them to sing a wider range comfortably (in upper primary, nearer A below middle C up to F above the C above). Teachers often feel less confident modelling higher pitches in singing due to their own fear of 'high' notes and this can lead to children struggling to match the lower pitch of adults, sounding weaker and less confident or even shouting as a result. Male teachers should sing in their own range and allow children to take their time learning to transpose to their own natural range.

Diverse performance

We commonly think of learning songs for performance, to share with an audience, to learn until perfected, to showcase the song and the singers. However, in many cultures singing together works more in an informal setting, as it might in a folk club or at a party, where someone starts to sing, others tap a beat or clap along, gradually joining in with more and more phrases of the song. One reflection on such an experience transformed our thinking about performance, song learning, making and teaching. (See Case study 6.2.)

Case study 6.2: Reflections on intercultural musicking

I recently had the opportunity to work with sixty children in KS2 in Kenya. Their teachers were also present. I began teaching songs with my 'Western' mindset, using pedagogy learned over the year, but always assuming we were wanting to learn a song, learn it well and prepare to perform it to an audience at the end of the week.

When it came to an opportunity for the children and their teachers to share some Kenyan songs, I observed how the small group would sing their idea a few times, with more and more of the 'audience' joining in each time round. At a certain point everyone got onto their feet and danced and sang. The piece gradually sped up until there was a real sense of party about it, and then everyone seemed to know when it was time to bring the singing to an end, not abruptly, but gently and almost merging into laughter and commentary about the moment. The singing was part of the social expression of the group and of the moment. I remember experiencing a similar moment in Senegal last year, and while both of these countries have groups who rehearse very seriously for high-level performance in regional festivals, they none-theless commonly express their connection through informal learning and sharing by osmosis. It was so good to be reminded of this and of the value of sharing by simply doing. This also leaves room for some 'freestyle' ad-libs or joyful call outs to lift the music, if the song can be lifted in this way.

This can be a wonderful way to lead singing in the classroom, or in assembly, and makes a cultural change from the common practice of 'I sing, you sing' until a song is learned. Try the following:

1 Invite the group or assembly to join you in a body pulse or simple rhythm; tapping knees if sitting, clapping with just one or two fingers or making a gentle chest tap for a deeper sound.
2 When everyone is together, sing the song, or if it's more extensive, the chorus of the song. Emphasize the last line.
3 Sing again, but as you approach the last line, make a gesture to invite everyone to join in as they keep their pulse.
4 Keep building this up until most, if not all, are singing the whole chorus together.

Without having to give instruction or repeat line-by-line rote learning activities, everyone can come to know the song by gentle osmosis.

ASSESSING *FOR* CREATIVITY THROUGH SUNG PERFORMANCE

Performance has the potential to validate the effort of children's learning, celebrating music, the community of singers and individual and collective contributions. Once children are confident in the piece they are singing, plan an opportunity for them to perform (in their class, to another younger class, in assembly, etc.). Below are practical steps which, taken over time, lead to increased confidence to perform.

▪ **Assessing for learning**: Once a part, or all, of a song is learned, divide the group into two halves. Ask one to sit and face the 'stage' and ask the others to set themselves on the 'stage' area to perform the section of the song being worked on.

▪ **Assessing communication and participation**: Invite the audience to feel a part of this performance, exploring with them how much better people will perform if they feel supported and encouraged, rather than criticised or negatively judged. In watching and listening *in silence*, internally willing the singers to do their best, they are likely to be rewarded with a better performance and they can share in its resulting success. Swap over groups. Ask children to listen for the words, to assess how the melody communicates ideas, whether everybody is listening to each other and singing together. Do they look confident? What about their posture? Do their faces communicate the words? Who is your gaze drawn to and why?

▪ **Assessing musical memory**: Towards the end of a rehearsal or song learning session, ask if there are any singers who feel confident to perform it from memory. Allow these few to step out in front and sing for the rest, going through the same feedback process at the end. This will develop a culture of confidence to perform and self-assess for learning.

▪ **Assessing staging and performance character**: On occasion, try to arrange for a microphone to be set up in the session and go through the same invitation process for individuals to come up and try the song solo.

▪ **Assessing creativity**: Listen to different recordings/versions of the piece they are singing. Discuss with the young singers how the renditions vary – how would they assess the creativity involved in the arrangement?

At each step, there has been no coercion, only opportunity and encouragement for everyone to share the responsibility for each other's learning and growing. In this way, children control their own steps towards performance and are far more likely to enjoy fully the sense of achievement and validation that it brings.

CONCLUSION

Creative teachers seek to find ways to engage with their pupils in enriching, collaborative and meaningful ways. They follow some key principles, *themes* and *threads* that are highlighted in this chapter. Creative teachers:

- See themselves as learners and model the risk of learning something new.
- Foster ownership, identifying pupil agency as key in building communities of musical practices.
- Understand learners' cultural and subcultural groups, watching and listening for the group dynamics and drawing from these cultures to develop meaningful music making in classroom contexts.
- Thrive off the unusual and the risky and expect learners to surprise them – as in the case of Sue who stood back and trusted the pupils to create their bike sound piece.
- Model humility and involve themselves in music experiences as a teacher *and* a learner. Their role is facilitator, guide, questioner, collector and synthesiser of ideas; with the benefit of their adult experiences they have the authority to make decisions so that there is a clear outcome within time limits and agreed frameworks.
- Have an overwhelming belief that everyone can sing and find ways to engage the whole community in a safe and trusting environment. They are passionate advocates for singing as essential in the life of all school cultures.

Singing is good for you and everyone can sing; no matter how many people have told you otherwise, no matter how many times you were told to mime or find another hobby, no matter what the sound, no matter whether alone or together. What matters is that you find ways to inspire the young people in your care to feel the sense of joy and connection which creative singing and singing together can bring. We invite you to:

Stop the words.
Open the window in the centre of your chest,
And let the spirits fly in and out.

(Rumi, translated by Coleman Barks, 1995, p. 34)

SOME RECOMMENDED CHILDREN'S SONG SOURCES

The Sing Up website (http://www.singup.org) has a substantial bank of contemporary and traditional songs representing diverse musical cultures. The British Council has developed a bank of songs to demonstrate cultural variety. Many nursery rhymes and solid, basic starter songs to work with creatively can be found here. For example, see:

Twinkle Twinkle Little Star
The Grand Old Duke of York
Old Macdonald Had a Farm

Old King Cole
Oranges and Lemons
The Wheels on the Bus
Humpty Dumpty

See also:

The Big Book of Nursery Rhymes & Children's Songs: 169 Classic Songs Arranged for Piano, Voice and Guitar (2004). London: Chester Music.

https://schoolsonline.britishcouncil.org/classroom-resources/world-voice/bebo-yo

NOTES

1 See the CUP website for a free downloadable PDF copy of this seminal study in which you can find out more about the musical song worlds of young children.

2 See Figure 1.1 in Chapter 1, which features the threads and themes that are woven through the chapters.

3 http://www.doreenrao.com

4 http://www.youtube.com/watch?v=rqnNu3u-Apw (Brazilian children performing body percussion).

5 http://en.wikipedia.org/wiki/Ostinato

6 http://www.youtube.com/watch?v=yq7G9Cx7pkw (Honda car advertisement)

7 Another simple tool for creating the score, if schools have iPads, is to use an app/programme called Singing Fingers (see http://singingfingers.com), which explores sounds and how they work together when notated.

8 http://www.youtube.com/watch?v=pp1WX1pF-uc and http://www.solidharmony.co.uk ('On Yer Bike', Solid Harmony, June 2007).

FURTHER READING

Aróstegui, J. and Ibarretxe, G. (2016) Intercultural education and music teacher education: Cosmopolitan learning through popular music. In P. Burnard, E. Mackinlay and K. Powell (eds.) *The Routledge International Handbook of Intercultural Arts Research*. Abingdon, UK: Routledge.

Barks, C. (1995) *The Essential Rumi.* San Francisco: Harper.

Burnard, P., Mackinlay, E. and Powell, K. (2016) *The Routledge International Handbook of Intercultural Arts Research*. Abingdon, UK: Routledge.

Campbell, P. (1998) *Songs in Their Heads: Music and Its Meaning in Children's Lives*. Oxford: Oxford University Press.

Davies, C. (1992) Listen to my song: A study of songs invented by children aged 5–7 years. *British Journal of Music Education*, 9(1), 19–48.

Hennessey, S. (2000) Overcoming the red-feeling: The development of confidence to teach music in primary school amongst student teachers. *British Journal of Music Education*, 7(2), 183–96.

Jackson, J. (ed.) (2014) *The Routledge Handbook of Language and Intercultural Communication*. New York: Routledge.

Rao, D. with Pearson, B. (2005) *Circle of Sound: Voice Education: A Contemplative Approach to Singing Through Meditation, Movement and Vocalization*. London: Boosey & Hawkes, pp. 54–7.

Welch, G. F. (2003) The importance of singing. In A. Paterson & E. Bentley (eds.) *Bluebirds and Crows: developing a singing culture in and out of school*. Matlock, UK: The National Association of Music Educators (NAME), pp. 2–5.

<table>
<tr><td>CHAPTER
7</td><td></td></tr>
</table>

EXPLORING NEW MEDIA MUSICALLY AND CREATIVELY

Alex Ruthmann

INTRODUCTION

Innovations in new media and ICT are inspiring children in their creative play at home and in schools (Somekh, 2007). Today's computers, both desktop and mobile, can now be considered musical instruments in and of themselves (Ruthmann and Dillon, 2012; Thibeault, 2012), and are inspiring new practices that integrate sound, image, touch and video as the medium and method of musical expression.[1] These practices parallel the emerging trend that today's youth are now more often going to YouTube to find and listen to music, rather than listening to MP3s and CDs.[2] With the growing prevalence of mobile devices like iPhones, iPads and smartphones, our children now have access to powerful music-making applications and new models of creative musicianship *at their fingertips*, providing new avenues for creative engagement within and outside of our music classrooms.

This chapter provides an introduction to projects and tools for exploring the creative dimensions of new media with primary pupils. I begin with an introduction to creative musicianship with new media, followed by an overview of tools for creating and being creative with new media. These tools are discussed in the context of practical projects and creative strategies for teacher and pupil exploration within primary classrooms. The first project I share focuses on a mobile app for Apple's iDevices[3] – the application Singing Fingers,[4] which enables children to 'finger paint in sound' connecting physical gesture, drawing and sound. The second project focuses on creative performing, improvising and composing experiences with the Scratch multimedia programming environment[5] created by the Lifelong Kindergarten Group[6] at the MIT Media Lab.

WHAT IS NEW MEDIA MUSICIANSHIP?

New media musicianship is a broad collection of creative musical practices where video, images and sounds are interactively used as the medium for musical expression. Today, artists such as Kutiman[7] browse YouTube for videos and remix them using video editors into completely new musical compositions. The band Pomplamoose[8] has pioneered the genre of the *video song* where all layers of the musical texture recorded in their songs appears via split screen technology in the video, providing a window into contemporary music recording production techniques. Choral composer Eric Whitacre invites and crowd-sources singers from around the world to submit videos of their singing, which are stitched together into his multimedia Virtual Choir[9] performances. One of the common aspects across these three examples is that music, image and sound are present together in both the final product and throughout the creating process.

The innovative practices and technologies described and linked to throughout this chapter provide a glimpse into ways children use these technologies to make music with media they find culturally valuable and relevant (Ruthmann and Dillon, 2012). Children can more easily take on the musical roles of curator, video editor, producer, remixer and programmer of musical media with these technologies. New web-based and mobile tools open access to children's music-making experiences using interactive webpages running on a computer or mobile device they have at home or at school. The simplicity of not having to download expensive and complicated music production software affords children and their teachers access to musically complex creative media-making experiences producing digital stories, creating animations and designing musical instruments, video games and interactive soundtracks. For example, the Scratch visual programming environment[10] is home to over 3 million child-created interactive multimedia projects; over 500,000 of them include creative use of music and sound.

The tools for exploring new media musicianship can be sub-categorised into tools for social media musicianship, video-edited musicianship, tangible media musicianship and computational media musicianship. *Social media musicianship* tools include blogs, wikis and social networking sites where music is discussed, shared and collaboratively created, such as online music notation platform Noteflight.com and audio remixing platform Indaba.com.

Video-edited musicianship tools are available online and via mobile apps where children can remix and edit videos as the musical medium. YouTube's interactive video editor, Smule's MadPad[11] application for mobile music video sampling and interactive websites like InBflat.net provide children access to basic creative video editing in musical contexts within Internet browsers and on their mobile devices.

Tangible media musicianship tools harness children's touch and gesture as the central method of exploring and being curious with musical media. Examples of these technologies include the iPod and iPad app Singing Fingers (discussed later in this chapter), the interactive MakerBloks[12] and LittleBits[13] maker/synth kits, and the MaKey MaKey invention kit, where children can easily turn the physical environment around them into a musical instrument.

Computational media musicianship tools engage children in making music through computational, mathematical and pattern-based processes. The Scratch multimedia programming environment, as well as the interactive musical media websites aQWERTYon,[14] GroovePizza,[15] Fresh Ed Annotator,[16] Bohemian Rhapsichord[17] and Girl Talk in a Box[18] engage children in building, designing, remixing and making their own musical instruments, games and music.

The common thread across all of these categories of new media musicianship is that children are new producers, designers and creators of musical environments, in addition to the traditional roles of performer and listener. These tools provide opportunities for students to use their voices, sounds and the environment around them as musical instruments inside our classrooms and also at home. It is incumbent upon us, as teachers, to encourage and study these practices and develop new pedagogical strategies that foster our children's musical agency and learning. I encourage you to take plenty of time to explore the linked websites, tools and videos yourself to experience firsthand these new tools. If our children have access to these tools and are making music with them in their free time, it is our responsibility to get to know them and make space for them within our classrooms.

CREATIVE STRATEGIES FOR SINGING FINGERS

Singing Fingers is an interactive media application that allows young children to 'finger paint' and play with sound. When the application is loaded, the user is presented with a blank drawing surface. The user simply sings or makes sounds while touching and drawing along the surface of the mobile device (see Figure 7.1). When you have finished singing and drawing, the application automatically turns into playback mode, where the user can retrace their drawing, performing back the drawing they recorded. The user can touch or trace the drawing forward, backward or anywhere colours are drawn on the screen. If you do not like what you've recorded, you can wipe the screen and start again. And, if you really like your creation, you can save it and share it for playback and interaction at a later time.

Drawings made with Singing Fingers are also designed to be performed via multi-touch. This feature enables you to play chords with your drawings or even a multi-part drum kit if you record non-pitched sounds. Melodic sounds are mapped to the colours of the rainbow, which correspond to each note of the chromatic scale. For example, a pitch in any octave is always the same colour. Non-pitched sounds show up in various shades of grey. This visual and musical design distinction opens up many possibilities for creative visual, musical and gestural expressions with Singing Fingers.

sing & draw

touch & listen

■ **Figure 7.1** Singing Fingers.

Finger painting in sound

Activity 7.1 Finger painting your first music with Singing Fingers

1. Invite children to sing a song they know.
2. Using one iPad, invite the class to sing a phrase of the song and select a pupil to draw while the class sings the song.
3. Invite children to come up and try different ways of performing the drawing. What happens when you trace it fast? What happens when you trace it slow? Forwards? Backwards? Stopping and starting?
4. Ask the children if they can figure out why certain notes are different colours. Do they notice a relationship? Can they explain the reason behind it?
5. Clear the screen and draw a staircase while singing an ascending scale. Each step of the staircase should display as a different colour. Lead the children in the song again and ask them to think of the first note. Invite a confident pupil to find that note on the staircase. Work with that pupil and the whole class in finding and performing the melody of the song they just sang on the drawn staircase.
6. Invite children to come up and perform parts of the melody while the whole class sings.

Activity 7.1 is designed as an orientating, whole-class introduction to Singing Fingers assuming that you only have one mobile device available. As the teacher, you have the opportunity to model not only how Singing Fingers works, but also to model and introduce creative thinking and performance of the drawing. Because Singing Fingers is also a visual drawing tool, it is ideal for experimenting with and reinforcing concepts such as pitch relationships, rhythm, timbre, tempo and texture, many of which are visual and gestural metaphors for sound (higher, lower, shorter, longer, slower, faster, etc.).

In addition to using Singing Fingers to record and perform melodies, it is great for recording and performing percussive sounds and rhythmic ostinati. A possible extension to Activity 7.1 is to record vocal percussive sounds emulating a drum kit. Invite children to think of sounds and record and draw them on Singing Fingers. You with the pupils could then perform a rhythmic accompaniment to the song you sang using Singing Fingers.

Another strategy that is useful with primary pupils is to pre-record and draw various musical examples. Sometimes it is easier for younger pupils to work with drawings that have already been created, rather than go through the process of creating the drawing and then performing it. An idea you might consider is to record melodies that have different pitch contours on the Singing Fingers screen:

■ Record and draw a melody that ascends.
■ Record and draw a melody that descends.
■ Record and draw a melody that ascends and descends.
■ Record a melody using only one pitch.

At this point, you can invite children to look at the four straight lines you drew and recorded. Ask them if they see any visual differences between them. Before you perform them, ask them to hypothesise what they think the lines will sound like when traced. Invite the children to trace the lines and test their hypotheses about the melodic contour. What happens to the melodic contour when you trace the line backwards? Singing Fingers can be a wonderful platform for musical problem solving,[19] hypothesising and exploring one's curiosities[20] in music and sound.

Singing Fingers provides an environment where children can be creative and explore the musical possibilities of their own voice. It is a space where children can make their musical ideas visual, audible and tangible, and easily share them with others. As a teacher, having access to children's musical ideas across multiple forms of representation provides additional insight into their ideas, challenges and learning process. The opportunity to learn and experiment with music and gesture through exploratory play can lead to deeper creative engagement with music.

Beyond just performing

With Singing Fingers, children can explore multiple musical roles. The most obvious role is that of the *performer* and *curator* of the sounds that accompany the drawing. Children either generate the sound themselves through singing, speaking or making other types of sounds, or they can have others create the sounds while they draw. Once the drawing is on the screen, pupils take on the role of *improviser*, exploring and experimenting with the drawing, looking for interesting sounds and patterns. Once the drawing is set, it becomes a platform for *composing* and *arranging*, either alone by the pupil or as part of a shared duet or trio small ensemble with other friends. The drawings can be saved for use by other children in the class or in other classes.

Once you and your pupils have had some beginning experiences with Singing Fingers, invite them to create their own free drawings and compositions.[21] For older, more experienced pupils, it may be easier to share mobile devices and integrate them into small group work. Singing Fingers works well in duets or trios of children, as they can all interact with the drawings. Singing Fingers also lends itself to integration with classroom singing, collaborative performance with other classroom instruments and improvisatory works. Pupils can all start from the same starting picture or can be asked to create their own, based on their level of comfort and experience with music and Singing Fingers.

Activity 7.2 Design your own instrument

1. Invite children to imagine an original musical instrument. To help get their ideas flowing, ask them: If you could design your own personal musical instrument, what sounds would it make? How would you play it? What would it look like? Provide blank sheets of paper and coloured markers for pupils to explore and draft their ideas. This is useful if you have a limited number of mobile devices with Singing Fingers available.

2. Invite children to create, draw and record their instrument into Singing Fingers. If you have multiple mobile devices, this can be an individual or partner project. If you only have one, or a few, you can make this a whole-class or small-group project.

---

3. Once children have created their instruments, give them time to explore the instruments and to make changes. As with any musical instrument, it takes time and practice to master it. Be sure to provide enough time so that pupils can explore the creative possibilities of their instruments.

4. Invite children to create an original composition with their Singing Fingers instrument and rehearse it.

5. Invite children to present their instrument to the class and give them time to perform the composition they created with their Singing Fingers instrument. Be sure to have them save their drawn instrument for archiving.

CREATIVE STRATEGIES FOR USING SCRATCH

Scratch is a free, visual programming environment created by the Lifelong Kindergarten Group at the MIT Media Lab.[22] This environment was created as a means for children to 'remix' and 'play' with computer code in the same way that DJs and turntablists remix, play with and recombine musical samples and drumbeats. Also inspired by LEGO building blocks, children are asked to *imagine*, *program*, and *share* blocks of computer code, creating simple to very complex interactive computer programs and animations as a result. Rather than just being *consumers* of technology and games, Scratch enables children to be the *designers*, *producers*, and *creators* of the games. Additionally, the Scratch website serves as an online community of practice for both Scratch users and teachers to upload, discuss and share the projects they create.

Kafai, Peppler and Chapman (2009) profiled children's use of Scratch in afterschool *computer clubhouses* in greater Boston, Massachusetts. Their work documents how Scratch and the clubhouse teachers and environment inspired children to think of themselves as competent, creative and critical thinkers and learners. In the clubhouses, this was accomplished through an approach to the design of Scratch and the children's experiences where they actively build and design the tools with which they work.

Scratch is designed so that primary school age children can easily enter into computer programming experiences, while providing enough complexity to enable the creation of sophisticated projects by motivated pupils. This is, in part, accomplished through careful design and by putting the processes of play and remixing at the centre of the learning experience.

While Scratch is a general purpose programming environment designed for kids, it has a strong set of musical and sonic capabilities.[23] The music and sound blocks (see left side of Figure 7.2) enable children to work directly with musical concepts such as pitch, melody, duration, rhythm, tempo, tone colour, form, texture and volume, among others. Children can record in and edit their own sounds and sound effects, or they can create drumbeats and musical riffs, sequences and songs that accompany and interact with their animations and computer games. As a result, Scratch is a sophisticated, yet accessible, platform for musical and computational play that can foster creative expression among primary school age children.

Getting into Scratch

With the metaphor of 'remix' at the centre of the design of Scratch, children are encouraged to first visit the Scratch website (http://scratch.mit.edu) to browse and play one of the over

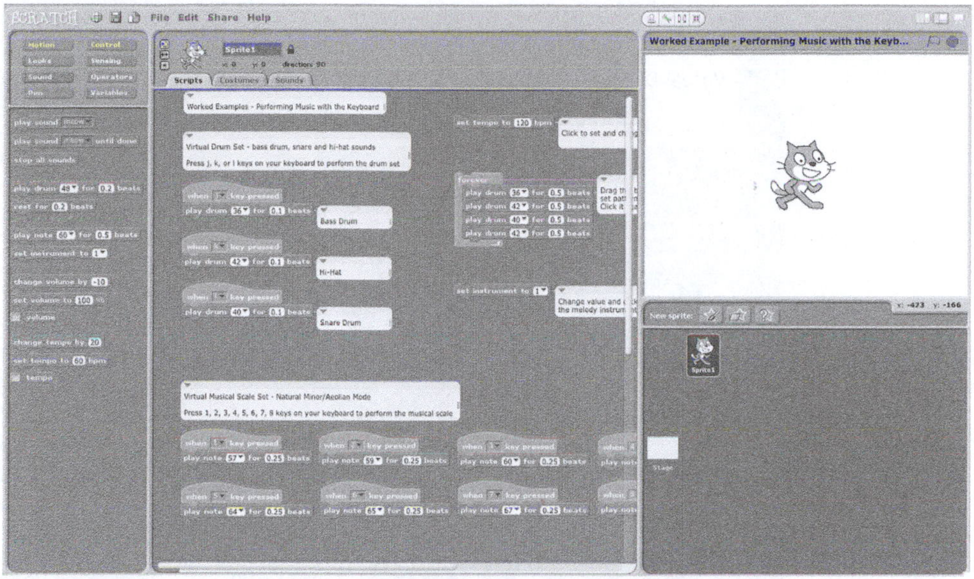

■ **Figure 7.2** Screenshot from Scratch 1.4.

10 million projects created by kids across the world. Once children find a project or game that they like, they can simply click a button to literally 'see inside' the project, which exposes all of the programming code, animations, sounds and images that were used in its creation.

A simple introduction to working with Scratch is for pupils to replace the images and sounds of the main objects (called 'Sprites' in Scratch) in one of the Scratch games with their own, using Scratch's built-in image and sound editors. Pupils who are more experienced with Scratch can further play with, explore and remix the inner code to any project as a way to learn how it was created or to make it their own. Though one can begin with a blank project and start from the ground up, this can be intimidating to pupils (and teachers!) who are new to computer programming. Starting in the 'middle' by remixing existing programs is often the most accessible entry point for primary age pupils.

There are many tutorials and related resources for getting started with Scratch available online. Many of these can be found on social media sites, such as YouTube and on the educators' page for Scratch at http://scratched.gse.harvard.edu. I encourage you to search out introductory tutorial videos to watch and also to connect with other primary educators working with Scratch on the ScratchEd site as you explore the project in this section of the chapter.

Making music with Scratch: performing with a keyboard

The project I am sharing with you starts with the principles of creative musical play and sound exploration. To begin with, download and open the example Scratch program – ScratchMusicKeyboard.sb[24] – in your version of Scratch. In this project, we're starting

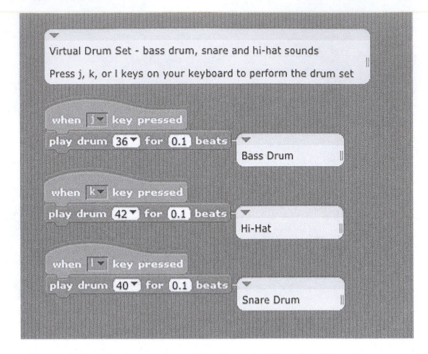

▨ **Figure 7.3** Code for a keyboard drum kit in Scratch: When the 'j' key is pressed, play
   drum sound '36' for '0.1' beats.

with a small, working program that turns your computer keyboard into an interactive drum
set and melody player. You can choose to start from the example program, or open a new
Scratch file and duplicate the code, as shown in Figure 7.3.

When you've downloaded and opened the ScratchMusicKeyboard.sb file in Scratch,
take a moment to view the first set of blocks (see Figure 7.3) and press the 'j', 'k' and 'l'
keys on your computer keyboard. If your volume is turned up, you should hear the three
basic drum set sounds of a bass drum when you press the 'j' key, a hi-hat when you press
the 'k' key and a snare drum when you press the 'l' key. This simple set of Scratch blocks
maps the computer keyboard keys to perform three drum sounds when the keys are pressed.
In Scratch, the blocks can be read similarly to regular language. For example, you can
convert the top set of two blocks into the following statement:

Take a couple of minutes to play around with those keys and drum sounds. Can you
find and perform a drumbeat?

The yellow blocks in Scratch are referred to as 'event' blocks. In this case, they are
'listening' for when a specific key on the computer keyboard is pressed. If it is pressed,
Scratch detects that *event* and does what the next block in line tells it to. In this case, each
of the three 'when __ key pressed' blocks is connected to a 'play drum' block. Whenever
one of the specified keys is pressed, the 'play drum' block plays the sound of the specified drum.

In the ScratchMusicKeyboard.sb project file, the 'j', 'k' and 'l' keys are assigned
to the drum sounds and the drum instrument values of '36' (bass drum), '42' (hi-hat) and

'40' (snare drum). Other drum sounds can be selected by clicking on the black triangle to the left of each number and changing the values in the 'play drum' block. This action brings up a list of many different drum sounds that can be used and assigned to various keys on the keyboard. Additionally, any key on the keyboard can be mapped to any sound in Scratch.

Remixing the Scratch drum set

While it is possible to create interesting drum rhythms using just a bass drum, hi-hat and snare, encourage your pupils to explore additional sounds by remixing and duplicating the existing ScratchMusicKeyboard.sb code. Pupils are also not limited to only three drum set sounds at a time. They can create additional sounds by dragging a new yellow 'when __ key pressed' block to the screen and connecting a new purple 'play drum' block. By repeating this process, pupils can build an entire percussion orchestra in Scratch for their own creative play and performance.

This example harnesses the interactive aspects of computer programming. Computers take input from various devices (such as mice, touch events and keys) and put those actions into motion to do various things, in this case to play musical sounds.

Creating and exploring riffs, patterns and melodies

Just like with drum sounds, melodic pitches can be also mapped to keys on the computer program. Take a look at the example code a bit further down on the screen in the Scratch-MusicKeyboard.sb example. In this example, the number keys on the computer keyboard are mapped to the pitches of a minor scale. Take a moment to press the numbers 1 through 8 on your computer keyboard and listen to the result.

Just as the drum set sounds and computer keys could be changed, so can the musical pitches. Again, by clicking on the black triangle to the right of the note value in the 'play note' block, you can change the pitches in the scale (see Figure 7.4). Convert the scale from a minor scale to a major scale by adding 1 to the 'play note' values under the 'when 3 key pressed' and the 'when 7 key pressed' blocks. Changing these values from 60 to 61 and 67 to 68, respectively, will create a major scale across the number keys on the computer keyboard. Take some time to see if you can find a melody or short musical riff using the number keys.

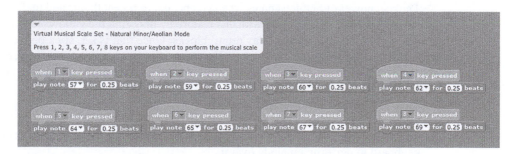

■ **Figure 7.4** Code for performing minor melodies with the keyboard in Scratch.

Tips for play and further exploration:

- Duplicate the blocks to add more notes to the scale.
- Adjust the existing values to create new scales.
- Play around and try to find a melody or musical riff or pattern that you know.
- Try performing a melody *and* a drumbeat at the same time, or with a partner.
- Assign the same keyboard key to multiple notes to create chords.

Listening for patterns and building loops

Computers are great at doing repetitive tasks. We can write a very small piece of code that tells the computer to do something over and over, and it will do that for us. The computer never gets bored repeating a task. We can harness this power of computers to our advantage when working creatively with music. Professional musicians spend hours practicing in order to learn to play and perform well the music they play. In fact, I'm sure you spent some time practicing the drumbeat and melody patterns you found above before you felt successful.

Patterns and sequences are key concepts in music. They are everywhere, from the riffs and drumbeats we find in popular songs to the repeating rhythms of Kendrick Lamar and motivic development of Beethoven. Below is a basic four-sound drum set pattern with a bass drum on beat 1, hi-hat on beat 2, snare drum on beat 3 and hi-hat on beat 4:

| 36–42–40–42 | 36–42–40–42 | 36–42–40–42 |
| J – K – L – K | J – K – L – K | J – K – L – K |

Take a moment to practice and perform the pattern above in tempo.

The pattern you just practiced above has been re-created as a connected set of blocks in Figure 7.5. If you connect multiple 'play drum' blocks together, you create a *sequence* of blocks, which in turn performs a musical sequence of drum sounds. Take a moment to duplicate and click on the above set of blocks in Figure 7.5. When you click on the blocks, Scratch will play drum 36 for 0.5 beats, drum 42 for 0.5 beats, drum 40 for 0.5 beats and finally drum 42 again for 0.5 beats. If you want the beats to be performed at a faster or slower speed, change the value of the 'set tempo' block and be sure to click the block after changing the value.

The real power of Scratch comes when you need it to repeat things and perform code blocks over and over. You can play with this feature by dragging the yellow 'forever' control block around the four purple 'play drum' blocks. Once that is set, click on the yellow block and your drum set pattern will repeat *forever*, until your computer loses power or you click on the yellow block again. You can use this feature to set up a regular drum pattern accompaniment.

Tips for play and further exploration:

- Start a drum set loop going within a 'forever' block and use the number keys on your keyboard to perform a melody over it.
- Create a more complicated drum pattern by adding 'play drum' blocks within the 'forever' block.

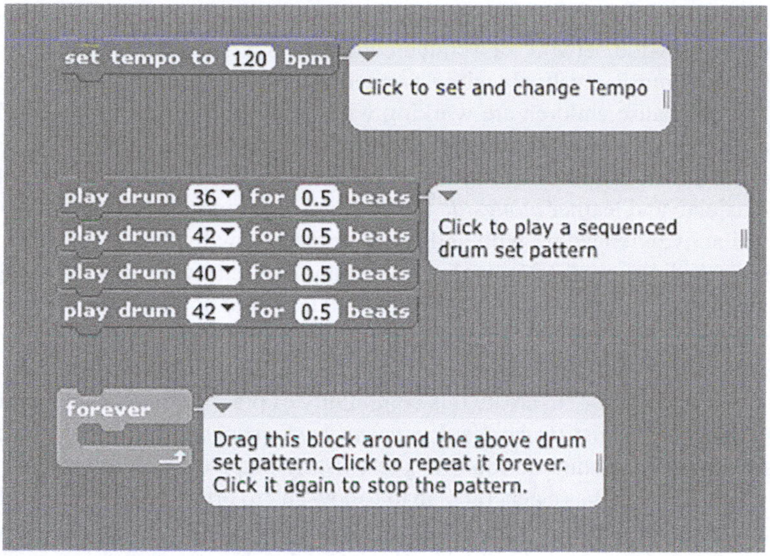

■ **Figure 7.5** Code for sequencing drum sounds in Scratch.

■ Change the 'beats' values to create different rhythms.
■ Drag 'play drum' blocks in and out of the 'forever' block while the loop is going to create variety and to explore different patterns.
■ Apply the same 'forever' block repetition technique to 'play note' blocks to create *melodic* riffs and patterns.

CONCLUSION

In this chapter, you have read about tools and projects that explore tangible media and computational media musicianship. The same creative threads and themes discussed in other chapters throughout this book also apply to new media musicianship. New media tools provide access to new communities of musical practice and help to scaffold pupils' musical expression. All of these tools engage pupils as makers, designers and curators of musical instruments and experiences. In these roles, children have new opportunities for musical agency through participation in the design of instruments and environments for musical exploration, performance, improvisation and composition in addition to the simple use of these engaging tools. And, these tools provide opportunities for creative musical experiences any time pupils have access to a mobile device or a computer, at home or at school.

In Singing Fingers, timbre and melodic contour are made audible, visible and tangible for children. This shifting of representations can help strengthen children's understanding of musical concepts and music-making skills. Singing Fingers is designed in ways that allow the students to participate in music making and creating at multiple levels and with any sound imaginable. This aspect is further developed within the Scratch environment as a platform for musical interaction, creativity and interdisciplinary connections with maths and computing. The sheer volume of student-created projects on the Scratch website and the worldwide network of Scratch educators is a great resource for beginning your work teaching music creatively with new media.

Because children are working with these tools on their own outside of school, the challenge then is for the teacher to cultivate a culture and community of new media musicians inside and around their classroom. This requires that the teacher take on the role of musician and learner *alongside* their pupils, creating spaces for pupils to share their music and actively engaging with and learning these new media musicianship practices. These new media musicianship tools enable you to extend your pupils' engagement with your music curriculum outside the physical and temporal bounds of your classroom and provide a space for students to bring their own musical ideas, *familiar and unexpected*, to the classroom.

One strategy to create this community of practice is to adopt a process advocated by ethnomusicologist Bruno Nettl: *musical cartography*.[25] When confronted with new technologies, it is natural to look for pre-existing maps to guide the way. In fact, one way to view this book is as a general map to follow and to orient you to the possibilities of learning and teaching music creatively. However, in order to facilitate creativity, one needs first-hand experience traversing the landscape and making one's own map. This is strengthened for pupils when the teacher sets off with their pupils on that same journey of creative exploration and collaborative map-making.

Now that you've read through this chapter, take time to review the tools and projects described and view the website links. Explore these yourself, make your own music with new media and think about what connections you might make to your curriculum, your musicianship and the interests and proclivities of your pupils. Document your own creative exploration with these new media musicianship projects and read other accounts of teachers sharing the findings of their own action research projects with new media technologies (e.g. Finney and Burnard, 2007; Somekh, 2007). Join online communities of practice focussed around primary classroom issues[26] – many of these communities have dedicated discussion groups around technology and new media. They are a great place to discuss your challenges and interests with other like-minded educators.

The tools for making and creating music have always been changing. Our children are making music with new media on their own, finding their own way and discovering new pathways for musical expression. Join them on their journey and create maps together helping them achieve deeper levels of musical understanding, expression and creativity with new media.

WEBSITES AND APPLICATIONS

Singing Fingers	http://singingfingers.com/
MadPad	http://www.smule.com/madpad/
aQWERTYon	https://musedlab.org/aqwertyon/
GroovePizza	https://musedlab.org/groovepizza/
Fresh Annotator	https://musedlab.org/freshannotator/
Bohemian Rhapsichord	http://bohemianrhapsichord.com/
Girl Talk in a Box	http://static.echonest.com/girltalkinabox

InBflat Project	http://www.inbflat.net/
Scratch	http://scratch.mit.edu/
MaKey MaKey	http://www.makeymakey.com/
Scratch Music Projects	http://scratchmusicprojects.com/

NOTES

1 See Kutiman's 'Mother of all funk chords' (www.youtube.com/watch?v=tprMEs- zfQA), Lasse Gjertsen's 'Amateur' (www.youtube.com/watch?v=JzqumbhfxRo), and Pomplamoose's 'Hail Mary' (www.youtube.com/watch?v=fYy2p_0DVMU).

2 Smith, E. (August 14, 2012) Forget CDs: Teens are tuning into YouTube. *Wall Street Journal*. Available at http://online.wsj.com/article/SB10000872396390444042704577587570410556212.html.

3 iPad, iPhone, and iPod Touch.

4 http://singingfingers.com/

5 http://scratch.mit.edu/

6 http://llk.media.mit.edu/

7 http://thru-you.com/

8 http://pomplamoose.com/

9 http://ericwhitacre.com/the-virtual-choir

10 http://scratch.mit.edu/

11 www.smule.com/MadPad

12 www.makerbloks.com/

13 https://littlebits.cc/kits/synth-kit

14 https://musedlab.org/aqwertyon/

15 https://musedlab.org/groovepizza/

16 https://musedlab.org/freshannotator/

17 http://bohemianrhapsichord.com/

18 http://static.echonest.com/girltalkinabox/

19 For more practical ideas exploring musical problem solving in primary music education, see Wiggins, J. (2010) *Teaching for Musical Understanding* (2nd edition). Rochester, MI: Center for Applied Research in Musical Understanding.

20 For practical strategies facilitating children's musical curiosities, see Greher & Ruthmann's (2012) summarisation of the work of Jeanne Bamberger.

21 If you have multiple mobile devices, it is helpful to have several headphone splitters and headphones to keep the sound levels low enough for optimal recording.

22 Scratch can be accessed at http://scratch.mit.edu.

23 For more examples of projects and information on teaching music with Scratch, visit http://scratchmusicprojects.com and http://performamatics.org.

24 You can download the ScratchMusicKeyboard.sb file that accompanies this chapter at http://alexruthmann.com/ScratchMusicKeyboard.sb.

25 See Nettl, B. (1960). Musical cartography and the distribution of music. *Southwestern Journal of Anthropology*, 16(3), 338–347.

26 http://www.facebook.com/group/musicpln.

ENHANCING CREATIVITY THROUGH LISTENING TO MUSIC

Regina Murphy

INTRODUCTION

Listening is the keystone to developing a musical ear and it provides one of the most accessible entry points for enhancing creativity. Listening to music can bring joy, energy or tranquillity, inspire action, evoke memories or provide an impetus for dance. A major creativity theme that weaves through this chapter is the idea that active listening provides a way of connecting with both the familiar and unexpected features of a piece of music. In whole-class music listening, the teacher is completely immersed in the process and thus is well positioned to embark on creative and exciting explorations with his or her class.

In this chapter we will explore creativity through the avenues of listening, visualising, moving and talking about music. Beginning with listening, we will also learn about approaches to creating new music with children, whether starting with music they already know, entirely new pieces or with the children's own music. Listening closely and analysing structures, melodies and creative ideas helps children think about how they can make music of their own. Over time, they will come to appreciate that composers tend to play around with ideas – as Mozart did on the piano with the tune 'Twinkle Twinkle Little Star' in the 1780s or, some centuries later, as John Cage did in his composition with various household items to create 'Living Room Music' in 1940.

As in previous chapters in this book where the threads of creativity are woven through the teaching and learning processes of the teacher and the pupil, the creative approach is also essential to listening to music. The imagination can take flight in an active listening lesson, as we shall see, and the possibilities for exploration and experimentation are also limitless. Once again, the teacher is pivotal in the creation of an environment that allows for open-ended thinking, curiosity and diversity of interpretation. The teacher and the pupils also share the creative experience in a very special way since they both encounter the music simultaneously and can savour its rhythms, melodies, style, mood or tone colour in shared listening moments.

LISTENING CREATIVELY TO MUSIC AS A TEACHER

As a teacher you encounter music in innumerable ways. Interests can be diffuse and diverse – from early childhood experiences at home, through school and college years, and throughout your teaching career as you teach new music, listen to a group perform, participate in music events for secular or spiritual purposes or simply express an opinion about a recording or a live concert. But it is possible to get stuck in a kind of groove too, and to confine yourself unwittingly to a favourite set of recordings or radio stations.

Activity 8.1 Reflection on listening

▦   How often do I really listen to music, apart from background music?
▦   What kind of music do I listen to?
▦   Am I conservative or predictable in my listening choices?
▦   Do I need to be more adventurous in what I choose to listen to?
▦   How does music affect me?

Music surrounds us and indeed it is used in many subtle ways in our environment, which we may or may not be conscious of as we go about our everyday lives of travelling to work, eating, shopping for food or clothing, listening to advertisements or sitting in waiting rooms (de Nora, 2000). Music from other cultures finds its way easily into the listening surroundings, and the boundaries between different genres, traditional and modern, often overlap or blend with each other so that it can be hard to distinguish what one is listening to, even when we try to listen carefully. Children too, are not excluded from the varying types of music in the world around them – their music can come from a very rich tradition, but it is likely to be restricted to their cultural worlds and, for the urban child, is more likely to be influenced by visual rather than aural media, depending on their contexts.

How is listening to music creative?

Listening to music is like the internal operation of the external process of singing, playing, improvising and composing. If you want to learn to play a piece, you will instinctively listen to it millions of times. If you want to sing it, you might try singing along with the words until you know them exactly in time and in pitch with the soundtrack. To be creative, you have to internalise the music until it is yours and then you can invent your own things to do with the music. So first we see that the creative teacher listens closely and thus becomes very familiar with the music and with its possibilities before exploring it with others. This is similar to exploring a poem with a class – where the teacher strives for a good understanding of the work before presenting it to the class for discussion.

But how does one become good at listening to music?

Activity 8.2 Becoming a creative music listener

▦   Find a few minutes in your day for listening to music, either as part of your commute to work or after hours. Think of yourself as 'getting out more' – out of your usual listening habits and entering a special world of music listening.
▦   Set yourself a challenge of finding a genre or a composer that is unfamiliar to you. You've probably listened to lots of popular music and music by great

---

Western composers, but how many living composers do you listen to? And do you know any female composers? Maybe you know one or two songs from a single opera – but have you tried listening to other opera pieces, or a whole opera itself? And what does the term 'world music' mean to you?

■ Give yourself a chance to listen to the music, but you don't have to understand it in great detail – just be affected by it in some way and enjoy the creative space that it affords.

■ As you listen, you can make associations with the music and imagine a dream world of your own. On the other hand you can try to figure out what is happening in the music by looking out for some features – is there a melody that is repeated, or even a whole section, or just some part that is varied? Does the music have a recognisable beat? Is there a rhythm pattern that recurs? Are there many instruments playing? What kinds of effects are they trying to create? Is there one instrument leading and another following? Are they having some kind of musical conversation? What kind of shape do you imagine the music to be? What kind of light and colour?

■ Allow yourself many opportunities to listen to the music if you can and to 'listen out' for different features each time – such as following the direction of a melody line and how singers or players are interpreting it, noticing individual instruments playing or falling silent or sounds merging with other instruments. If you had to choose the most interesting part of the music, think about what section it would be.

■ With a lot of classical music it's very easy to find many different recordings of the same piece. Listen to one other interpretation and decide which one you prefer and why. (There are endless amateur and professional recordings on YouTube.) Soon you're on the way to developing your creative musical imagination – and to becoming a music buff!

The key to creative listening in the classroom is being familiar with the music in advance. You do not have to have expert knowledge about the music, nor do the children, although researching information about the composer and the music is worthwhile and can happen subsequently. Finding and selecting music for listening can come from any number of sources, be it your own private collection, digital radio, online collections belonging to national agencies, digital music shops or online video such as YouTube. (A list of sources is provided at the end of this chapter.) Most classrooms are busy places and it is good to select the music in advance and decide how much of it you're going to use.

HOW TO SELECT MUSIC FOR CLASSROOM LISTENING

For background listening, the music can drift along for several minutes and need not have a particular focal point. (This is sometimes referred to as 'piped music', 'elevator music' or 'muzak'.) But for close listening, where you want the children to engage creatively with the music and learn something special, every second counts; in such cases, even 20 seconds can provide plenty of material. This brings us to the criteria for selecting music for listening. Music listening pieces for the classroom should be:

■ Short
■ Surprising and varied
■ Colourful and unique
- in character, style or instrumentation;
- in how it facilitates a creative approach by the teacher; and
- in how it enables a creative response from the children.

Short pieces

Short pieces of music provide very good opportunities for listening to music several times, which is important if the children are to get know the music during a regular lesson in the classroom. Even 30 seconds can provide a lot of listening 'information'. An excerpt can be used if a piece is long, and the full recording can be listened to at a later stage or at home. Research shows us that listening to music several times also develops a liking for the music and an increased understanding.

Surprising and varied

Music that shows a variety of speed/tempo or loudness/quietness, or that has striking contrasts in sections, in the use of instruments or other aspects, works well for creative music listening because it is easier to follow than long, flowing pieces. Surprises and variety also enable children to identify a feature quickly and to locate it in the music, before or after other parts. In that way, the listening experience can be made more concrete and represented in other forms. Selections of music can also be varied for different lessons, even if they share a common theme – for example, 'The Cuckoo' in the piano piece by Louis-Claude Daquin and 'The Cuckoo in the Depths of the Woods', from *Carnival of the Animals* by Camille Saint-Saëns.[1]

Colourful and unique

The sounds of different instruments or voices lend themselves to different kinds of questions about the special colour (or timbre) of a piece. A piece of music by a rock group will have different qualities to a choir singing unaccompanied, different again from a honky-tonk piano or a French horn playing with an orchestra. The words we might use to describe the music will also stretch the imagination.

Each piece can allow for different ways of exploring the music, such as through discussion, listening and creating a dance or writing a script for a play. The uniqueness of the music will also facilitate different ways in which children can respond to music. Likewise, if we want to facilitate different kinds of responses, the kind of music that we choose in the first instance is important.

Of course it is possible to listen to interesting marching music over the course of a whole year, or music by Mozart only, but by thinking about the unique quality of a piece of music, a teacher can think creatively about the kind of palette that is being presented to the children and the kind of interpretations that are facilitated.

The uniqueness of a music selection will also be governed by cultural context of the children in the class and how the teacher might like to affirm or expand cultural identity. A creative teacher is one who is mindful of inclusive practices and sensitive to minority cultures and traditions, yet knows how to challenge the limitations of cultural norms by presenting music that is in some way 'new' to the child listener. 'Colourful' music will have:

▦ Contrast in loudness and softness.
▦ Contrast in speeds, getting faster or slower.
▦ Contrast in instruments – one or many; different kinds of instruments or voices.
▦ Parts that change and transform into something else.
▦ A pattern that is played and then a new pattern comes.
▦ A repeat of something that is heard earlier.
▦ A recognisable melody.
▦ A quirky rhythm.
▦ A conversation.
▦ A dark or light mood.
▦ Music that inspires different images, feelings or memories.

A yearly plan for classroom music listening might include any number of learning objectives and span a range of musical genres and styles to support such learning. There is no magic formula to generating a creative curriculum for music listening. Indeed, in some schools, certain pieces might be prescribed for cultural, historical or policy reasons, but a creative teacher will consider creative ways of exploring a familiar piece of music, as we shall see in the next section.

ENGAGING CREATIVELY WITH THE MUSIC

Once a teacher has selected some pieces for listening, it's important to involve the children in the musical experience from the beginning. Stopping and starting a piece of music can be frustrating, but by having an entire short excerpt, it is possible to play the whole piece through and enjoy it as a complete listening experience.

The teacher's role is to organise the activity and the children, start to pose questions at the right time and direct the children's attention towards the music. The creative teacher will be a good observer, participating in the children's explorations, guiding the children towards a better understanding of the music and explaining and mediating what the lesson is about.

There are a number of ways of exploring listening with children which are illustrated in many listening resources on the web or in published materials. Many lesson plans involve the children in 'closed' type approaches and responses, such as:

▦ Is the music fast or slow?
▦ Where is the slow part?
▦ Can you clap when you hear the drum in the music?
▦ How many times can you hear the triangle being played?
▦ What is the name of the group of instruments that you hear at this point?
▦ Follow the listening map in your book and use two colours to show the parts where it is loud or soft.
▦ Write the names of the instruments that you hear in the correct order.

These questions and the related activities are important for ensuring that children are following the music and can accurately describe the structure or feature of the music at particular points. However, there is little room for creative engagement if this is the *only* approach. An alternative and more creative way of exploring the music listening experience is to ask questions such as:

- Can you tell me what is happening in the music?
- Is the music the same all the way through?
- Why do you say this?
- How would you show that in a drawing/dance/script/using LEGO blocks?
- Can your group make a dance to match the music? What gestures will you use? Why?
- How can you show in your story that the music changes?
- Can you explain why you have used different colours and patterns in this part in your drawing?
- Is there a way of showing the special character of the music in the images you have selected?
- Is the music similar to any music you have heard before? Why do you say so?

The teacher's questions are vital for directing the children's attention towards the music and for encouraging the children to justify their responses. This fosters an open and creative approach that permeates other aspects of music making and indeed other aspects of learning across the curriculum.

LEARNING MORE ABOUT THE MUSIC

As a teacher you don't have to have advanced knowledge or feel compelled to impress such knowledge on young children to enable them to listen to music creatively. Rather, the important element is to foster an open style of questioning and to value the children's responses. Encouraging them to express their opinions and justify their interpretations leads to more sensitive understanding and this is also fostered in a classroom of trust where individual children can also express views about pieces, including their personal preferences.

Preparing for listening

Equipment for listening has evolved in sophisticated ways – from cassette tapes to digital recordings – and while some yearn for the quality of sound produced on vinyl records, in the classroom the principle remains the same: use the best quality equipment that you can muster to convey the breadth of sounds in the music to all parts of the room. Additionally, to facilitate independent and focussed listening, sets of high quality headphones are important, especially for use by younger children. In this way pupils can listen independently (and silently!) in the classroom if necessary while others are working in cooperative groups and discussing their responses to a piece.

Choosing the moment to share information

Children do not need a lot of theory or detailed historical knowledge about the music in order to engage with it, especially if there are surprises and contrasts in the music that excite them from the start. Neither do they need the title of the piece or the name of the composer – at least at first – that can come later.

For example, a teacher could say, 'Here is a piece of music, what image does it create in your mind?' (take for example Rimsky-Korsakov's 'The Flight of the Bumble Bee' played on the flute or 'Spinning Song for Cello' by David Popper – recordings of which are easily available on YouTube). The children might think of insects or racing cars or something wobbling around off balance. After the children have listened to the music, discussed what is happening in it a few times and made suggestions for a title, then the teacher could share the composer's title with the class. The children could then discuss whether or not they felt the title was a good one, or if their own one was better.

A similar approach can involve the children in studying bumblebees (or spinning tops) and creating a piece of music that tells us something about how they move, fly, eat and sting. After the children have invented their music, rehearsed and performed it for the class, the teacher could then introduce Rimsky-Korsakov's piece and let the children compare their music with that of the Russian composer, deciding which one they prefer and giving reasons for their opinions.

Information about the composer herself or himself can also be introduced at appropriate moments. Stories from contemporary composers about how they came to write a piece of music and devised its title can be found on the composer's own website or through links with the contemporary music information centres.

Listening as a whole group to the whole piece is a good way to start a listening experience, following that with discussion to clarify aspects of the music or to give the children pointers for the tasks ahead. For particular pieces of music, the point at which the music itself is introduced can be built up in a series of preparatory activities – such as learning to play a melody from a longer piece or making a new composition based on a given structure. A technique that composers use quite frequently is a 'musical sandwich' – something regular, something different, something regular again (often known as ABA form, with a letter for each part, and showing how the first part 'A' is repeated). The children can explore making music with this kind of structure, for example by experimenting on a xylophone, making patterns such as a 'walking tune', a 'gliding tune', and then repeating the 'walking tune'. While proposing a structure for the composition the teacher remains open to unusual ideas from the children and fosters their curiosity. Later, they can listen to a piece of music that has the 'musical sandwich' or ABA structure (e.g. 'Radetzky March' by Johann Strauss Sr.) and the children can talk about what they recognise or notice in the music, their sense of anticipation having been whetted by the previous activity.

GENERATING CREATIVE RESPONSES

In the example above, we saw how listening to music and generating a response is a form of creative problem solving – figuring out what is going on, making comparisons with something encountered previously and making mental images before representing the music in concrete form. In this respect, it is possible to see how listening to music can create cognitive demands, as much research attests, but more importantly the child is drawn into the process and begins to develop a sense of ownership of both the music and the process of engagement.

Continuing the creative approach initiated by the teacher, the children can be guided to respond to the music in a number of ways but at all times connecting their response to the music itself. They can choose to make imaginative associations with the music – letting the music affect them in some way and imagining a mood, feeling, story or picture that would match the music – or they can be guided to focus on structural elements in the music. These would include features such as the overall patterns and structure of the music, the shape of the melody and rhythms, the particular sounds of the instruments and whether they are played singly or together.

The children's responses can relate to activities within music and to learning in other areas of the curriculum. As we can see, the responses can be verbal, artistic, physical, musical or digital. Creative teachers will balance the types of responses expected from students – diverging from written activities into responses that involve creating a dance or movement sequence.

Opportunities for movement in music help develop understanding of the natural structures in music – much like sentences in reading. Learning about structural features and inventing notations (as we see in Chapter 9) can provide stepping stones to musical reading and writing. These emphases are not new and can be found in the philosophies of some of the great music educators such as Zoltán Kodály, Carl Orff and Émile Jacques Dalcroze. Their ideas are still being adapted to twenty-first-century classrooms, to new forms of music making and to the digital worlds of young children today.

Habituating the children to creative listening responses can be developed with very short pieces, for example by drawing the shape of a piece of music that is just 10 seconds long. 'Drawing' music lies very close to the first stage of inventing notations as we shall see in Chapter 9. As well as that, short activities can be organised quickly in busy class-rooms where time is precious, but they can be very effective in sharpening listening skills and focussing attention (see Table 8.1).

■ **Table 8.1** Responding creatively to music

Speaking writing	Discussing, improvising a drama – in pairs or groups, creative story, poetry, script writing, stories
Reading	Studying, researching a composition, composer, period, genre; reading others' written responses
Art making	Drawing, e.g. using lines to show melody, rhythm, texture; colour to show mood; mask making, using clay, paint, collage, puppetry
Construction	Using bricks, blocks, train tracks, pebbles; connecting clips to show structures
Movement	Finger play, hands and feet; facial expression to show mood, surprising elements; creating a whole dance or march in groups to accompany a piece; making up a dance whilst sitting; creating a mime
Performing	Figuring out the melody on a xylophone, chime bars or recorder; finding the tune 'hidden' in the instrument; playing along; figuring out the rhythm pattern and playing along on a tambour
Composing	Creating new music response, in the same style; making an accompaniment; songwriting
Improvising	Playing along with the music and extending it
Curation	Finding 'more like this' or 'similar but different'; making a list of favourites
Digital manipulation	Creating a visual interpretation or presentation to accompany a piece; remixing clips

Activity 8.3 Show me the music

■ Play two short excerpts for the whole class (or increase to three for added difficulty).

■ Using a personal listening device and headphones, let one child listen to the music and then show what is happening in the music through movement.

■ The other children have to guess which piece he or she is listening to.

■ The children have to justify their reasons for interpreting the music and the movement the way they do.

As in many creative endeavours, there are no absolute 'right' answers – just interpretations that work either more or less effectively than others. This idea is also developed further when we come to look at assessment in Chapter 11.

Encouraging the children to explore music by developing 'musical maps' (Blair, 2007) has been shown to be an artistic and useful way of enabling children to demonstrate their music listening in concrete ways. A similar strategy is to create puzzle cards that match the music – either with symbols, lines, dots or patterns – and let the children work in pairs or groups to solve the 'musical puzzle'. Other variants that can be featured in puzzle cards include fragments of notation, dance patterns, pictures of instruments, musical terms and signs or single words (Espeland, 1987, 1991; Murphy and Espeland, 2007).

Case study 8.1: Puzzle card listening

Mrs. Jackson selected a short piece of music for her class to listen to: the 'Viennese Musical Clock' from the *Háry János Suite* by Zoltán Kodály. She chose it because it was classical music and because it illustrated orchestral playing, but most of all because she liked the way the excerpt is full of variety – a strong beat, an identifiable, quirky melody, a part that repeats, a middle section that is quite different and then a repeat of the first part again, with some differences towards the end – and all packed into 2 minutes. Mrs. Jackson made some notation puzzle cards for the children – but not using standard notation. Instead, what she presented were graphics that suggested something about the shape of the melody and the sounds of instruments. At that stage of the year, the children could not read music, but they had talked about different ways in which music could be written down or notated. In this lesson, Mrs. Jackson was asking the children to think about the music from the other way around – by giving them notation first and asking them to work in groups to match it with the music. At first the children were too busy organising themselves in their group and didn't seem to be listening to the music. But she persisted in asking them questions to probe their understanding and explain what they were doing. Every time she asked if they were finished they pleaded with her to play the music just one more time – not realising that they had listened to it several times already. Her creative approach was working! Mrs. Jackson realised that even 2 minutes of music could be full of interesting listening challenges.

Cooperative learning

Many activities can be approached using cooperative learning strategies (Gillies, 2007). This is where the children work together in small mixed-ability groups to solve a given problem related to the music and achieve the task set by the teacher. The members of the groups are interdependent; they encourage and support each other in the learning, participate equally and take responsibility for their own share of the work. As each individual child's engagement with the music will differ, the children will need to be accountable for their work, individually and as members of the group, explaining and justifying their solutions and demonstrating their approach to the other groups with conviction. In this respect, children's agency and ownership of the music learning experience is nurtured.

Engaging deeply with the music

Once the children have prepared and presented their responses to the music and shared their explorations and justifications with the rest of the class, opportunities for engaging more deeply with the music can take place. This can happen in a number of ways: through extension activities, discussion and reflection and, most importantly, through returning to the music again some weeks later to listen to the music afresh, with new insights gained from other music activities that have happened in the meantime.

Case study 8.2: Instruments in dialogue

Paul chose a piece of Breton music to play for his class. They had been playing folk tunes on the tin whistle and he thought it would be good to hear other wind instruments. The music provided an opportunity too for the children to think about music as a conversation between two instruments. At first the children found the sound of the *bombarde* (big bagpipe) and *biniou* (little bagpipe) very strange. But Paul persisted with questions that encouraged the children to say what was happening in the music.

John said that it seemed as if the instruments were talking to each other and that it sounded as if two people were having an argument; it reminded him of when he and his friends are talking about which football team they follow, and when his younger brother interrupts in his squeaky voice. Paul then asked the children to write a dialogue that would match the music and so John used lots of exclamation marks in his. Later, Paul felt it was the right time to tell the children that the music came from Brittany in France. Then Orla told the class that she saw two people playing 'sort of bagpipes' in the campground when her family was on holidays in Brittany the previous year, and that she would bring in a photograph of the musicians in their costumes to show the class. Conor wondered if these pipes were like the *uilleann* pipes[2] that his dad plays at Comhaltas music club. Some of the children wanted to listen to the music on the headphones one more time. Paul thought it best to read the dialogues aloud another day so that they could continue the discussion about Breton music.

NURTURING CREATIVE LISTENERS IN A 'FLIPPED CLASSROOM'

Flipped teaching, or reverse teaching, refers to a form of learning that allows pupils to use technology to learn outside of the classroom so that the teacher can utilise classroom time for extension of the basic lesson and higher order teaching.[3] Rather than what happens in a traditional classroom, where the teacher typically introduces the lesson, sets a task and assigns follow-up homework, in a flipped classroom, the teacher might post a video of a lesson and encourage the pupils to undertake private study outside of class time. Given the wide access to music and children's individual tastes in music (Boal-Palheiros and Hargreaves, 2001) it is worthwhile encouraging the children to become 'curators' of their own music and to search for and listen critically to music that appeals to them.

Children can be guided to become critical and creative listeners through the activities described previously. In addition, some Internet-based resources can be particularly useful.

Activity 8.4 Adjudicators

Choose a piece of music that the children have listened to earlier in the year and have an affinity with in some way. (It works best as a solo piece.)

- Find two different recordings of the piece on YouTube.
- Explain to the class that they are going to a concert to hear two performers playing.
- Members of the class are designated the adjudicators.
- Play the music and have the adjudicators give their opinions as to which one they prefer by giving reasons for their choice.

The World Music Network website includes a section titled 'Battle of the Bands' where members can upload their best original track (see additional resources section at the end of this chapter). Older primary school children may be involved in junior garage band activities outside of school, but even if they do not post music, they can be involved in the public voting on the site for their favourite music. This is a useful way of developing the children's individual agency as creative listeners and music critics. Creating a class YouTube channel of favourite links can also provide a doorway to music curation and empowerment of young audiences.

Too often, parent–teacher communications focus exclusively on formal learning in literacy and numeracy, while discussion on music is confined to showcase, seasonal events or end-of-year concerts. The rich learning that takes place in music lessons can be lost if it is not recorded in some way, connected with homework and reported at the end of the term. Music listening lends itself easily to listening in other contexts, especially at home, where parents and children can enjoy music together. Given opportunities, children can follow up with their parents and request that they listen on their own devices to longer excerpts, or to music that is similar in style or purpose.

CONCLUSION

The skilled use of questioning and a facilitative and open-ended approach to the teaching and learning experience are essential for finding creative 'solutions' to musical 'problems' and gaining active engagement from the children. By organising the activity and children, putting the right questions at the right time, directing the children's attention towards the music, observing closely what is going on, participating in the children's explorations, guiding the children towards a better understanding of the music, explaining and mediating, and by assessing the children's expression and their ability to relate to the music, the teacher has the potential to nurture the children towards artistic music making. At times the teacher is also the person who is 'silently receptive' to the children as they work, conveying an open attitude to their creations and explorations and accepting the variation in their solutions.

SOURCING A RANGE OF MUSIC FOR CREATIVE LISTENING

World Music Network

Using informative text combined with playlists and video content, World Music Network (http://www.worldmusic.net) guides listeners through music from around the world. With text excerpts courtesy of the *Rough Guide* books, this site is a great resource and introduction into world music, especially from minority cultures.

International Association of Music Information Centres

IAMIC (http://www.iamic.net) is a global network that provides links to an international network of almost forty organisations that document, promote and inform on the music of their country or region in a diversity of musical genres. Many member sites feature free resources for teachers as well as a host of audio and video clips, interviews with composers and information on where to get original scores.

Jango

Jango (http://www.jango.com) is a free Internet-based streaming radio service and music search engine that can provide customised music feeds with detailed information. By building on the user's listening and search history, the search engine can make recommendations based on preferred genres, styles or artists.

Comhaltas

Comhaltas Ceoltóirí Éireann (http://comhaltas.ie/music) is an Irish traditional music non-profit association and cultural movement with hundreds of local branches around the world. The website includes archives of many audio and video sessions of different instruments and players of all ages, as well as daily clips of live music from around Ireland and worldwide.

BBC

The website http://www.bbc.co.uk/music features video excerpts from many BBC performances in various genres.

iTunes

iTunes is a digital media player produced by Apple that can be used on various Mac devices and others that use Windows operating systems. Amongst other things, it is used for playing, downloading, saving and organising digital music and video files, and for accessing the iTunes music store, where it is possible to listen to an excerpt from a track before making a purchase.

Spotify

Spotify (http://www.spotify.com) is a music streaming service that offers digitally restricted streaming of selected music from a range of major and independent record labels. Music can be browsed by artist, album, record label, genre or playlist as well as by direct searches.

Pandora

Pandora (http://www.pandora.com) is another online streaming radio station that enables you to create your own stations based on what you like. It also enables you to discover new artists and to create new playlists based on your recent choices.

Naxos

Naxos (http://www.naxos.com) is one of the largest independent classical record labels in the world. It is known for its specialisation in classical music but it also includes other genres among its collections, such as Chinese music, jazz, world music and the early years of rock and roll. The company also distributes streaming web radio and podcasts and produces listening guides and booklets for listeners.

SoundCloud

SoundCloud (http://www.soundcloud.com) is an exciting portal where listeners are introduced to recordings of new and emerging works by various users and artists who freely share their work. Here the most popular works that are trending can easily be identified and listeners can also search by artist, genre, track, etc. From a social media perspective, by following users, one can stay abreast of new releases and mark them for storage in a personal music collection.

DEVELOPING YOUR KNOWLEDGE OF MUSIC

Open Yale courses

Open Yale Courses (http://oyc.yale.edu/music/musi-112) is a project of Yale University that provides free access to full video and course materials, including a course in music listening.

SOURCES FOR CREATIVE MUSIC LISTENING FOR CHILDREN

Carnegie Hall Online Resource Centre

Includes music excerpts, listening guides, games and activities (http://www.carnegiehall.org).

Classics for Kids

Features excerpts from many of the most popular classical music pieces (http://www.classicsforkids.com/music/).

NOTES

1   Both pieces can be found on YouTube. *Carnival of the Animals* is widely available in various recordings.
2   See http://comhaltas.ie.
3   Alvarez, B. (2012) *Flipping the Classroom: Homework in Class, Lessons at Home.* National Education Association. http://neapriorityschools.org/successful-students/flipping-the-classroom-homework-in-class-lessons-at-home-2.

CELEBRATING CHILDREN'S INVENTED NOTATIONS

Rena Upitis

INTRODUCTION

We have already seen that creative approaches to music making involve some key elements: teachers who are committed to children's learning and are themselves interested in learning new things, teachers who can take risks and are curious about children's interests and teachers who are able to use a wide variety of teaching methods to reach the pupils that they teach. Creative practice also includes the ability to link ideas across disciplines and approaches, to connect with pupils' lives, to encourage pupils to ask questions and to provide an environment where pupils can work individually and with others. In order to learn in these ways, the classroom culture has to be one that promotes emotional and intellectual engagement, has the resources needed for learning and ensures that students feel safe and valued while, at the same time, they are encouraged to take risks with their learning. These are the same types of conditions that foster creativity in any discipline, but especially in music, where the teacher may be learning alongside with the pupils.

In this chapter, we will explore the kind of classroom environment needed to support children as they learn to write and read music creatively. In looking at the environment, we will explore not only the types of resources and activities that support creative work, but also the ways that the teacher can model creative approaches and demonstrate trust towards the pupils. We will also examine a few open-ended activities that teachers introduce to help young pupils develop their own notational systems, including examples produced by primary school children. Throughout, the interaction between musical performances and notational systems will be described, showing how ideas are linked and developed further. Another link that we will examine is the relationship between invented music notations and invented notations in language. Finally, we will look at how invented notations can be bridged to standard notational forms through composition and performance.

WHAT ARE OUR EXPECTATIONS FOR READING AND WRITING MUSIC NOTATIONS?

From birth, children learn that language is important. They are constantly bombarded – overtly and covertly – by the sounds and the symbols of language. While most of us hear music every day, music symbols are far less evident in everyday life. Many of us can go through days at a time without seeing a treble clef or notes on a staff. But it is nearly impossible to spend a day without seeing a sign with words, or a newspaper, book or text on a computer screen. Children watch adults and older children interact with print every day – while driving, reading recipes or answering text messages on their mobile phones. The same simply cannot be said for reading music. No wonder so many of us find the idea of reading music daunting! From the early years we simply haven't been exposed to notation as often as we have been exposed to print.

There is another complication with music that we don't have with print. The music that young children are exposed to in formal teaching settings – and even at home – is often limited to 'children's songs', that is, songs that have been determined as developmentally appropriate for children. The music of older primary children is similarly limited, usually to whatever is offered in the school curriculum, coupled with the iTunes and YouTube selections they listen to with their friends. In contrast, children are exposed to language that is far more complex than 'children's language' – that is, a few simple words or language from limited genres. No wonder they learn to communicate through the written and spoken word more easily than through musical symbols.

From an early age, and right through school, we both encourage and expect children to use language to communicate. We encourage original utterances from children, praising even the earliest resemblances to adult forms. For example, the phrase 'Do by delf' as an approximation for 'I'll do it by myself' will elicit cries of glee from parents and older siblings. Not only is children's novel speech praised, their early attempts at writing (or scribbling) are also celebrated. In contrast, children's novel music making is rarely given the same consistent attention – if it is even noticed in the first place.

But when children are immersed in an environment rich with possibilities for musical creation, they develop an astonishing variety of symbols and strategies to notate rhythms and melodies. These charming notations can be of familiar melodies or of their own compositions. Children's creative notations often include the use of pictures, icons, letters, words, numbers, straight lines, squiggles, music symbols, abstract symbols and colour to create engaging and effective systems of recording the music that they hear.

SETTING THE STAGE FOR EXPLORING NOTATIONS CREATIVELY

Nothing scares a teacher more than the feeling of being ill-prepared to teach music. Usually this fear comes from the inability to read standard music notation – admittedly, an important part of music making in the Western world, but hardly a deal breaker. Many extraordinary musicians lead full and successful musical lives without ever reading a note of music. That said, our musical worlds can be incredibly enriched through music notation, giving us access to more music for performance and a deeper understanding of musical structure and form.

Learning to read music is not as daunting as one might think, especially if it is done in ways that mirror the acquisition of language. For those classroom teachers who have yet to learn to read music, many will find that they can learn along with their pupils, using the same creative kinds of activities and approaches that the pupils engage in to discover how sound and symbol are related. There are also many web-based notation tutorials that will be enough to get you started – even an hour or two will yield a lot of learning. And even if you don't read a note of music, your abilities as a teacher will be enough for you to lead the activities that are described in this chapter.

We will now explore four related activities that can help pupils develop their own musical notations. In the first instance, the activity centres on a familiar melody. In the second, the notational task involves a melody that is presented to the pupils, but is unknown to them. In the third activity, the task is for the child to compose, and then notate, an original work. The last activity shows how a group composition can be created, notated and read by other members of the class. All of these activities have been used successfully – and with a great amount of fun! – with pupils aged 6 through 16; right through the primary grades and beyond. The notational examples depicted here were created by children aged 7 through 12. As each example is described, some of the dimensions of creative practice featured are highlighted.

Notating a familiar melody

Just as there is an urge to sing and move in the early years, there is also an urge to depict – through drawings – the songs that children know how to sing or make up on their own (Figure 9.1). Teachers can capitalise on this urge in creative ways by encouraging pupils to

■ **Figure 9.1** A child's invented notation for 'Twinkle, Twinkle Little Star' with pictures of the stars and moon and the title of the song.

extend the traditional idea of notation to include all sorts of drawings and symbols, thereby linking ideas across disciplines.

A powerful way of exploring musical notations is to ask children to create ways of notating a melody that is already familiar to them. Give them lots of enticing materials and plenty of time to explore, working on their own and working with others.

One melody that is almost bound to be successful for this task for children up to the age of 8 (or older if they don't feel 'insulted' by being asked!) is some variation of the tune for 'Twinkle Twinkle Little Star'. I say 'some variation' because with a little bit of rhythmic tweaking, the same melody is used for the 'Alphabet Song' and for 'Baa Baa Black Sheep'.

Activity 9.1 Notating a familiar melody

Step 1

- Introduce the melody by singing or playing.
- It is a good idea *not* to tell children what it is – that way, they can decide for themselves whether they hear 'Twinkle' or the 'Alphabet Song' or 'Black Sheep' – or all three.
- Let the title become something of a guessing game on the side and encourage pupils to listen closely to the melody.
- If you are using this activity with older children (10 years and up), one way of making it more accessible is to tell them that this melody, in fact, is used for many popular songs for younger children, and they might want to try and name them all.

Step 2

Next, the children are given all sorts of materials to notate their melodies, including:

- Pencils
- Crayons
- Coloured felt markers
- Plain paper
- Manuscript paper (with staff lines)
- Coloured paper
- Scissors
- Glue or tape

A variety of materials suggests that there are multiple ways of notating the song, with many 'right' answers. In addition, a variety of materials can inspire ideas that children might not otherwise have had, such as using colour to depict different notes or features of the music. The verbal instructions given to the children for the task also reinforce the idea that any type of symbol can work.

Step 3

When the children are settled (having a plethora of materials to choose from can take a bit of additional time!), the teacher makes this invitation: 'I'm going to play you a melody that you've heard at least a thousand times before! I'd like you to write something down so that you could remember it later, say, a week from now, or show to a friend who could play it from what you've written or drawn. You can use anything you like to show the melody – lines, dots, pictures, words, music notes, numbers, drawings – anything'.

This exercise invariably results in a wide variety of invented notations. A child who hears 'Twinkle Twinkle Little Star' may offer a page full of stars. Another child may offer the alphabet as a depiction of what they heard – the 'Alphabet Song'.

Some children will hear more than one possible melody, as depicted in Figure 9.2, where one child has drawn both a sheep and a star. In all of these cases, the children have successfully shown that they have identified the melody and that they can find a way to depict that melody so that they can recall it once again. Some children, in fact, may well be capable of producing more sophisticated notations. However, in the case of 'Twinkle Twinkle Little Star', children may simply draw a few stars (see Figure 9.3) or write the word 'twinkle', claiming that others would be able to recognise the song because 'anyone would know that's supposed to be Twinkle Twinkle Little Star' (Upitis, 1990b, p. 95).

■ **Figure 9.2** Sheep and star, signifying 'Baa Baa Black Sheep' and 'Twinkle Twinkle Little Star'.

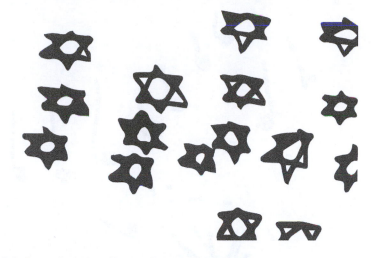

■ **Figure 9.3** Stars depicting 'Twinkle Twinkle Little Star'.

Some children may combine musical symbols with drawings. It is common to see a series of notes or even someone singing a song, along with the stars. Children using these notations show us that they can both name the song with their notation and show that it is music. Here are two examples:

■ **Figure 9.4** Singing 'Twinkle Twinkle Little Star'.

■ **Figure 9.5** Star and musical notes.

Another approach is depicted in the notation here, where the child has elected to use manuscript paper (because this is a music activity, after all), and produces what looks like rather abstract scribbles. When asked about this notation, the child said that she was 'writing music'. And so she was.

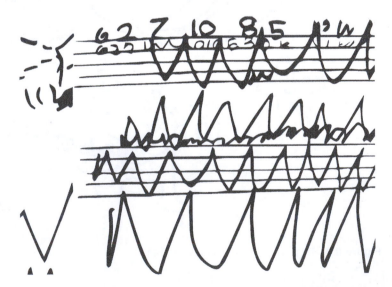

■ **Figure 9.6** Writing music.

■ **Figure 9.7** A graphic notation for 'Twinkle Twinkle Little Star'.

In the final example we see a style that, in fact, shares many features of standard music notation. The shorter lines are for faster notes and the longer lines are for slower notes. The lines that are lower on the page correspond to lower pitches. In fact, if you begin reading this notation from the top left, you will soon see that it is a very accurate graphic representation of 'Twinkle Twinkle Little Star'. Later in this chapter, we'll explore how notations like these can become stepping stones for learning to read and write in standard notation.

Notating an unfamiliar melody

Notations for unfamiliar melodies often yield a great variety of symbol type and use and offer an intriguing window to children's cognitive processes. Most often, children use icons (e.g. pictures of drums, other instruments or people singing or making music), words, discrete marks for pitches and/or durations (such as in the 'Twinkle' examples above) and continuous lines indicating either the direction of the pitches in a melody (e.g. a line moving up the page as pitch rises) or mood (e.g. a dark jagged line to indicate music that sounds dramatic or angry). Once in a while, children will use letters for pitches or even standard notation symbols for pitch and duration, but this is usually the case only for children who take music lessons outside of school. Children occasionally use numbers as well, either to count the number of discrete events or to supplement another notational form. For instance, after one 9-year-old notated an unfamiliar melody using discrete marks, he added a string of numbers across the top. When asked what these numbers meant, he answered, 'Oh, I just put them there. They're numbers'.

The use of discrete marks to indicate pitch and the number of events is by far the most popular method employed by most pupils. Children using this method understand that this approach has great promise to yield information about a melody, particularly if there is a combination of type of symbol and placement on the page that mimics the way that notes would appear on a staff. As one child commented, 'If I get the marks in the right place, they'll get it, won't they?'

■ **Figure 9.8** Notation for an unfamiliar melody.

How does one encourage children to notate pitch and/or rhythm in more sophisticated ways than in most of the examples that were shown earlier for the familiar 'Twinkle' melody? Well, in precisely the same way as for the familiar tune! Again, the teacher should provide an array of markers, paper and other materials for creating notations. Sometimes teachers will even provide materials such as string, yarn, ribbon and straws, encouraging children to build notations that are three-dimensional in form.

As for the notation of a general melody, the instruction on the part of the teacher should include the idea that the notation is being created to 'remember the piece a week from now' or to 'show it to a friend'. By using these directions, the teacher is making it clear to the pupils that the notation has a function: for remembering or sharing a piece with a known audience.

Here is an example of a notation created in response to hearing an unfamiliar melody. The tear drop shapes at the top indicate that it is a sad melody (it was in a minor key) and the horizontal lines represent the melody, while the sharp peaked shapes represent chords.

Notating an original composition

In order to notate an original composition, the children first have to create one. A sure-fire way of producing a composition is to have children work in pairs, each with an instrument of their choice. The instruments should include traditional instruments found in many primary classrooms (Orff xylophones, drums, clave sticks, etc.) as well as instruments the children have made themselves or objects that make interesting sounds but aren't considered conventional instruments, such as bits of copper piping.

The children are then invited to explore the kinds of sounds they can make with their instruments (prepare for a rather loud – but almost never chaotic – classroom experience for this exploration stage). Once children have played on their instruments for a while, they

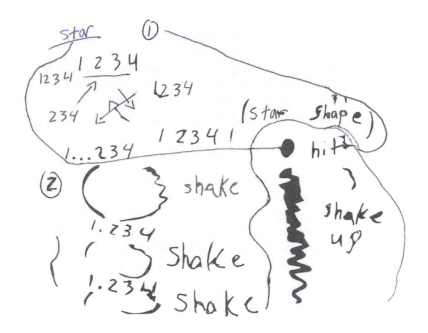

Figure 9.9 Composition for two tambourines.

are invited to create a composition for both instruments, and then to write it down so that another pair of students can play their composition using the same instruments. This means that the audience for the notation becomes a real one: it will be another pair of pupils in the classroom. The teacher then watches the group, and once two pairs of children are ready to exchange instruments and notations, they begin exploring the compositions as well as the notations. Often, children will be completely delighted to see that their peers can read their notation. Sometimes, the notation will be misread, leading to much laughter and exclamations of this sort: 'Oh! I see why you did that. Here, let me change this,' followed by a subsequent modification to the notation itself.

This activity can be repeated many times and, over time, both the notations and the compositions themselves become more complex and interesting. Pupils can compose and write on their own as well, or in larger groups than the original pairs. However, beginning with pairs is a good idea, as it means that pupils are less vulnerable than they might be if the teacher asked them to compose and notate a piece on their own.

Case study 9.1: Encouraging a child to clarify meaning of symbols through repeated questioning

Rena: I notice that you use [this symbol] to mean two different things. Sometimes it means play two notes together, sometimes it means play two notes in a row. How can you tell, from your music, which one to play?

Joel: Well, it isn't different, but I just showed you.

Rena: What if you didn't show me?

Joel: You mean what happened if you weren't here and you wanted that two notes together? And I was with them [i.e., a different person]?

Rena: No, you weren't with the person either. All the person had was your music.

Joel: You mean me and you were away and I was outside playing?

Rena: Yes.

Joel: You mean how would they know not to do this [plays the other version]?

Rena: Yes.

Joel: You see, someone is obviously in the house.

Rena: What if there was no one in the house?

Joel: Well, I always come in for a drink, and I'd notice them. I'd come out of the kitchen with my cup full of juice and come in here with my class, I mean my cup full of juice, and all I'll do is sort of like, and you know, watch and stuff and sit around and *turn around and show them.*

Adapted from Upitis (1992, pp. 55–6).

This activity is more than a way of engendering music notations. In fact, even if the teacher didn't ask the pupils to notate their pieces, many would do so in any case as the *need* to develop a notational system almost always develops when children are invited to compose their own music. It is this function of notation – as a means of making a permanent record of one's creations and sharing them with others – that makes notational systems most meaningful to pupils. In the two prior activities, the notion of audience was introduced by asking children to notate the pieces for an imagined friend. When notating original compositions, the idea of audience becomes paramount.

The notion of audience is an important one in these ways. First, children are less likely to use music symbols (whether they themselves read music or not) if they know that the person who will be reading their notation is not fluent in standard notation (Upitis, 1990a). If the notation is being created for an unknown audience, pupils will frequently ask, 'Does the person know notes?' or something to that effect.

Sometimes, the teacher might stress that the notation is being created for an unknown future audience, which can lead to frustration on the part of the pupil (but charming conversations!). Case Study 9.1 is an example of an exchange with a 6-year-old who had developed a notational system with an ambiguity. As the conversation develops, it is clear that this pupil can't yet imagine composing a piece for an unknown performer.

When children first try to record their compositions through notation, the notations are not very sophisticated – in fact, they look much like the examples that have been shown for the previous activity. This is not at all surprising, since pupils only need to write down enough to capture the essence of the piece. That is, if the purpose of a notational system is to preserve a composition, then the notation only needs to go so far. Some children, for example, will only notate pitch in some fashion and not bother with rhythm, because they can remember the rhythm of the piece once they reconstruct the pitches. And some children will simply draw a 'memory' of making music, as in the delightful example here.

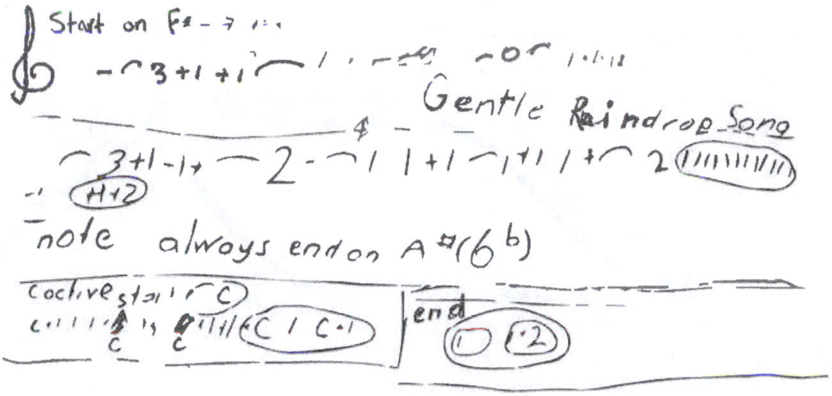

■ **Figure 9.10** 'Gentle Raindrop Song'.

But after leaving a piece for a few weeks, or after someone else tries to read the notation – and does so incorrectly – the need to refine or develop the earlier notations arises. Indeed, the notations that children develop can become incredibly complex and difficult to read unless one understands the system that they have employed.

The example here is a case in point: the notation for the 'Gentle Raindrop Song' is perfectly suitable for giving both pitch and rhythm information, but is extraordinarily difficult to read! At this stage, introducing some of the features of standard notation makes good sense. In fact, children will often embrace standard notation when their invented notations have reached this point. The 10-year-old who composed the 'Gentle Raindrop Song', upon learning about notes on the staff, speculated with sheer glee, 'Wow! I wonder who thought *that* one up!' There are two important things about this comment. One is that the child actually *wanted* to learn how to read standard notation, partly as a result of creating his own compositions first. And the second point is that even though the desire was there, it was still a struggle – learning to read is a process, whether we are learning to read print or music. But it is infinitely easier when the desire is there.

Creating and notating a group composition: soundscapes

The soundscape activities described herein are based on the work of Canadian composer R. Murray Schafer.[1] Schafer developed the term as part of his documentation of the ways that acoustic environments have changed over time and across cultures. In his book *The Tuning of the World (The Soundscape)*, he examines the topic at length. Many classroom teachers in Canada, the United States and the United Kingdom have developed activities that are inspired by Schafer's work and give children an opportunity to deepen their understanding of their environments as well as of musical forms and structures. One example is of a soundscape depicting the natural sounds of California.[2]

Soundscapes can be created with the most readily available materials – the human body. But they can also be composed by using traditional instruments, nontraditional instruments and electronic instruments and recording devices. Over the course of the year, the teacher might invite students to create several soundscapes in small groups, moving from simpler manifestations to more complex extensions of the idea.

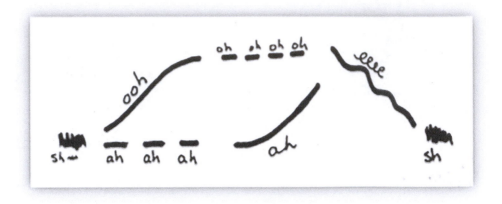

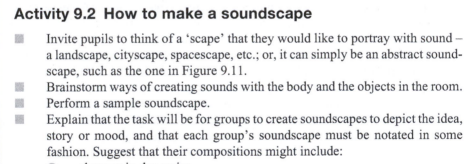

■ **Figure 9.11** Simple abstract soundscape using the voice for instrumentation.

Here is an example of an abstract soundscape made entirely with vocalised sounds. This soundscape is for two groups of performers. Everyone performs the 'sh' and 'eeeee' parts, with the group splitting in two for 'ooh' and 'ah'. When the lines rise on the page vertically, the voices also rise.

Activity 9.2 How to make a soundscape

■　Invite pupils to think of a 'scape' that they would like to portray with sound – a landscape, cityscape, spacescape, etc.; or, it can simply be an abstract sound-scape, such as the one in Figure 9.11.

■　Brainstorm ways of creating sounds with the body and the objects in the room.

■　Perform a sample soundscape.

■　Explain that the task will be for groups to create soundscapes to depict the idea, story or mood, and that each group's soundscape must be notated in some fashion. Suggest that their compositions might include:

    ● changes in dynamics

    ● solo and ensemble sections

    ● audience participation (marked specifically in the notation).

■　Divide the class into groups of five or six, set a time limit (15 minutes is good for the first one), and explain that at the end of the time, each group will per-form their pieces with the class participating where indicated. (Pieces can be audio recorded for future use and/or for assessment purposes.)

■　Provide each group with a strip of mural or butcher's paper (three metres long), coloured markers and sticky tape for posting the notation on the wall.

There are many ways to extend this activity. An obvious one is to use a greater variety of sound makers, such as rhythm instruments, pitched instruments and a greater variety of found objects. Teachers might also wish to include electronic sounds, such as prerecorded material or material that the students record and manipulate with samplers and sequencers. It is possible to use a greater variety of materials for the notations, such as paint, streamers, ribbons, wool, icicles, corks and pipe cleaners, which add to the visual complexity and appeal of the soundscape, so that the work becomes more of a mixed-media artefact. In that vein, words can also be added, either acoustically or electronically created.

For this activity – as for the other three described previously – the goal is to explore music and the vast possibilities of associated symbols to describe music. Because we want children to use language fluently, both in written and oral forms, we expect them to be readers, writers, critics and creators. If we want children to use music as a way of convey-ing meaning and emotion, then they should be musicians in the fullest sense. We must expect – and provide conditions for – children to be improvisers, composers, notators, performers, listeners, critics and creators.

LINKING IDEAS: BRIDGING INVENTED AND CONVENTIONAL NOTATIONS

We have seen that children's notations of music employ a huge variety of symbols – strings of numbers or letters, words, mathematical symbols and operations, icons and placement on the page. Children use standard music notation symbols as well, though not necessarily in standard ways. How can we link these notations to more conventional forms?

Just as there are stages in the writing of language and learning the conventions of spelling,[3] so too are there stages in developing invented notations into more conventional forms of music notation. Research on children's writing of text, where children's invented spellings and structuring of text are examined, has enabled teachers to develop better meth-ods to help children become enthusiastic and competent writers. One aspect of this approach involves using children's invented spellings, somewhat akin to their invented music nota-tions, to enable them to develop conventional spellings; invented spellings are fine to a point, but will not suffice in the longer term (some of the earliest – and still the most intriguing work in the area – appears in Gentry, 1982).

While the learning of a language cannot be equated isomorphically with the learning of music, there are parallels in the development of both systems. In the very first stages, children create symbols that don't form words or music (e.g. using scribbles that approxi-mate writing or strings of letters or making shapes that look like notes on manuscript paper, but have no musical meaning per se). Later, they begin to represent some of the musical information – something like the stage of semi-phonetic or phonetic spelling. In the exam-ple below, we see a young child who can represent pitch accurately using letter names, but doesn't provide information about rhythm – in a very real way, this is equivalent to the stage of spelling also contained in the notation where 'quick' is spelled 'cwic', and 'you got to rest here' appears as 'you go to rest ere'.

We have seen that when children use instruments where letter names are marked on the instrument – such as Orff instruments – or if they already know the names of the notes on the piano it is natural for them to make use of that information in their notations. This use of letter names forms another great bridge to standard notations. In the example here, the child has used the piano to create a melody and is already familiar with the names of the white notes on the piano. However, he did not know the symbol for the F#, and so, drew a knife, telling his teacher, 'It is a pirate's knife. And a pirate's knife is *very* sharp!' This provided a way to introduce the '#' symbol, which the child then began using in subsequent notations.

To help children make the transition from letter names to notes on a staff it is effective to begin with their actual compositions, rather than trying to teach the notes in an abstract or discrete manner. This was done with the notation here, where the teacher showed the child

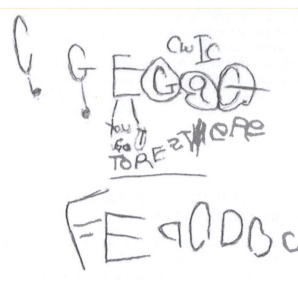

■ **Figure 9.12** Semi-phonetic spelling and an equivalent stage of music notation.

the pitches for the notes F, A, E, D, G and C, because they appeared in her piece. When she then transcribed the piece into standard notation, she added the note names below the staff notes. While this is arguably redundant, it certainly serves to reinforce the notes, and over time, the letter names diminish and eventually disappear altogether, as shown in Figure 9.14.

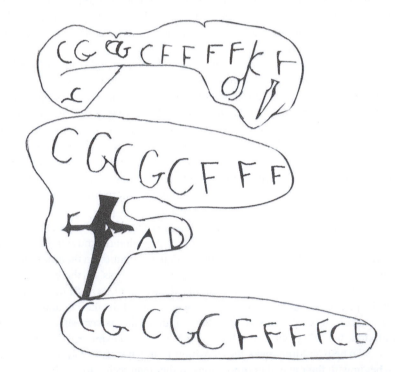

■ **Figure 9.13** Pirate's knife for the sharp symbol.

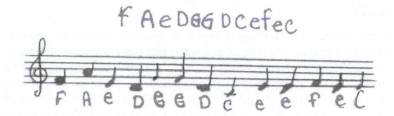

■ **Figure 9.14** Combining note names with notes placed on the staff.

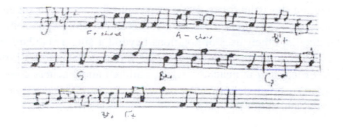

■ **Figure 9.15** Notated and illustrated composition.

The last example (Figure 9.15) is of a notation where the child has successfully represented the melody using notes on the staff with a treble clef. Then she has illustrated the composition as well. This approach represents yet another level of engagement on the part of the child, where she has not only effectively composed a piece, but has further enhanced the creative work with a drawing.

SUMMARY

In this chapter, we have seen a variety of notations created by children in the context of activities introduced in classroom settings that support creative thinking. With this kind of approach to writing and notation music, children's abilities to notate information about rhythm, pitch, texture, dynamics, mood and harmony will increase with age as they become more versed in symbol systems in general. Their abilities to notate may be even more impressive if they take music lessons outside of school where conventional systems are explored.

Regardless of whether pupils have supplementary music lessons outside of school, all primary aged children can benefit from the activities described in this chapter, helping them develop a creative approach to notation and expanding their musical horizons. By acknowledging the value of multiple notational forms – both invented by children and more standardised versions – teachers and children can expand the boundaries of their understanding and their uses of notations beyond a single standard music notation. Ultimately, a broad understanding of notational forms will support a broad understanding of music and of learning in general – where children and teachers come to appreciate many genres and make creative links between different forms of music making and the complexities of social and cultural values.

NOTES

1 Learn more about Schafer's work at www.patria.org/arcana/arcbooks.html.
2 Hear a Californian soundscape here: www.museumca.org/naturalsounds.
3 Read more about invented spellings at www.readingrockets.org/article/267.

FURTHER READING

Barrett, M. S. (2006) Inventing songs, inventing worlds: the 'genesis' of creative thought and activity in young children's lives. *International Journal of Early Years Education*, 14(3), 201–20. doi:10.1080/09669760600879920

Blair, D. V. (2007) Musical maps as narrative inquiry. *International Journal of Education & the Arts*, 8(15). Available at www.ijea.org/v8n15/

Campbell, P. S. (2010) *Songs in Their Heads: Music and Its Meaning in Children's Lives*. New York, NY: Oxford.

Kaschub, M. and Smith, J. (2009) *Minds on Music: Composition for Creative and Critical Thinking*. Lanham, MD: Rowland & Littlefield Publishers, Inc. in partnership with MENC: The National Association for Music Education.

Lee, P. N. (2013) Self-invented notation systems created by young children. *Music Education Research*, 15(4), 392–405. doi:10.1080/14613808.2013.829429

CHAPTER 10

INTEGRATING THE PRIMARY CURRICULUM

Regina Murphy

INTRODUCTION

Integrated learning shows potential for improving student learning across a range of subject areas (Burnaford, 2007; Goff and Ludwig, 2013; Ludwig, Marklein and Mengli, 2016; Rabkin and Redmond, 2004) and this chapter focuses in particular on the theme of teaching for creativity through integrating music across the curriculum. Integration occurs through making connections within music making activities of listening, improvising, composing, singing, playing, appraising, responding and moving, as well as across school subjects, working with the unexpected and the familiar to generate new knowledge and understanding. Integration provides a way of connecting, deepening and consolidating learning across the curriculum and can maximise the available time for creative music making. Teachers can sometimes feel that there is 'not enough time' to integrate meaningfully – and indeed, research suggests that curriculum overload is a reality in many countries at primary level,[1] – but as Parsons (2004) affirms, an integrated curriculum is not simply about timetables and the length of the school day, but about creating meaning and understanding through learning.

In this chapter we look at the roots of curricular integration, benefits of integration and contemporary definitions that are applicable to music teaching in the primary classroom. Next we explore ways in which music learning in one aspect can be further enhanced in another dimension – focussing in particular on one of the teaching ideas that features in several chapters in this book by way of example. After this, we look at how music can be integrated into a broad thematic development that honours both the subject of music as well as the conceptual understanding of the other subjects. Finally, we draw the ideas together to emphasise how creativity intersects in the integration endeavour and is realised in ways that are both concrete and compelling.

ROOTS OF INTEGRATION

Subject integration is a feature of many arts curricula worldwide, yet it is not always fully understood nor its potential maximised. If done well, an integrated approach can enrich the teaching and learning of school subjects for both the pupils and the teacher. Parsons (2004) suggests that the kinds of changes in society and problems that we face require us to be able to deal quickly and effectively with large amounts of complex information from different sources. Our need to integrate information in our personal lives is as important for daily living as it is for our teaching. Consequently, children need to learn to be adaptable and flexible, and to process information from different sources in ways that bring meaning to their lives, thus enabling them to see the 'bigger picture' and engage creatively with it.

The concept of the integration of the whole child has its roots in the progressive era of education at the beginning of the twentieth century led by the American philosopher and educator John Dewey and other 'progressive' educators who rejected the narrowing of the curriculum at that time. Among other things, they called for greater respect for the diversity of abilities and interests and the development of engaged citizens who could participate actively in affairs of their community in an effort to achieve the common good. This emphasis on holistic development led to the emergence of the term 'child-centred' education. It is also interesting to note that the progressive educators called for greater attention to the emotional, artistic and creative aspects of human development, and regarded experience and aesthetic experience as the basis around which education should revolve (Bresler, 2002).

However, it is important to remember that good intentions of integration were not intended to undermine the value of the disciplines, as Dewey (cited in Parsons, 2004) believed that each discipline brought important knowledge to the goals of education. Bresler (2002) observes that the notion of integration reemerged in the 1960s and 1970s during a period of social upheaval and when concern for students' experiences began to outweigh the more rigid demands of curricula at the time. Once again, the arts assumed a more desirable status. As Bresler reports, the educational beliefs of Harry Broudy and Elliot Eisner began to have an impact. Broudy believed that the purpose of education was the development of the imagination whilst Eisner advocated arts integration through an expanded view of 'forms of representation', which emphasises our ability to interact with the world and draw meaning from it beyond verbal and numerical modes.

Integration is also commonly associated with constructivism, which some (e.g. Bruner, 1996) regard as a philosophy that spans several disciplines, such as arts, sciences and languages. The child is encouraged to actively construct the meanings of what is learned, inquiring into topics of interest and relating what is learned with what is already known, thus becoming an active meaning maker. Generally speaking, the children integrate based on their own understanding, not on what the teacher demands.

The relationship between the teacher and the pupil is central to any model of integration that builds on social constructivist principles. This relationship is characterised as one of collaboration – while the teacher might have the initial suggestions, the children will help determine the topics and flow of activities, the ongoing research, the related projects and criteria for assessment. Negotiation of curriculum is a key feature at this point. Children must grapple with having to take responsibility for their own learning, sharing their emerging constructs and engaging in lively discussions with others. The teacher's role then is one of facilitator rather than transmitter of knowledge as the pupils construct meanings for themselves. In this regard, the entire effort resonates with principles of creative learning where pupil agency is fostered and valued, and where unusual ideas, curiosity and questioning drive the inquiry and the negotiation of new knowledge.

BENEFITS OF INTEGRATION

Recent research points to the benefits of integrated learning in schools (CUREE, 2009).[2] Cross-curricular approaches prove to be most effective when they are either centred around a particular theme/dimension or when they are connected to the school-based curriculum and with young people's wider experiences outside of school. This type of cross-curricular learning can have a positive impact on pupils' motivation, discursive language and potential to collaborate with each other. Russell and Zembylas (2007) support this view in relation to arts education in particular, noting that qualitative studies and anecdotal evidence suggest strongly that an important, possibly long-lasting benefit to children of an integrated curriculum is a positive change in attitude towards school itself.

At a European level, advocates for the implementation of a cross-curricular approach make the case that cross-curricular learning should:

- Require that pupils pull together appropriate knowledge from a range of subjects and relate it to everyday life;
- use concepts as the intellectual building blocks and as essential aids to the categorisation, organisation and analysis of knowledge and experiences; and
- use participatory and experiential teaching and learning styles.

(CIDREE, 2005).[3]

In her studies of integration in arts education in the US, Bresler found various models in operation, the most prevalent being what she termed the 'subservient' integration style. In this model, music (and other arts) served the other curriculum areas in a nonreciprocal relationship. A more egalitarian model was seen very rarely. However, the best models of integration that Bresler (2002) observed were where integration occurred through a variety of strategies.

Strategies in teaching for creativity through effective integration

- Posing broad questions, identifying common issues and themes;
- introducing artistic ways of seeing;
- analysing and communicating to expand inquiry;
- scaffolding and modelling ideas rather than using didactic methods;
- foregrounding child-centred approaches;
- using strategies reciprocally across other subjects;
- using portfolios, projects and performances for assessment;
- encouraging the presentation of concepts and ideas;
- using a variety of modes of representation – music, movement, visuals;
- enabling individual and group projects;
- encouraging independent research and public communication; and
- fostering higher order thinking.

(Adapted from Bresler, 2002)

MODELS OF INTEGRATION

In addition to Bresler's (2002) model of integration, several other frameworks for curricular connections have been proposed. Models which support mutual integrity of subjects linked to an overarching concept are referred to as 'equal development' (Nixon and Akerson, 2002) or producing an 'elegant fit' (Burnaford, Aprill and Weiss, 2001).

▨ Table 10.1 Three models of integration (Russell-Bowie, 2009)

Service connections	One subject servicing learning in another subject
Symmetric correlations	Two subjects using the same material to achieve their own outcomes
Syntegration	Subjects working together synergistically to explore a theme, concept or focus question while achieving their own subject-specific outcomes as well as generic outcomes

In considering arts contexts in particular, Russell-Bowie (2009) proposes three models or levels of integration that enable subjects to work in meaningful ways to achieve authentic outcomes. She argues that each approach is valid in itself when used creatively by a teacher to nurture children's learning. The models can be used at different times in sequence with each other, depending on the focus, the music in question and the overall musical purposes underpinning them. Russell-Bowie refers to the three models as 'service connections', 'symmetric correlations' and a specially coined term which she calls 'syntegration' (see Table 10.1).

Russell-Bowie explains that in the 'service connections' model material in one subject is used to reinforce learning in another. An example of this is where the children sing a song to help remember the letters of the alphabet, or chant some number patterns. Similar to Bresler's notion of subservience, music learning is not advanced in such contexts, although learning in the other subject may be reinforced. The second model, 'symmetric correlations', occurs where there is a greater consciousness of the inherent learning opportunities in each subject and an explicit effort is made at realising these opportunities in authentic ways during the course of each lesson. For example, in singing the 'Alphabet Song', the children might be asked to hum it first (to warm up the voice at the start of a longer singing lesson) or to sing it silently in their heads (to develop 'inner hearing') and then to sing the correct letter aloud on a given signal. Another example of this model is seen in the 'Alphabet Dance' in Chapter 5 of this book. In the third model, 'syntegration' involves the use of broad themes or concepts that can be developed discretely within each subject as well as across subjects. Additionally, learning in all subjects is enhanced by virtue of the shared understanding and deeper meanings that are created through multiple experiences of the same concept from different perspectives. The approach also provides opportunities for problem solving, close observation, analysis, research, collaboration, inquiry and synthesis – or, in other words, higher order learning.

Integration within music itself

A special kind of integration can also occur with the subject of music itself and this is one that should not be overlooked. Music teaching in primary schools is often supported by more than one teacher – the class teacher primarily, but often a specialist teacher or an external teacher for instrumental teaching, choral music or dance. It is important that the class teacher, who may either observe, interact or plan with the external teacher, is aware of the strategies and starting points that each one uses and finds creative ways of building on them in his or her own teaching. Across this book, we see many authors using a familiar idea – in this case, 'Twinkle Twinkle Little Star' – as a starting point for creative exploration; from humming, singing, deconstructing the melody, playing, inventing nota-tions and listening to different interpretations, to a child or visiting musician playing or searching for Mozart's piano version on YouTube. This idea of starting with the known provides a safe and secure place to begin, but there are also possibilities to enrich learning in one aspect through development and extension of another. For example, the vocal crea-tivity of Kymberly Evans singing the 'ABC Medley' is more fully appreciated and enjoyed when all the other creative avenues have been explored and it provides a natural stepping stone into appreciating the creativity of jazz arrangements even for the very young.

Activity 10.1 Integrating and extending musical ideas using 'Twinkle Twinkle Little Star'

Singing	Humming as a warm up; analysing the structure; inventing new words; varying the melody
Playing	'Finding' or figuring out the notes of the tune on an instrument (e.g. on a set of chime bars, C, D, E, F, G, A); playing the rhythm, varying the rhythm
Inventing notations	Drawing the tune; moving from associated ideas towards the shape of melody and later bridging invented and standard notations
Listening	Listening to a performance on a string instrument (e.g. inviting a child who learned an instrument using the Suzuki method to perform for the class; noticing rhythmic variations in the 'Twinkle' tune)
Listening	Listening to 'ABC Medley' in a jazz singing style (e.g. performed by Kymberly Evans on *Jazz Baby Session 2*, available on iTunes)
Listening	Listening to 'Ah! Vous dirai-je maman', the French version of 'Twinkle' and arranged into twelve variations by Mozart (YouTube); 'finding' the tune as you listen
Music reading	'Ah! Vous dirai-je maman' (Mozart); looking for piano performances on YouTube that include images of the notes (called a 'score'); following the shape of the tune as the right hand or left hand plays

---

Integration as storytelling

Another set of possibilities for integration is found through storytelling methods. Linda Pound and Trish Lee (2011) illustrate this very effectively in the book *Teaching Mathemat-ics Creatively*, where they build on Kieran Egan's (1986) framework for creating powerful stories. The model involves identifying important features in the story, finding the binary opposites, organising the content into story form, arriving at a conclusion that resolves matters and evaluating the success of the learning at the end. Egan makes the point that binary opposites are pivotal in many traditional stories. We can immediately think of several significant ones, such as the notions of 'good versus evil', 'fear versus safety', 'exclusion versus inclusion', 'war and peace' or 'bravery versus cowardice'. Using any of these as an entry point it is possible to explore the binary opposites in a country's myths and legends and to illustrate these through composition. Opposing ideas make for concrete and accessible starting points in music making, for example: bad witch and good witch – playing loud and soft; being alone or in a crowd – single notes and groups of notes. By beginning with such polarised opposites and then linking some ideas in between, it is possible to build up a series of interactions that flow into an entire musical story.

Integration using picture books

Children's picture books can also provide a very accessible stimulus for developing and interweaving pictures, text and soundscapes. As an art form where the illustrator and author often work in tandem to suggest a larger narrative or subtext, the process of examining details in the pictures (that are not mentioned explicitly in the text) or teasing out the dialogue in the text that is not illustrated by the pictures can prompt many musical ideas. In addition, the 'problem' that drives the story forward is succinctly contained within a concise resource. Such exploration of the problem, dialogue, character, setting, plot, etc. can sensitise children to hidden meanings in the text and metaphorical ideas, and complement the development of creative skills explored in reading and writing (Cremin, 2009a).

Journeys, transformations, characters in conversation and larger-than-life characters provide rich material for exploring musical ideas. Classic texts include, for example:

- Ginsburg, M. (1974) *Mushroom in the Rain*
- Rosen, M. (1989) *We're Going on a Bear Hunt*
- Sendak, M. (1970) *Where the Wild Things Are*

Texts developed as a series also allow for extended composing ideas:

- Carle, E. (1969) *The Very Hungry Caterpillar*
- Child, L. (2000) *I Will Not Ever NEVER Eat a Tomato*
- Dodd, L. (1983) *Hairy Maclary from Donaldson's Dairy*
- Thomas, V. and Paul, K. (1987) *Winnie the Witch*

CREATIVE INTEGRATION

The following examples illustrate more extended forms of integration through units of work that could span several weeks or months, depending on the age group, with the possibility of leading to Russell-Bowie's outcome of 'syntegration' as a result. The first one explores the topic of rain as one that has immediate links with environmental issues and the importance of water. However, its tangible qualities are foregrounded in musical expression and many creative possibilities are identified.

The second theme is a more abstract, conceptual one – time – that immediately evokes connections with mathematics and history. The unit certainly warrants a thoughtful approach, although the inclusion of rock music brings a contemporary flavour and is a reminder to the teacher of the need to find connections between children's exposure to music outside of school and the more formal approaches that prevail within schools.

Activity 10.2 An integrated unit on the topic of rain (adapted from Murphy and Espeland, 2007)

Overview

The familiar idea of the sound of raindrops is captured in the opening composing activity and used as a bridge to the listening and responding task which comes later. Songs about rain feature in many cultures and here they provide a link to music in the movies as well as to the singing tradition of South Africa.

Rain – either in its absence or presence – is an important issue in sustaining life in communities everywhere. The focus of this theme therefore is broad enough to facilitate many links across the curriculum, while also allowing for many creative opportunities for creative music making.

Resources

Percussion instruments; recording equipment; recordings of listening pieces; song lyrics/sheet music; art materials; writing materials; atlas; Internet-based research sources.

Supplies of instruments differ in schools, but it is surprising how much can be hidden away, waiting to be rediscovered and played.

Introduction

The teacher leads the discussion by talking about experiences of rain in summer, reading the poem 'Spring Rain' by M. Espeland and inviting the children to share stories of their own experiences of rain.

A cross-curricular integrated theme can begin with any subject. In this instance it begins with poetry.

A discussion on spring rain can link to environmental issues, seasons, the necessity of water and the water cycle itself.

Spring Rain
One drop –
and then another.
Spring rain.
Many drops that gently fall.
One drop –
perhaps another? then suddenly –
stillness.

Poetry can provide both an artistic stimulus and an exciting opportunity for creative work in music and other areas.

(For further ideas on using poetry, see Chapter 9 in Teaching English Creatively, *Cremin, 2009b.)*

Composing task

■ The teacher encourages the children to share ideas and suggestions about how to compose music to fit with the ideas in the poem, and how they might use the percussion instruments (or whatever is available) to make a short piece.

■ The children are organised into groups, encouraged to try out different instruments and sound sources to create the idea of raindrops.

■ If time permits, the children can write their compositions using graphic notation.

Once the groups are established, the teacher can begin interacting and asking questions to sharpen focus and guide the children in their creative decision-making, e.g.
What has your group decided to do?
Why did you choose these instruments?
How have you used the poem as the basis for your composition?
What mood or feeling do you want to show in your music?
How do you plan on making the music interesting to listen to?

Sharing compositions
- The children rehearse their compositions and perform in turn for the class.
- Compositions may be recorded in audio or video for reviewing later.
- Performances in class can vary between playing the music and reciting the poem separately or together, or other options using technology.

Listening task
The next phase of the unit focuses on listening.
- Music that evokes raindrops is chosen, e.g. Hovland's 'Raindrop Study' or Chopin's 'Raindrop Prelude (Op. 28, No. 15)'. Both pieces were composed for piano, although the Chopin piece is also played on classical guitar.
- The music is played for the class and the children are invited to comment.
- The composer's work is compared to the pieces created by the class.
- Discussion may focus on how the piece suggests a picture of raindrops.
- Some of the composer's techniques may also be described in simple terms.

Singing
Many songs about rain are found in collections for younger children. A classic song that features raindrops is 'Raindrops Keep Falling on My Head' by Hal David and Burt Bacharach (from the movie *Butch Cassidy and the Sundance Kid*) and is suitable for middle-senior primary children. Even though the words suggest that the rain brings the 'blues', the song has a light, carefree style that rejects any notion of moodiness:
Raindrops keep fallin' on my head
And just like the guy whose feet are too big for his bed
Nothin' seems to fit
Those raindrops are falling on my head, they keep fallin'

The teacher invites the children to talk about their work and each other's work and reflect on the process. The atmosphere is one of trust and openness at all times. Questioning is again probing and might focus on the connections between the text in the poem and the music, how the instruments are played and the tonal colour of the instruments.

Questioning will also feature at this stage of the process, allowing scope for the children to develop their own relationship with the music, e.g.
What are the similarities and differences between this music and ours?
How has the composer 'built up' his composition?
Do the notes vary between high notes and low notes?
How does the composer create the effect of rain in the music?
What can we learn about rain from this music?

As well as linking with singing activities and performing, the song allows for discussion on songs that feature in movies, especially those that seem to capture the atmosphere of a movie very well.
At this point the children could also inquire more into famous songwriters, such as Burt Bacharach.

Linking singing and listening

Listen to 'Rain Beautiful Rain' performed by Ladysmith Black Mambazo. This performance of a prayer for rain by a male voice choir from South Africa transports the children to another context for learning about rain from a different perspective.

The interchange between listening and performing heightens awareness and appreciation of art forms as the children move from one mode to another.

Linking with other subjects

The climate, music and culture of South Africa and other countries or climates where rainfall is scarce can be researched to bring a deeper appreciation of the song.

Art, poetry

In art, the children can paint a picture or make a collage based on the music or the poem 'Spring Rain' that reflects the character of the poem and music (or extends it in some way).

The sense of open inquiry from one subject to another, while preserving the integrity of each subject and each dimension of music, leads to new understanding and appreciation of the topic as a whole.

Geography, language

Explore scientific terms and metaphorical terms to describe rainfall, e.g. 'thundery showers', 'raining cats and dogs'.

Research projects can explore cities in the world that have high or low levels of rainfall, as well as comparing rainfall tables in cities within the country where the children live.

In addition, the use of judicious questioning to guide discussion and exploration fosters creativity in music and teaching for creativity.

The second thematic unit explores the concept of time through music, English language, mathematics, science, history and film. Although the topic is very broad, the connections with creative activity serve as motivational factors to sustain curiosity and learning across the different subject areas. An overall aim of this unit might be to develop an appreciation of time and things 'of their time', recognising not only the invention of the pendulum clock, the imagining of a time machine, the experimentation with cinematic effects in the film, the cleverness of short story writing and the role of diaries in recording life at a particular moment, but more importantly the artistic and creative contribution that various innovations made to creativity in music, and how this has endured (Figure 10.1).

Music Listening
Time – Intro (excerpt)
(Pink Floyd, 1973)

Music Reading and Appreciation
Beat, rhythm, note values

Rock and pop music over time
Rock instruments

Drama/Mime
Group task: connecting to the opening sequence of Pink Floyd's *Time*

Music Singing:
Moving On
(Gary Moore, 1992)
Turn! Turn! Turn! (To Everything There is a Season)
(Pete Seeger, 1959)

Mathematics
Computing time

'Time'

Science
Pendulum clocks, discovering how they are made

English
Diary writing;
letters for a time capsule

Film/novel
The Time Machine
(HG Wells, 1895)

Language(s)
saying, idioms, proverbs and quotations about time

Art
Looking at depictions of clocks
The Persistence of Memory
(melting clocks)
(Salvador Dali, 1931)

Exploring time in a short story:
After Twenty Years (O. Henry)

History
Timelines
Memorabilia of time in school;
Digitised presentation of artefacts and significant moments

Composing
'Music for the end of school' – a timeline of significant events

■ **Figure 10.1** An integrated unit based on the theme of *time*.

Activity 10.3 An integrated unit on the concept of time (adapted from Murphy and Espeland, 2007)

Overview

Two classic pieces of rock music are used in different ways to celebrate the end of the school year and to inspire creative ideas for the children's own music making as well as on the theme of 'time'. The use of clocks in the introduction to the piece 'Time' by Pink Floyd provides a stimulus for discussion as well as creative music making. At the end, Gary Moore's 'Moving On' adds energy and builds excitement surrounding what lies ahead. As well as linking to all sorts of creative ideas, the choice of Pink Floyd, Gary Moore and Pete Seeger provide opportunities to discuss music over time, what is considered innovative, interesting or enduring, what is valued in rock and pop music in the present time and what may be listened to in the future.

Resources
Recordings of 'Time' (excerpt from opening clock section) by Pink Floyd; 'Moving On' by Gary Moore; and 'Turn! Turn! Turn!' by Pete Seeger

Clocks; weights and pendulums; maths units on time

Pink Floyd is a rock band that was formed in 1965 in Cambridge, England. The band is famous for experimenting with new sound ideas, having psychedelic lyrics and amazing performances.

Introduction: Listening
Discussion and questioning focuses on the timbre (sound of the clocks) and texture (layers of sound) of the music and how these can be shown through movement.

The children's listening task is to work in groups of four to make a mime which shows the character of the music and how it develops and ends.

The long introduction at the beginning of Pink Floyd's 'Time' with clocks chiming and alarms ringing provides an unexpected introduction to the piece of rock music.

Development and sharing
The music is played many times for the children while they sketch ideas for their mime and rehearse it with each other.

Once each group is satisfied with their preparation, they present the mimes for each other while the music is being played.

Discussion can focus on the mood of each mime, narrative elements and gestures and how they relate to the music.

The children should be able to show how they worked out the sound of clocks that feature in the music.

*Creative questioning guides the structuring of the mime,
e.g., Is there something exciting in the music?
Are all the instruments playing at the end?
How do you show this? Have you a particular place or time in mind for the setting of your mime?*

Performing
In this lesson the children listen to and later sing the rock music of Gary Moore and the song 'Moving On'. Though depicting a different era, mood and genre, Pete Seeger's 'Turn! Turn! Turn!' provides another useful stimulus for thinking about time through music.

The collective experiences of listening and singing, and extended activities in other subject areas, prepares the creative space for the final composing activity.

Composing
The final activity involves creating an original piece of music that captures the years of primary school. The children focus on selected events and try to convey the idea of time passing in the music (through use of pulse or steady beat).

The final piece of music can be presented as a timeline, matched with a digital presentation or series of drawings and writings, as a personal creation by the children.

CONCLUSION

In this chapter we explored some of the theory behind curriculum integration and its roots in broader educational movements such as progressivism and constructivism. Whilst there is much satisfaction to be gained from integrating subjects effectively, for both teachers and pupils, it does not happen without some consideration of the overarching purposes and conceptual links that inhere in the chosen subjects. The challenge in integrating any two subjects through a single concept, topic or idea is to maintain a creative tension between the substantive topic which may involve language, mathematics or science, and the other subject which may be more concerned with forms of expression – as in the case with music. As Parsons (2004, p. 787) observes, 'When these two elements are taken seriously and coordinated into one enterprise, the curriculum is integrated'. In the illustrated examples we have seen too that disparate activities can be enhanced through their careful alignment under a unifying theme. Ultimately, when children leave the classroom and return enthusiastically the next day with new ideas, artefacts, discoveries and questions, we know that our integrated teaching has been both meaningful and creative.

NOTES

1 National Council for Curriculum and Assessment (NCCA). (2010) *Curriculum Overload in Primary Schools: An Overview of National and International Experiences*. Research Report. Dublin: NCCA.
2 Centre for the Use of Research and Evidence in Education (CUREE). (2009) *Building the Evidence Base: Learner's Survey Final Report*. Coventry: CUREE.
3 Consortium of Institutions for Development and Research in Education in Europe (CIDREE). (2005) *Cross-Curricular Themes in Secondary Education*. Available at www.cidree.org.

FURTHER READING

Alexander, R. (ed.) (2010) *Children, Their World, Their Education: Final Report and Recommendations of the Cambridge Primary Review*. London: Routledge.
Davies, D. (2011) *Teaching Science Creatively*. (Chapter 4: Cross-curricular starting points). Abingdon, UK: Routledge.
Dewey, J. (1934/1980) *Art as Experience*. New York: Perigee.
Egan, K. (1986) *Teaching as Story Telling*. Chicago: University of Chicago Press.
Jones, S. M. and Pearson Jr., D. (2013) Music: Highly engaged students connect music to math. *General Music Today*, 27(1), 18–23.
Ludwig, M., Marklein, M. B. and Mengli, S. (2016) *Arts Integration: A Promising Approach to Improving Early Learning*. Washington, DC: American Institutes for Research.
Miller, B. A. (2013) Joining forces: A collaborative study of curricular integration. *International Journal of Education & the Arts*, 14(SI 1.9). Available at www.ijea.org/v14si1.

Additional resources

Learn about the relationship between art and sound, music and movement in the performance art information for children at the Tate Gallery, London: http://kids.tate.org.uk/create/art_and_performance.shtm
Arts integration resources: www.artsintegration.com

CHAPTER 11

ASSESSING CREATIVELY

Regina Murphy

INTRODUCTION

Assessment is integral to music curricula, to music teaching and learning and to music making of all kinds the world over. Undertaken effectively, assessment can bring a shared vision of teaching, learning and creativity in the school, generate high expectations for learners and teachers alike and enable all to move forward consistently towards higher goals and fulfilment in music learning.

Assessment is part of day-to-day teaching and learning in all subject areas and, over time, teachers become highly skilled in noticing details, in recognising the slightest improvement in a child's work or in sensing a reduced effort in the completion of a task. However, assessment receives something of a 'bad press' in many settings as it becomes associated with its unloved counterpart – testing – bringing with it a host of imagined pressures, such as demands for higher standards and greater accountability. Whilst the associations with testing tend to accompany specific aspects of curriculum, such as literacy and numeracy, assessment in music is sometimes considered less relevant in the overall management of teaching tasks simply because formal testing is not required. Yet, to underplay the role of assessment in music teaching is to undermine the many dimensions of teaching and learning that form part of creative music making. At the heart of assessment lies the impetus to improve, to transform our artistic efforts into something more beautiful, more elegant, more satisfying and, ultimately, to experience the joy of greater achievement. Assessment tools and strategies can lend support to this endeavour.

This chapter explores some of the tacit assumptions in music assessment and focuses on the importance of making assessment tangible and visible such that it benefits both the learner and the teacher more explicitly. The threads and themes of creativity that are alluded to throughout this book are as relevant here as in other methodological aspects, in particular the notion of profiling agency and creating a community of musical practice. An underlining creativity thread for teachers too is 'watching and listening to children' as a highly enabling strategy.

WHAT DO WE MEAN BY ASSESSMENT?

The term 'assessment' has been broadly defined to encompass a wide range of *methods* for evaluating a learner's performance and attainment, including formal testing and examinations, practical and oral assessment, classroom-based assessment undertaken by teachers and informal observations (Gipps, 1999, p. 356). Assessment can also be thought of as the *process* of gathering, recording, interpreting, using and communicating information about all aspects of a learner's development to facilitate decision-making (Airasian and Russell, 2007). Later in the chapter we will look more closely at some of the methods that are ideally suited to music teaching and learning. Assessment is concerned with:

Methods	Processes
Observations	Gathering
Classroom assessment by teachers	Recording
Practical tasks	Interpreting
Examinations	Using
Testing	Communicating

WHAT ARE THE PURPOSES OF ASSESSMENT IN MUSIC EDUCATION?

Assessment serves many functions depending on the learner, the context, the time of year and the capacity of the teacher or school to support the learner as further progress is made. Assessment can happen on a day-to-day basis to help the teacher decide what the young musician needs to do next and what kind of tasks to set. So, the purposes of assessment are many, but for music teaching in school they mainly serve formative, summative planning and accountability purposes.

Assessment to summarise

The kind of summary assessment that provides a synopsis of what has been achieved is known as *summative assessment*. Normally it occurs at the end of a unit of work or at the end of term and it is useful for recording information systematically and reporting on progress in music.

Assessment for planning

Assessment plays an important role in the teacher's planning as it is used to help make decisions about how the class should advance within the particular music teaching context. Knowledge gleaned from assessment will have implications for preparing new material, for supporting or challenging children's abilities, for gathering other resources and creating further music-making opportunities.

Assessment to enable progression

The most important purpose of assessment in music is to enable the child to make progress over time. A teacher who reflects on his or her teaching and how the child is learning is in a strong position to identify what the learner needs to do next. This type of continuous assessment 'feeds forward' to future learning and can be described as *formative assessment*. It is effective in ongoing teaching and making daily progress.

Connecting planning and assessment

Think about a lesson that you plan to teach soon.

■   How will you know if you have succeeded in teaching what you have in mind?

■   How will your pupils know if they have succeeded?

■   If you assess their learning, is the assessment for them or for you?

FORMATIVE ASSESSMENT AND ASSESSMENT FOR LEARNING (AFL)

One of the most influential pieces of research evidence to emerge in recent years on effective assessment are the studies of formative assessment (Black, Harrison, Lee, Marshall and Wiliam, 2004). Black and Wiliam (1998) reported that where formative assessment is used well it can help low achievers more than other children. Their research shows that frequent informative feedback (rather than infrequent judgmental feedback) can be beneficial to children and especially when they are deeply involved in how classroom assessment happens, how records are kept and how the information is passed on. Having knowledge of their own learning in the form of self-assessment by children is also very valuable. Black and Wiliam conclude their study as follows:

> Thus self-assessment by pupils, far from being a luxury, is in fact *an essential component of formative assessment*. When anyone is trying to learn, feedback about the effort has three elements: redefinition of the *desired goal*, evidence about *present position*, and some understanding of a *way to close the gap between the two*. All three must be understood to some degree by anyone before he or she can take action to improve learning.
>
> (Black and Wiliam, 1998, p. 141, emphasis in original)

To reinforce the messages specifically for policy makers, implicit in the Black and Wiliam review, the Assessment Reform Group (1999) coined the term 'Assessment *for* Learning' (typically abbreviated as AfL). Assessment for learning is defined as 'the process of seeking and interpreting evidence for use by learners and their teachers to decide where the learners are in their learning, where they need to go and how best to get there'.[1] The '10 principles' of assessment for learning are that it:

■   is part of effective planning;
■   focuses on how pupils learn;
■   is central to classroom practice;
■   is a key professional skill;
■   is sensitive and constructive;
■   fosters motivation;
■   promotes understanding of goals and criteria;
■   helps learners know how to improve;
■   develops the capacity for peer and self-assessment; and
■   recognises all educational achievement.[2]

The principles underpinning the work of the Assessment Reform Group have generated interest among curriculum and assessment providers in several countries and regions, such as Australia, Hong Kong, Scotland, Wales, Northern Ireland and the Republic of Ireland. In England, the Office for Standards in Education, Children's Services and Skills (OFSTED) traced the role that AfL has played in improving teaching, learning and pupils' achievement in primary and secondary schools in England. They found that the most important factor in effective AfL was the very clear whole-school vision of teaching, learning and assessment developed by senior staff, their high expectations of teachers and an agreed drive towards consistency (OFSTED, 2008). In music education we see that AfL strategies are advocated by music educators (Fautley, 2009) and have begun to be used more widely.

One could say that an overarching principle in the AfL approach is the use of assessment in the classroom as a tool to improve pupils' learning. But the nature of feedback in the assessment process is critical. The purpose of feedback information is to alter the achievement gap, and that if information about the gap is merely stored without being utilised to alter it, it is not feedback. The learner is at the heart of the assessment process, and if given specific feedback tailored to the nature of the assessment task, then he or she will gradually come to realise what the teacher expects in high quality work and the strategies needed for improving.

CONSIDERATIONS IN ASSESSING MUSIC CREATIVELY

Valuing diversity of musical cultures and contexts

All musical experience is culture-specific and in contemporary classrooms the range of differences among children is vast and includes, for example, differences among children in multicultural communities as well as differences in monocultural communities from different backgrounds. There can also be many differences in a class according to gender, access to instrumental or vocal tuition, exposure to a variety of forms of music and preferences for different kinds of music and different traditions. For some, the idea of teaching music and assessing it in the face of such diversity could seem daunting, especially as teachers traditionally like to be in control of their subject knowledge and manage how the curriculum will evolve over the course of a year. A creative teacher, however, will embrace such diversity and create a climate where the work in the classroom is valued and nurtured and where individual taste is also respected.

Embracing the complexity of music

Music is a complex area of learning and there is no one prototype or analogy sufficient to cover all of the possibilities for potential musical performances or experiences. This means that in order to assess music, a teacher should seek a range of perspectives on musical problem solving through multiple musical experiences. As we see across the chapters in this book, there are many opportunities for doing just that, through children's play, improvisations, listening encounters, performances, invented notations and technological explorations. The chapter on integrating music (Chapter 10) suggests further possibilities for looking at musical activity from multiple perspectives.

Maximising the range of skills and experiences in the classroom

In the day-to-day classroom setting, participation in music lessons outside of school tends to have a high bearing on assessment outcomes within school. Children taking music lessons outside of the main curriculum gain skills and experience through the protocols of performance. This experience has traditionally been associated with graded examinations in instrumental and vocal performance, with many technical, interpretative and repertoire requirements for examinations and public competitions. On the other hand, in composing, structure and progression are far less apparent and less widely studied, and external benchmarks are less commonly understood and therefore, in the world of classroom composition, either in progress or at a terminal point, approaches to assessment can be inconsistent and difficult to compare (Fautley and Savage, 2011). Again, a creative teacher will be mindful of the musical identities and levels of expertise of the children in his or her class and will look at how high level skill in one aspect of music can infuse more diverse, improvisatory styles in another – and vice versa. Each classroom and each school can thus be a unique community of musical practice that draws from multiple music experiences between home and school.

Case study 11.1: Creating a community of musical practice that supports assessment

It's Friday morning and Olivia, a senior teacher in a Dublin primary school, is leading the assembly in whole-school singing. The assembly hall is full of children aged 8 to 12, sitting on low benches and surrounded by their class teachers. It's a semi-public event, with occasional movement of other administrative staff through the back of the hall as they go about the normal school duties, trying not to disturb the singing activity. Olivia begins with the old favourites, 'Oh When the Saints' and 'Trasna na dTonnta' ('Over the Waves'), both rousing tunes. The children are relaxed but enthusiastic, enjoying seeing their friends in other classes in the hall and sharing the special feeling of singing as part of big group. The sound seems to fill the school to the rafters!

Olivia starts to revise the new song they started last week, but the tone is not very good and voices seem strained. Although everyone is looking at her to sing as beautifully as she normally does, Olivia has no hesitation in asking Rosemary, a much younger teacher, for a second opinion. 'I don't think that sounded right, perhaps we should try a different key. What do you think Rosemary?' Immediately, 130 pairs of eyes light up and turn to face Rosemary. She is surprised to be asked for an opinion in front of the children and all the other teachers, but the question is genuine, and she knows that despite all her years of experience, Olivia is open to learning from others and will value her expertise. 'I think you could start a tone lower, and that will help when you get to the middle part,' she offers, and then sings the short passage. 'OK, let's try it everyone!' Olivia responds eagerly. The children face Olivia again, keen to try this suggestion. They are used to being invited to express their opinions about the singing and how to make it better, but this is the first time they were aware that the new teacher, Rosemary, liked to sing as well. Everyone's opinion matters – they learn that in class – so why shouldn't other teachers have a view about music too?

WHAT ARE SOME PRACTICAL APPROACHES TO ASSESSING MUSIC?

Several researchers in music education (e.g. Brophy, 2000; Spruce, 2001) recommend the collection of a wide range of data on classroom activities. In terms of formative assessment, such data enables teachers to thoughtfully reflect on pupil learning and effectively plan successive learning experiences. Portfolios can be used as a practical assessment tool. Rubrics help provide a more fine-grained idea about what goes into a portfolio. Finally, a dialogic approach to feedback and questioning builds momentum in the teaching, learning and assessment cycle. We will now look at each of these approaches in turn.

Portfolios

Portfolios can be used as an assessment tool to record children's efforts and accomplishments through a collection of authentic samples of work. They can be used as an alternative to music tests or grade examinations, or in conjunction with other summative measures in order to give an overall picture of the learning and a framework for the pupils and teachers to review what has taken place. The individuality of a portfolio is especially suited to music-making contexts and can complement AfL strategies.

Drawing from over forty years of expertise in arts assessment at Project Zero at Harvard University, Mills (2009) looks at the concept of a portfolio as a route to assessment and proposes two main types: a 'learning portfolio' and a 'best works' portfolio. Both of these models can be used in classroom, small group or individual music teaching settings. A learning portfolio can work as a 'behind the scenes' record of events. It can be used in a formative way for documenting children's learning at various stages and showing progress over time. The learning portfolio could include illustrative examples of authentic music making, such as recordings taken of music at different times of the year showing how the child created a new piece or practised an existing piece for performance. A learning portfolio could also include a series of recordings of pieces of music and a child's growing ability to respond or appraise the recordings. This would show growth over time as well as the child's own reflection on the learning.

In contrast, a 'best works' portfolio is more 'front of house'. It can contain a showcase of the final performances, creations, illustrations, reflections, written assignments, test results, annotated scores or evaluations, including peer or self-evaluations. A best works portfolio serves a summative function and can be used to illustrate the totality of a child's achievement over a period of time and to determine his or her readiness to continue to the next stage or class.

Portfolio reflections

The incorporation of reflective writing is essential to portfolio development and is often overlooked in the compilation of portfolios.

Reflective writing with senior primary children

For senior primary pupils, portfolios are a way of helping them to thinking critically about what has been accomplished, about their own strengths and weaknesses and about what they need to do in order to improve. Developing metacognitive strategies, or 'learning to learn', is vitally important in enabling the child to take responsibility for his or her learning and fostering the ability to self-regulate. Such disciplined thinking is important for the development of all kinds of musicians. They need to be intrinsically motivated and to have the ability to work independently or collaboratively so that they can sustain music making in a whole variety of contexts. Guidelines can ensure that pupils avoid formulaic approaches or simply writing something to please the teacher. The teacher should specify the surface features, such as the word length and style, but also the deeper, more substantive issues such as key questions, analysis of components, comparisons with other interpretations and synthesis of the whole experience.

Reflective writing with young children

Reflective writing with young children can also be prompted through reminding them of the learning intentions. Shirley Clarke (1998) developed useful acronyms to help younger children remember learning intentions. These are WILF (the dog) and TIB (the cat). These are used widely in the teaching of various subject areas to help children to focus on self-assessing their work and they suit music teaching contexts very well.

WILF the dog

The teacher prompts the children: 'What I'm looking for . . .' (WILF the dog), this reminds them to think about their immediate task with their own specific learning goals.

TIB the cat

When the children know something and want to connect it to a specific learning goal, they can explain by saying: 'This is because . . .'

USING TECHNOLOGY TO SUPPORT ASSESSMENT

Up until relatively recently, the process of audio or video recording a child's work could have been considered quite labour intensive, typically involving special cameras, cassettes or disks, connecting cables, expensive software, compatible disks for copying and burning files and ultimately devoting many hours to the process. In recent years, much of this work has been simplified through advances in digital video technology and social networking sites as we have seen in Chapter 7. Mini digital video cameras in particular are very accessible and in many instances it is possible to connect directly to a computer wirelessly or via a USB connector, store the files securely in the cloud and begin viewing or editing straightaway. Smartphones and tablet computers such as iPads make the task even simpler. Digital documentation created in this way can capture the context, be sensitive to diversity and enable different ways of showcasing different achievements. It can also facilitate the development of skills in self- and peer-assessment and it makes for a very exciting and integrated teaching, learning and assessment environment.

Assessment rubrics

Hale and Green (2009) advocate the use of assessment rubrics as a way of framing expectations and of providing the children with a precise guide for their work. A rubric is a scoring guide that can provide sets of descriptions of different aspects of a task or performance and at different levels. Rubrics can also be a valuable component in pupil portfolios.

Two types of rubrics are found in the literature: analytic and holistic. Analytic scoring rubrics divide a performance into separate aspects with a separate scale for each one. On the other hand, holistic scoring rubrics use a single scale to evaluate the process as a whole, encompassing all the aspects that contribute to a task. Both types can be used effectively for different types of music making. For example, an analytic rubric could be used for assessing a composing task that had several prescribed elements, whereas a holistic rubric could be used to assess the performance of the composed piece.

The use of rubrics can also be beneficial for providing a language for peer-assessment and self-assessment. In developing creative approaches to assessment, the learners must be at the heart of the process, and for music, becoming a self-directed learner is the key goal. The creative teacher will also be mindful of his or her own growth as a music learner and be open to finding ways of improving teaching, learning and musicianship.

Case study 11.2: Valuing openness to ideas, curiosity and questions in peer-assessment

Six weeks to the end of the term and already the grade 6 pupils have started to ask Mr. Stevens about the Battle of the Bands competition, and if it's going to be the same as last year. Some of the groups have been practicing already: looking up tracks, lyrics and various arrangements on the Internet, comparing performances and deciding who will do what part. Mr. Stevens reflects on last year's event and its rules; the children could choose any song they wished, but it had to be approved by the teachers (in case of inappropriate lyrics) and they weren't allowed to use backing tracks. Any instruments had to be played by the children themselves. David, Karolina and Shauna want to use the rubric for band performances that they developed in class together last year, with some changes now that they are all a bit older. It was useful for practising and for figuring out ways of making the music sound better. Karolina wonders if singers should try to imitate famous singers or just sing in their own style, and David is concerned about how to make a bass guitar sound really big on an improvised instrument. Mr. Stevens poses a lot of questions about what makes a good group performance, even if everyone does not play an instrument. In the end, the class makes a list of features that they think are important and they save it in a special music folder on the interactive whiteboard so that it can be revised later.

FEEDBACK: THE ESSENCE OF ASSESSMENT FOR LEARNING IN MUSIC

As discussed earlier, feedback is a critical component of formative assessment, and research has identified its importance in learning general music theory as well as in more specific aspects, such as composing (Murphy, 2007). Furthermore, Fautley and Savage (2011) observe that assessment practices should not have an exclusive focus on state-level requirements to the detriment of supporting pupil learning in composing. In responding to pupils' compositions, Reese (2003) recommends that the teacher's response must first be directed towards how the child created the whole work and its overall expressive character before appraising the details of melody, rhythm, harmony, etc. Next, he suggests focussing on the pupils' readiness to receive criticism and leaving space to moderate responses as necessary. Most importantly, Reese draws attention to the dialogic nature of the relationship between child and teacher and its balance of give-and-take. He suggests that neither a primarily directive, didactic approach nor a heavily facilitative, heuristic approach is sufficient on its own. In this respect, the self-regulative aspect is two-way for pupil and teacher, and this is also an important dimension of creative teaching.

In a similar way, Younker (2003) steers clear of absolute assertions of correct/incorrect comments in providing feedback to pupils and instead recommends that the model of teacher–pupil relationship moves from one of master and apprentice to one of listener and responder. Here the teacher acknowledges, understands and values children's roles in an interactive relationship where feedback and insight is only offered as required, whilst the child is encouraged to self-regulate and work independently towards the desired goal. Questioning is key in Younker's approach to assessment and she recommends both the use of Bloom's taxonomy for progressive questioning as well as the Socratic method for a more probing approach. Younker concludes that feedback is not about single right answers but real musical growth, suggesting that 'closure is not always necessary, nor is it always possible' (p. 240).

LOOKING OUT FOR ASSESSMENT OPPORTUNITIES

As a classroom teacher, it is natural to think, 'I'm just a classroom teacher, how would I know what to look for in music?' Yet, a classroom teacher is an expert educator, and one whose skills in observation, noticing details in student work and internalising knowledge of student progress become more refined each day. Transferring these skills to music teaching contexts is just a short step. During the teaching of singing, there are many things that a teacher can undertake:

- Find out if all the children are able to show the difference between their speaking voice and their singing voice.
- See how the children can cooperate in the making of a simple chant or rap.
- Be aware of how individual children clap or slap to keep the beat.
- Notice if children can sing with confidence and expression and participate fully in the spirit of a song.
- Find out if children can maintain their own part in singing partner songs, when singing in a large group, in pairs or individually, after practice.

Although not every school may offer, or wish to offer, the services of a music specialist, music teaching in primary schools is often collaborative – involving another teacher or teachers in a year group, a person who assists with accompaniments or an occasional artist visitor to school. So whether the classroom teacher is working alone or with others, there are many opportunities to exercise skills in gathering assessment information in music when the children are playing instruments.

Things to look for during playing and improvising

- Be mindful of how children participate in creative exploration on familiar and unfamiliar instruments.
- Observe when children can come up with a new melodic line as part of a given structure.
- Let the children take turns playing a two-note accompaniment to a song and see if they are choosing when to change from one note to the other.
- See if the children can perform a piece alone with confidence and expression, after practice.
- Notice how children invent their own parts.
- Encourage the children to create their own assessment rubrics and see if they can use them to guide self- and peer-assessment.

All observation is a form of data gathering that can feed into formal or informal conversations with parents, anecdotal notes on music progress or more formal end-of-year reporting. Group or solitary activities where there are written artefacts as part of the process provide very rich data.

Things to look for during listening

- As the children illustrate short musical excerpts, notice how they represent musical features in their drawings.
- See if the children identify different sounds in their environment and invent ways of illustrating them vocally or on an instrument.
- Observe the children's problem solving strategies as they listen to a piece of music and solve a musical puzzle.
- Be mindful of the children's responses to the music through discussion and writing and how they justify their opinions with reference to the music.
- Notice the commitment children make to curating their own digital music collections and why they select particular pieces.

In all music activity, improvising and composing affords the most freedom for learners. But freedom in the classroom need not be synonymous with a need for restrictive management of classroom behaviour. Rather, the creative teacher will seek to establish a classroom ethos where each individual's efforts are respected and valued, and where creativity can flourish.

Things to look for during composing

- In composing, look for ideas in sound and musical expression that reflect the character the child is trying to convey.
- Notice how the children respond to each other's compositions and their growing musical awareness.
- Look for cooperative group work and how this contributes to the making of the composition.
- Observe how ideas explored in one aspect of music are explored creatively in another.

■ See how the children invent symbols or begin to use standard symbols to notate their own compositions.

■ Encourage the children to record and then notice how they evaluate their compositions, making note of their comments.

CONCLUSION

In this chapter, we have seen how assessment can commence in various ways, be it as part of a singing lesson or throughout an extended listening task. Assessment for learning contributes meaningfully to children's learning and to teachers' planning. It identifies the teacher as a responsible and committed professional who cares for the learning of his or her pupils whilst encouraging the pupils to assert control of the purpose and pace of their progress in music.

However, there is a danger that the best intentions can be lost in the everyday challenges of teaching large numbers of pupils and the full diversity of their range of expertise, skill development, musical cultures and preferences. To avoid this, the teacher may share the learning intentions of each music lesson with the pupils, clarify with them the criteria that will be used to measure success of the intentions and engage in dialogue with them to establish whether and how success is achieved. The classroom teacher may not be expected to have all the solutions to the various musical challenges, but he or she can remain open to learning alongside others, including the pupils, and can be ready to guide, suggest or point in the direction for more sophisticated learning when necessary.

The combination of portfolios, assessment rubrics constructed in dialogue with the pupils and the judicious use of feedback can provide the basis for very formative learning for the child. Together with digital technology, assessment can be a lively and integral aspect of everyday teaching.

While assessment brings untold positive benefits for the music learners, it has unintended positive consequences for the classroom music teacher – for he or she will invariably become more open, fair, skilled at questioning, sensitive to pupils, cognisant of learning needs, humble in the face of great skill and, ultimately, even more creative in how he or she goes about his or her professional work.

NOTES

1 The Assessment Reform Group worked closely with teachers, teachers' organisations and local authority staff, as well as policy makers over a period of twenty-one years, to ensure that assessment policy and practice at all levels would take account of evidence from research (OFSTED, 2008).

2 Assessment for learning: ten principles, available in the publications section of the Assessment Reform Group's website, https://www.aaia.org.uk/blog/2010/06/16/assessment-reform-group/.

FURTHER READING

Brophy. T. (2000) *Assessing the Developing Child Musician*. Chicago, ILL: GIA.

Elliott, D. (1995) *Music Matters: A New Philosophy of Music Education*. Oxford: Oxford University Press.

Fautley, M. (2010) *Assessment in Music Education*. Oxford: Oxford University Press.

Additional resources

Designing rubrics

A good resource for creating rubrics can be found at http://rubistar.4teachers.org. Templates are provided for teachers to create, save and edit rubrics. Additionally, teachers may view rubrics that other educators have created for band, choir and general music.

Online resources

A selection of summative and formative assessment templates can also be found on the Carnegie Hall website: https://www.carnegiehall.org/ORC/Curriculum-Materials-List-View/#!sel=4294983037,4294982096

CHAPTER 12

USING A WHOLE-MUSIC APPROACH CREATIVELY

Rena Upitis

INTRODUCTION

In order to support creative music making in school, the school ethos itself must encourage music creation. The environment includes a wide variety of sound makers and symbols of music, even symbols that children don't understand. An environment for creative music making also requires daily interventions from teachers, emulating those that parents naturally undertake in teaching their children to speak. Finally, a creative school community involves a broad community of music makers. Adult musicians who both model and encourage playfulness with music all form part of the greater music community. In this chapter, we explore all three of these ideas, namely:

1   Setting up a classroom environment to support creative music making;
2   Providing meaningful, daily and directed support to pupils;
3   Interacting with a broad community of musicians and artists.

HOW SHOULD I SET UP MY CLASSROOM?

One of the marvels of the human experience is that children learn to speak, without formal instruction, in a remarkably short period of time. Because children are surrounded by the sounds of their own language from birth, because adults interact with children in ways that actively support the development of language and because we simply *expect* that all children will learn to speak, children learn to communicate through the spoken word. This book has been written on the premise that the same thing can happen with music – that children, taught creatively and in nurturing environments, can learn to 'speak' the language of music in the same sort of environment in which they learn to speak their mother tongue at home.

To some extent this idea of learning to 'speak' music already happens. There is overwhelming physiological evidence suggesting that music is meant to be part of the human experience. Researchers have demonstrated that even very young babies – across cultures – respond in predictable ways to rhythm and melody, leading to the conclusion that some parts of the brain are hard-wired to respond to musical stimuli (Cohen and Trehub, 1999).

And because of this hard-wiring, along with pre-school experiences with music, children enter school with musical preferences, with a bundle of tunes that they can sing and with an even larger bundle of melodies that they recognise. How can we ensure that the music experiences children have during their primary years build on the intrinsic pleasure they already take from music? And build creatively on the musical knowledge they already possess?

We have seen throughout this book that creative learning in, about and through music is more likely to happen when teachers make learning active and when they enable learning through social interaction. Creative learning also depends on multi-sensory experiences and practices that help pupils develop skills in self-regulation – so that they can take charge of their own learning. How does one go about setting up a classroom to do just that?

In order for children to engage with music creatively, they need opportunities to *play*. To freely explore. To direct their own learning, with the gentle guidance of their teachers. Some years ago, I described what I saw as the ideal setting for creative music making, calling it a musical playground (Upitis, 1990a). I remain convinced that this approach offers the richest possibilities for learning about music, for becoming a performer and for becoming a music creator.

There is ample research evidence attesting to the value of this approach. Late in the 1990s, early childhood music educator Katharine Smithrim conducted a study with extraordinary results. For 13 weeks children spent 20 minutes of each 30-minute music class engaged in free musical play (the other 10 minutes were spent singing and taking part in proscribed rhythmic activities). There were a number of instruments available, including xylophones, metallophones, glockenspiels, maracas, a rain stick, several drums, tie-on ankle bells, claves, chimes, headless tambourines, a guitar open-tuned to a C major chord, timpani tuned to an open C and G fifth and a piano.

The teacher observed the children's explorations and *only intervened if safety issues arose*. In other words, there was no direct instruction for these free exploration sessions. Many sophisticated musical behaviours were observed over the thirteen sessions, including the creation of complex rhythmic patterns that involved an internal shift between duple and triple metres – well beyond what would be modelled in most classes for young children. Long periods of absorbed activity were also observed, again in contrast to strictly teacher-led classes where activities are changed frequently to accommodate differing levels of interest. This research demonstrates that music play in group settings is not only satisfying for children, but that the range of activities that children learn from is far greater than might be the case in teacher-led classes alone (Smithrim, 1997).

While there is much to be learned from the peer teaching and modelling that arises from free musical play, this is not to say that the teacher no longer plays a role. Rather, it is to say that the teacher's role is expanded from demonstration alone to also include preparation of the environment so that musical play and peer teaching can occur.

So to prepare that environment – the musical playground – what should the teacher provide? Let's begin by dispelling the notion that the idea of a playground implies some sort of unstructured free-for-all. Playgrounds are, in fact, highly structured. There is structure in a park playground – the swings, monkey bars and open spaces – and these structures both enable and constrain the play that takes place therein. The same can be said for the structures of a musical playground, which might include a piano, a guitar, some beach balls, a computer, paints, markers, paper, costumes, puppets, shakers and home-made drums, copper pipes, metallophones, cardboard boxes and spaces for movement. Notice how different this list is than the one that Smithrim supplied for her musical explorations. But *both* of these lists hold incredible potential for creative music making; indeed, there is no single magical list that will ensure creative music making. What these lists hold in common are that the materials are all open-ended (there is no single way to use them), they can be used in combination, they cut across subject boundaries and there are limited numbers of each type of material ensuring that the materials will be used in creative combination by the pupils involved.

Providing materials, instruments and time for exploration is critical. But arguably the most important ingredient in the musical playground is that of trust. Teachers must trust that children will learn music, just as they learn to speak, and that much of that learning will happen through musical play. Just as in the playground in the park, children will sort out a set of rules that they all more or less agree to and abide by. The same thing happens when a group of children cluster around a piano.

But trust does not mean that the teacher doesn't play an explicit role. Clustering around a piano and exploring sound goes only so far. We now examine how the classroom teacher can support creative music making in a classroom that has all of the elements of a musical playground – materials that invite exploration and cut across subject boundaries, carry with them no single implied use and are provided in a joyful and trusting environment – and then how the teacher can take that play a step or two further.

I'M A CLASSROOM TEACHER, NOT A MUSIC SPECIALIST. HOW CAN I SUPPORT CREATIVE MUSIC MAKING?

Throughout this book, we have explored many dimensions of creative practice. For example, in Chapter 9 we focussed on aspects of pedagogy, such as rich resources and opportunities to work independently and with others. In this chapter, we examine some of the broader dimensions of creative practice, namely the role of the teacher as a curious and enthusiastic learner, the use of ICT, the integration of classroom practices with the broader school and artistic communities and the vital role that school leadership plays in supporting creative teaching and learning.

This particular section takes something of an 'iPod shuffle approach' to an extraordinarily rich topic, namely teacher-initiated ways of ensuring that children might engage in creative musical endeavours. The discussion here will be limited to three 'tunes' – the importance of the teacher as learner, sample activities that foster creative music making and web-based tools for creative musical explorations.

Teacher as artist-learner

Evidence abounds for the claim that the arts are important for experiencing the joy of creation, developing attention to detail, attaining fulfilment and learning ways of expressing thoughts, knowledge and feelings (Koopman, 2005). The most vibrant teachers experience the arts on a personal level that honours the very essence of artistic work. One way is to be involved in the arts in one's non-teaching time – whether that involvement is directly related to music, such as expanding one's listening experiences as we saw in Chapter 8 or learning to play the flute, or whether that involvement is with another art form, such as gardening, boat building, sculpting or cooking. The true power of music and other arts experiences lies in the engagement of the whole being. Teachers must themselves be thus engaged if the arts are to attain their transforming power in the classroom.

Uniting teacher and artist is not a new idea, but it is an important one. In an exploration of teachers' phobias about teaching music, one researcher suggests that, 'If the child is to feel the art alive within themselves, so must the teacher' (Franklin, 2000, p. 33). So the best advice may be to just try – join a community choir and see where the experience takes you, both personally and in terms of the new life that you bring to the classroom.

Sample activities

Find-a-sound

Children enjoy making sounds from various instruments – in fact, give them an instrument and it is nearly impossible to stop them from exploring the sounds they can make! By instruments, we mean traditional instruments (including the voice) and unconventional 'soundmakers' (such as copper pipes and cardboard cylinders), as well as technology that permits the active and playful manipulation of sound (e.g. the mobile application called Singing Fingers, which we saw in Chapter 7). Then ask the children to find some sounds.

Activity 12.1 Find a sound

What is the . . .

1. Softest sound?
2. Raspiest sound?
3. Highest sound?
4. Lowest sound?
5. Most unusual sound?
6. Sound that reminds you of water?
7. Sound that reminds you of sunshine?
8. Sound that makes you think about elephants?
9. Sound that reminds you of tractors?

The list, of course, is endless. Every creative teacher can introduce the 'find-a-sound' activity. It can be extended to improvisation, notation and composition explorations using some of the techniques described in Chapter 9.

Breaktime concerts

One deceptively powerful way of making music a part of the regular school landscape is the once-a-week Breaktime[1] Concert. It's short – 15 minutes – so it doesn't require 'good audience behaviour' for very long! It is important that concert attendance is *not* mandatory, allowing all sorts of concert-going patterns to emerge. Some children will come to every concert, some will come only when it is raining, some will come once or twice a year and some will never attend. This is as it should be (are adults any different?). If children are forced to come, they might never choose to come of their own free will given the choice at another time, and worse yet, it may negatively influence their interest in such events later in life. And even those pupils who don't attend know that the concerts are happening.

The teacher should encourage a great and eclectic variety of music – children playing instruments that they are learning outside of school, in-school impromptu performances, performances of works composed by pupils and solo and joint performances by teachers, parents, pupils, staff and visitors to the school. This means that there will be Italian arias and Mozart horn concerti alongside the impromptu works of the children, demonstrating powerfully how multiple genres of music are created and performed.

At the beginning of the year, the teacher might keep track of the bookings and post the programme the day before the concert in various key locations in the school. As the year unfolds, it is important that pupils take over the tasks of arranging the programme and printing the posters. And don't omit the posters – they are important, not only for informing the school population of the upcoming performances, but also to make the Breaktime Concerts seem more 'real' – and thus, a more valued experience. Children like to see their name in print. Children like to know that their musical contributions are valued and that they are for peers and adults to enjoy.

Body orchestra

The body orchestra idea is an extension of an introductory Dalcroze exercise where each participant is asked to say his or her name while at the same time 'playing' the name with some part of their body. So someone with a two-syllable name like Sally might lean her head to one side for 'Sal-' and then put her head back in the upright position for '-ly'. Immediately after each child performs his or her name, the group repeats the name, along with the movement, travelling around a circle until all of the names have been completed. Sometimes the teacher might begin by suggesting that the names be played with a particular part of the body (e.g. head, arms, legs); other times, the teacher may simply open up the choice to the pupils. The teacher may encourage the pupils to add a percussive sound as well, such as clapping or patsching. Like other successful activities of this type, there are many musically 'right' answers – and who better to judge how a name should be played than the person with the name?

> 'Let's take the Body Orchestra . . . do you learn anything from that?'
>   'No, it's just funny. Well . . . maybe you do learn something about polyphony and texture and beats and how to watch for your part to come in and listening for your part with the other parts and getting louder and softer and stuff . . . but mostly it's just fun'.
>
> (Upitis, 1990a, p. 11)

The body orchestra part comes in when more than one name is played at the same time. The teacher might strategically choose three names (one-, two-, and three-syllable names) in order that there are different rhythms to the names and also to ensure that the pupils she chooses are going to be comfortable having their name 'played' by other members of the class (most are!). Then the group is divided into thirds, with each section playing one of the names. The teacher begins by 'conducting' the orchestra, much as one would conduct three sections in an orchestra. The mood and texture of the piece can be dramatically modified by bringing in and stopping one, two, or all of the sections, and by varying the dynamic levels of each section or of the orchestra as a whole. Once the teacher has demonstrated how to conduct the body orchestra, children can take turns conducting – an incredibly enjoyable, creative act.

The body orchestra idea can be expanded further by adding a phrase after each name, instrumentation, harmony and melody (Upitis, 1990a). But even in its simplest form – with just three names – it has enormous potential for supporting music creation, and extensive musical training is not a prerequisite.

Web-based tools for creative music making

As we saw in Chapter 7, children's explorations in music can be greatly enhanced by the use of technology, as pupils tend to be more inventive and motivated when using technology in their creative work. The benefits of using music technology include more active involvement in music making on the part of pupils, as well as increased pride and enthusiasm for their music learning (Savage, 2012).

Despite the acknowledged benefits of using technologies to support music education, it is sometimes hard for teachers to use technology in their teaching. Teachers may struggle with using new technologies, while their pupils may find the tools relatively easy to use. Children may also have easier access to mobile devices and music software, and have a different range of knowledge and awareness of musical styles than their teachers. In the hands of a teacher who is ready to capitalise on these children's strengths, these characteristics can serve to strengthen children's music making, potentially engaging them more deeply and creatively. A teacher who remains open-minded, flexible and adaptable will also be ready to use technology creatively as it evolves both outside the world of the classroom and within.

WHAT ABOUT WORKING WITH OTHER MUSICIANS IN MY COMMUNITY?

Strong classroom teachers recognise the advantages of working with others to support every subject that they teach. In this final section, we explore ways of combining classroom resources with other resources in the school and community to provide a comprehensive approach to creative music making. Beginning with the work that can be done with music specialists and other teachers and moving to an exploration of the value of short-term visits and performing arts events, the chapter closes with a discussion of school-based programmes that serve as examples of how multiple communities might be engaged in the music making programmes, including two from the international arena and one that can be 'home-grown' in any school.

Generalist and specialist: partners in the dance

Over the past several decades, there has been a reduced commitment to arts education among policy makers and educational leaders. Even in schools with strong commitments to music and the other arts, the political pressure to raise standardised test scores and the lack of ongoing professional development serve to weaken teachers' efforts to teach music, particularly when music specialists are no longer present in schools. A recent Canadian report indicates that over half of the classroom teachers in Ontario – Canada's most populated province – do not have a background in music.

For teachers without a formal background in music, the entire music curriculum can seem challenging. But this need not be the case – especially if teachers have direct experience with an art form of some kind. Research shows that when teachers approach music from areas of personal strength, they are likely to bring excitement and passion to the classroom.

Music will thrive only if it is regularly scheduled *and* fully integrated into the school culture. Collaborations with specialist teachers ensure that children learn *in* and *about* music, working closely with classroom teachers to develop powerful music curricula that cut across subject boundaries so that pupils can learn creatively *through* music as well, although such purposes are not mutually exclusive.

It is this continued commitment of teachers – both personal and professional – that forms the backbone of creative schools. When committed teachers are supported by parents, administrators, artists and pupils; when teachers and their colleagues have the time and resources they require to do their jobs well and to plan and work cooperatively; and when teachers deeply understand the lifelong contributions that music makes to living and learning, only then will they be able to provide a rich music education – one that will develop the intellectual, emotional, physical and spiritual potential of the children they teach.

School-based programmes and arts partnerships

In order for music to thrive in primary schools and beyond, music must also thrive in the communities and practices that surround and support schools. One of the ways in which communities can contribute to music education is through school-based arts partnerships.

A publication titled *Creating Capacity: A Framework for Providing Professional Development Opportunities for Teaching Artists* was derived on the basis of interviews with educators and administrators involved in nine high-profile arts organisations in the United States (Gradel, 2001). The work delineates a continuum of artist involvement in educational settings. While the framework was developed in the United States, it applies equally well to other countries.

At one end of the continuum, artists may be involved in schools by giving performances or creating exhibits for pupils and teachers, but the artist is not expected to engage audiences in interactive learning experiences. An artist acting in this way is considered a 'performing artist'. Next in the continuum is the 'interacting artist', who, in addition to performing and exhibiting, engages audiences in pre-performance or post-performance discussions, possibly interpreting the artistic work within the educational context. Artist-teachers can be:

- performing artists;
- interacting artists;
- collaborating artists; or
- master instructional artists.

The 'collaborating artist' is engaged more deeply in the school setting, perhaps as an artist-in-residence who plans instructional and assessment strategies collaboratively with classroom teachers. At the other end of the continuum, the 'master instructional artist' contributes to curricular planning and acts as a mentor to other artists working in educational partnerships. Each of these forms of contribution has potential for helping teachers approach music in creative ways. If there is an opportunity in your school to host a musician-in-residence for a week or two, or if there is a new musical being performed at the local theatre, grab those opportunities! The wider the variety and the greater the number of interactions, the more fully the school becomes a thriving musical community.

Benefits of school–music partnerships

▪ Exposure to a wide variety of musicians and genres;
▪ deepening of musical experiences;
▪ more ways of being musically creative;
▪ brings expertise into the classroom;
▪ energising effects for school and community; and
▪ revitalising teaching and learning.

But beware: there can be challenges with arts education partnerships. Sometimes teachers and principals resist having 'outside' artist-teachers involved directly in the teaching of children. And even when schools embrace the talents of the local community, it is a complex matter to schedule visits, follow school protocols, develop curricula and assess the learning that has taken place.

Another potential problem with school-based artist programmes is that the presence of an outside musician leads teachers and administrators to feel that music is 'taken care of' – resulting in a lack of commitment to music education at the school level. Further, when arts interventions are introduced in schools, it often takes years to travel the road for a classroom teacher who conceives of herself as a novice in the arts to feel capable of conveying artistic or musical skills and knowledge in a classroom setting (Upitis, Smithrim and Soren, 1999).

Challenges for school–music partnerships

▪ Securing administrative support;
▪ finding adequate resources;
▪ providing professional development for all teachers;
▪ matching school expectations with the goals of the music project;
▪ finding planning time; and
▪ solving complexities of scheduling.

Despite the challenges associated with artist–school or artist–teacher partnerships, there is no question that these partnerships can be both successful and sustainable in the long term. All schools stand to enrich their offerings through well-structured partnerships. If potential challenges are acknowledged and acted upon in the early days, there will be a foundation for a strong alliance – an alliance which will likely continue after the initial champions move on.

Several models have been developed to increase the level of arts literacy in public schools in Canada through school-based arts partnerships, such as the national Learning Through the Arts (LTTA) programme spearheaded by The Royal Conservatory. Other

Canadian programmes include the Calgary Arts Partners in Education Society (CAPES) programme in Calgary, Alberta, and the national initiative ArtsSmarts, which seeks to promote active participation in arts activities of all forms through various projects that can be either school-based or community-based in nature. There are many school-based programmes throughout Europe as well, such as the school and community partnership between classroom teachers, dance instructors and dance artists in Kartanonkoski School, Vantaa, Finland (Anttila, 2007). These types of programmes bring new energy and life to schools with depleted arts programmes, and also provide important breadth and depth to schools that are already strong in the arts (Irwin and Chalmers, 2007).

Learning through the arts: a school-based partnership example

One of the most comprehensive arts education programmes in Canada – and certainly the one with the most extensive research – was developed by The Royal Conservatory of Music. Since its genesis in the mid-1990s, Learning Through the Arts (LTTA)[2] has become firmly embedded in schools across Canada. LTTA has received overwhelming support – millions of dollars in funding alone attests to the endorsement of the programme by both the public and private sectors.

> I think the arts are very important because when you were working with all those artists, you just think, 'WOW! There is so much more to art than you would have thought of before. It's not just painting, it's not just drawing, it's so much more'.
>
> (Grade 6 LTTA pupil)

Why has LTTA been so well received by teachers, pupils, parents and investors? First, the programme is an imaginative partnership between artists, teachers and the broader community, often involving full-school implementation. Second, the programme incorporates the arts as entry points for learning across the curriculum, so teachers can engage their pupils through the arts while at the same time enlivening the teaching of other subjects. Finally, artist and teacher professional development are key aspects of the work.

In the LTTA primary school education model, professional artists and musicians work directly with pupils, applying an art form to the teaching of concepts in another subject area. For example, a dancer might approach the teaching of a geometry unit through movement and modern dance.

The artists begin their work with the pupils after developing lessons and units with the classroom teachers, based on the curriculum requirements for each educational jurisdiction. Research studies on LTTA consistently show that the programme is positively received by pupils and results in more use of the arts by teachers, as well as increased administrative support for the arts. Other programmes that use the arts in conjunction with the teaching of other subjects have similarly demonstrated that positive changes occur for pupils as a result of such an approach.

The quality of the artist–teacher partnerships in the LTTA programme had much to do with its success as a professional development model for teachers (Kind, de Cosson, Irwin and Grauer, 2007). Teachers and artists who develop strong working relationships and a comfortable rapport learn a great deal from one another. As a result, artists positively respond to teachers' insights about education and child development, and teachers become excited about what the arts and the artists have to offer pupils.

Thus it is an intermingling of institutional, curricular, pedagogical and relational factors that contribute to the success of school-based partnerships in the arts. One could say the same about the mix of factors that constitute successful learning environments at all levels.

Musical theatre, pantomimes and variety shows

Musical theatre, pantomimes and variety shows are long-standing so-called extracurricular activities in many primary schools. Encompassing all of the fine and performing arts, musical theatre is one of the most comprehensive forms of art making and music making that is possible in the primary school context. Pupils act, dance, sing, tell a story and interact with one another, both in rehearsal and on stage.

Every single teacher in the primary school can contribute to musical theatre or other showcase performances, whether that teacher has extensive skills and experience in music or not. Taking part in primary school musical theatre encourages pupils to learn to trust one another, to take risks, to interact effectively with their peers, to form a sophisticated sense of creative identity and to gain ownership over the creative process and the product itself. Research shows that these benefits last a lifetime (Ogden, 2008).

Teachers are not mandated to organise musical theatre productions in most jurisdictions, and yet something compels them to do so. Perhaps it is because teachers see the benefits of musical theatre that they are willing to give up free time to provide the opportunity for their pupils. Further, parents and community members who have themselves participated in such activities promote and encourage youth to become involved in musical theatre.

The magnitude of musical productions, including the costumes, the tickets, the rehearsals, the make-up and the overall detail makes the experience real for the children. Indeed, the 'realness' of musical theatre is one of its key attractions. Musical theatre requires effective social negotiations between cast and crew, children and adults, school and community. Primary school musical theatre involves pupils, teachers, musicians, parents – on stage and backstage, in the audience and in the community – acting, singing, learning, building, advertising and selling tickets. Musical theatre is collaborative and creative music making at its best: group members work interdependently to create a performance that they value and learn from.

The Royal Opera House,[3] Covent Garden and the Metropolitan Opera Guild,[4] New York, offer a further extension of art forms that involve music and theatre through the programmes titled Write an Opera and Students Compose Opera, respectively. In these models, both institutions provide extensive professional development and outreach to participating schools and teachers with an enthusiasm for, interest in or curiosity about the arts and creative learning, and advanced musical knowledge is not required. The notion of 'opera' as an obscure performing art is completely demystified and the experience of creating a work from scratch is energising and fulfilling. The collaborations with artist-teachers and classroom teachers at all levels result in highly creative, pupil-led, artistic activity.

SUMMARY

Throughout this chapter, we have seen how the pillars of creativity can result in highly creative and satisfying approaches to music teaching and learning. These pillars – an open, inquisitive and curious approach on the part of the teacher, coupled with pedagogical stances that encourage questions and exploration, all in the context of a school ethos that promotes intellectual, social and emotional engagement on the part of pupils, teachers and the wider community – have shown themselves again and again throughout this book as the foundational conditions upon which teachers can ensure that pupils will learn music creatively. Learning in these creative ways will ensure that pupils enjoy a lifetime of rich music experiences.

NOTES

1   Also known as 'recess' or 'lunchtime'.
2   Learn more about LTTA through their website – download lesson plans and see classrooms in action at www.ltta.ca.
3   See www.roh.org.uk/learning/teachers/write-an-opera.
4   See www.metguild.org.

RESOURCES FOR FURTHER READING

Cornett, C. and Smithrim, K. (2000) *The Arts as Meaning Makers: Integrating Literature and the Arts Throughout the Curriculum*. Toronto, ON: Prentice Hall.

Jaffurs, S. (2004) The impact of informal music learning practices in the classroom, or, how I learned to teach from GarageBand. *International Journal of Music Education*, 22, 189–200.

Upitis, R. (1990) *This Too Is Music*. Portsmouth, NH: Heinemann.

Waldron, J. (2013) YouTube, fanvids, forums, vlogs and blogs: Informal music learning in a convergent on- and offline music community. *International Journal of Music Education*, 31(1), 91–105.

CHAPTER 13

TEACHING MUSIC INTERCULTURALLY
Posing questions, creating possibilities

Elizabeth Mackinlay

Today, as the boundaries between local and global communities disappear and the flow of information between them becomes instantaneous, the educational spaces in which we find ourselves as teachers have become increasingly culturally diverse. So too has the kind of access we have, as music educators, to the musics of the world. Intercultural performances and musical experiences present themselves to music teachers as important and meaningful ways in which to express and embrace the cultural diversity they see inside and outside the classroom. The intercultural encounter between musical ways of being, doing and know- ing, in relation to 'own' and 'other' cultures in a music classroom, overflows with a com- plex set of philosophies, politics and pedagogies. In this chapter I draw upon my work as an ethnomusicologist and educator to introduce some of the key concepts and questions which might usefully inform our work as music educators in the field of interculturality. In particular, my aim in this chapter is to explore:

- Defining what we mean by intercultural
- The intercultural music classroom as a contact zone
- The centrality of relationship to intercultural music education
- The pedagogical possibilities of adopting a whole-school, classroom and personal ethos to intercultural music education
- Ways forward to intercultural music education classroom practice

This chapter perhaps differs from others in this volume as it intends to challenge us, as music educators, to think deeply and carefully about the ways in which musics of other cultures enter into a dialogue with our own. Throughout the chapter, I ask us to step back and engage in moments of reflexivity about and around intercultural music education in our practice and classrooms. For me, this enables 'praxis', that is, reflection in relation to and within our teaching and learning worlds so that we might direct our actions as teachers towards transformation. As Maxine Greene (1995) reminds us, 'It is a matter of posing questions on both sides and of loving the questions that merge with one another, questions about living in the world and creating communities and collectivities' (Variations on a blue guitar, p. 159); in this spirit, I have included several reflective prompts to begin this ques- tioning process. However, I would first like to introduce and position my work and myself.

POSITIONING MYSELF AS AN INTERCULTURAL MUSIC EDUCATOR

She looks down the platform
And then at her watch
She is waiting for a train
Staring at the tracks she wonders where she has come from
And where she is going
She feels like she has been travelling
Since yesterday became tomorrow
And yet she senses there is still a long way to go
The screeching sound of metal on metal startles her
This is her train and it's time to climb aboard
Trying to remain invisible and unseen
She walks with her head down
Looking for the right seat
To place her self
She stumbles as the train lurches
And heavily sits down
Click clack click clack
Her mind reaches back to remember
The things she has packed in her suitcase
A PhD in ethnomusicology – check
A PhD in education – check
But what kind of music educator does that make her?
Click clack click clack back
To the dreaming board
A childhood memory of grandmothers singing softly
Two little girls in blue dear
Bright lights of a musical stage
The King and I and a bunch of sailors
And then a brass instrument in her hand
An orchestral song in her head
And a university music degree
To tightly hold
The train lunges to the left
She has to hang on tight to keep herself on the seat
Her body is moving to a different rhythm
She hears the melodies of mermaids
She hears their voices rising high above the ceremony ground
She hears stories of their strength, care and nurturance
She hears that song, dance, country and ceremony make women strong
And she feels as though she might have arrived
But the women singing around her are black
She is white-settler-colonial
Her husband is black and white
And their children black, white, black and white

She is not sure if she sitting in the right seat
Sometimes it is comfortable
But mostly she is not sure whether she is the driver or the passenger
She learns to trust the discomfort
She can see herself trying to take control
Her voice begins to sing a song she has always loved
With little people in little classrooms
Feet stamp, hands clap, voices shout
She gives her big heart to them
And they give theirs to her
Maybe she has found her rainbow
In a musical story she thought she had forgotten
Without warning the train begins to slow down
The dizziness of the past becomes the clarity of here and now
She is excited as she steps off the train
And she can't help but sing this songline because she knows now where she is going
To a classroom where dance, art, drama and music ground her
Where she can care and where she can love
Where teaching and learning touches hearts as well as minds
And the arts become locations of possibility for all of this and so much more

---

Activity 13.1 Becoming an intercultural educator

Having read this 'positioning piece', create your own three-word sentence creative writing piece, which describes your social, historical, political and cultural location as an intercultural music educator.

WHAT'S IN A NAME: DEFINING INTERCULTURAL

It is useful to begin by thinking about what the term 'intercultural' means and why it might be the preferred term to use when bringing music from different cultures into our music classrooms. Searching for an exact definition of 'intercultural' can be confusing because it is often used interchangeably with other words such as 'cross-cultural', 'transcultural' and sometimes 'multicultural'. Let's consider the differences between them. The term 'cross-cultural' implies that two or more cultures are related in some way, often for the purpose of comparison (e.g. a cross-cultural musical analysis). For this reason, the term 'cross-cultural' might be said to establish a binary way of thinking about 'us' and 'them', and 'own' and 'other' cultures. The term 'transcultural' differs in that it emphasises the crossing and therefore breaking down of cultural boundaries as two or more cultures become intertwined, encompassed or combined. Use of the word 'transcultural' seeks to foreground the understanding that cultures are dynamic and fluid, and that there is tension between similarity and difference. The term 'multicultural' on the other hand alludes to two or more cultures coexisting, with each culture retaining its unique cultural identity. The term 'intercultural' might, at its most basic, be usefully defined as 'having contact with, exposure to, and experience with different cultures' (Tsuda, in Alexander et al., 2014,

p. 16). However, unlike the other terms, 'intercultural' suggests that the encounter between cultures is exactly that – something that happens at the 'in-between' and on the borders. In my own music education practice, I prefer the term 'intercultural' because of the possibilities it holds for decentring dominant ways of knowing, doing and being in relation to music and opens up a space for dialogue where difference meets. Indeed, as arts educator and critical thinker Maxine Greene would suggest, those of us who are 'imaginative enough' to be present in such in-between places of difference and diversity are laying bare the possibility to 'open pathways to better ways of teaching and better ways of life' (1995, p. 12).

Case study 13.1: Playing the rhythms of life using 'bucket drums' in a drumming circle

In a grade 4 primary classroom, a music specialist is invited in to teach an 8-week drumming program as part of the 'Values Education' policy and program at the school. The music specialist is a trained West African djembe drummer, but she is not from West Africa and there are no West African children in her class. It is a large class and she soon realises she does not have enough djembes for all of the children to play one each. The school does not have the resources to pay to buy the djembes. The classroom teacher and the music specialist decide to improvise and purchase a class set of 'bucket drums' – 10 × 60 litre black plastic rubbish bins, 10 × 30 litre white plastic paint pails, and 10 × 10 litre blue washing buckets. They also buy thirty pairs of wooden drumsticks for the children to play the 'bucket drums'. The drumming program begins. The music specialist and the children sit in a drumming circle and she explains to the class that the drums are the 'heartbeat' of music and that they are going to play the rhythms of life. She explains to the children her understanding of West African drumming philosophy – that the drum is unity; in the drumming circle we are playing as one, no one is left out and no one is singled out and each and everyone becomes a musician with a unique part to play. The music specialist translates djembe hand playing techniques to the drumsticks and surfaces of the buckets. She then teaches the children the rhythms of West Africa and together they make music.

Activity 13.2 Reflecting on intercultural music education

What are some of the complexities of the intercultural music education in Case Study 13.1?

How would you describe it? Is it a cross-cultural, transcultural, multicultural or intercultural classroom?

Which word did you choose and why?

Which of these terms best describes your own practice as a music educator in an intercultural space?

THE INTERCULTURAL MUSIC CLASSROOM AS A CONTACT ZONE

It is useful for us to conceptualise an intercultural music classroom as a 'contact zone' that holds the possibility of presenting itself as a 'third cultural space' and 'cultural interface'. I will discuss each of these concepts in turn.

Let's begin with the contact zone. The *contact zone* is a concept made popular by anthropologist Mary Pratt, who described the contact zone as 'the social spaces where cultures meet, clash and grapple with each other, often in contexts of highly asymmetrical relations of power, such as colonialism, slavery, or their aftermaths as they are lived out in many parts of the world today' (1992, p. 33). As a particular kind of meeting place, the contact zone is a site for the intersectionality of cultures – an interactive and potentially transformative place where previously disconnected cultures are brought together through specific kinds of historical, political and cultural forces. The intersectionality of cultures in the contact zone makes it possible for new ideas, perspectives and understandings to be produced, and further 'permits us to give credence to alternative realities . . . to break with the taken for granted, to set aside familiar distinctions and definitions' (Greene, 1995, p. 3).

If we are willing to see the intercultural music education classroom as a contact zone, then it is useful for us to consider the concept of *third cultural space*. The notion of 'third cultural space' derives from Homi Bhabha's work on 'third space', which he explains as a location, grounded and based in the 'articulation of cultural difference' (2004, p. 56). A postcolonial thinker, Bhabha maintained that in contact zones, the flow of power and privilege is necessarily unequal; cultural texts and systems in the contact zone are crossed by difference: the ways in which cultures 'enunciate' themselves are different; and, combined, such unevenness results in the act of cultural representation often being misinterpreted and misappropriated into a Western or Eurocentric perspective. Bhabha suggests that a third space – a space which, like the contact zone, becomes a location for two or more cultures to meet – is therefore one that we have not yet seen (cf, Vass and Chalmers, 2015). It is culture created over because of the dialogue it opens up at the in-between of interculturality. In a third cultural space, the meaning and symbols of culture can be contested, 'reconfigured, rehistorisized and read anew' (Bhabha, 2004, p. 55).

Another valuable way of thinking about intercultural music education classrooms as contact zones is through the lens of the *cultural interface*. The cultural interface is a way of thinking about education as a contact zone developed by Torres Strait Islander teacher and theorist Martin Nakata (2007). While his work begins from his location as a Torres Strait Islander in relation to non-Torres Strait Islander peoples and cultures, there are three main ideas central to this model which are useful for our work as music educators. The first of these is the *corpus*, that is, the body of knowledge that is produced *about* non-Western 'others' by Western people. Within the corpus, 'others' are treated as objects whose identities and knowledges can be known, documented and represented. Of significance here is that often the gathering and reproduction of knowledge about non-Western 'others' serves an agenda located within the interests of the West, rather than the 'other' people themselves. The corpus was historically, and is today, produced by anthropologists, historians, travel writers, journalists and the media and makes its way into our classrooms as various kinds of authoritative texts.

Case study 13.2: Using electronic audio loops to compose a piece of digital dance music

It is term 3 in the year 9 music program and the teacher decides he would like to include some intercultural music experience in the upcoming unit of work on digital composition. The aim of this unit of work is for students to use electronic audio loops to compose a piece of digital dance music. In this unit of work students will listen to loop-based music genres such as hip-hop, techno and dance music; explore and analyse examples of music from these genres to understand how loops are used in music and in relation to concepts of beat, rhythm and time signatures; and explore and practise looping techniques and software. The teacher begins to prepare the resources the class will need for this unit of work and decides he will digitally sample some music examples for the class to use as this will save time. He knows that the didjeridu is a popular instrument in dance music and he borrows the school library recording of Alice Moyle's (1978) *Aboriginal Sound Instruments* to sample. He copies the tracks, which specifically feature didjeridu, and digitises them so that the students can further sample sections of each track to loop for their assessment work. The teacher returns the recording to the library. On his way back to his classroom, he remembers that he forgot to note down any information about the recording itself or the tracks he copied. The teacher decides it is not important, because after all, they are only interested in the sound of the didjeridu.

Activity 13.3 Reflecting on the intercultural music experience

Describe in your own words what the intercultural music experience is that the teacher is attempting to set up.

How do the teacher's actions and motivations relate to Nakata's concept of the 'corpus'?

What might this teacher have done differently?

The second important component of Nakata's cultural interface is *indigenous standpoint theory*. Indigenous standpoint theory draws on the notion that people as subjects rather than objects are socially located and that individual subjects are creators of knowledge about themselves – that is, the known becomes the knower and is given agency to create knowledge. Indigenous standpoint theory therefore directly contests the corpus and this means that, as music educators, we can begin to ask questions about the ways in which indigenous, non-Western and 'other' voices are heard in our representations of them in an intercultural music classroom. We can ask questions about whose standpoint is being privileged and whose standpoint is silenced in the musical and pedagogical moves we are making. We can also begin to ask questions about how such room might be made possible.

The third aspect of the cultural interface, which is significant for us is that, in as much as it is a space for possibility, it is also a space of tension. There is a constant *push-pull* between 'us' and 'other' as knowledges from Western and non-Western musical cultures come into contact. As teachers, we can become caught between the professional imperative to instruct and impart the musical knowledges of our own culture within an educational system which reflects and values our own ways of being, doing and knowing, and wanting to adopt an approach which inverts or at the very least includes 'other' ways of doing, being and knowing about music as the reference point. Indeed, Nakata insists that regardless of our subject location – indigenous, non-indigenous, Western or non-Western – we are all implicated in the cultural interface, and he asks us to consider the personal-is-political-is-pedagogical ways which engage in the 'push-pull' and the kinds of musical learning and understandings we make available to ourselves and those with whom we teach and learn.

Activity 13.4 Conceptualising the spaces in between

Here we have discussed the space of intercultural music education as a contact zone, third cultural space and cultural interface.

Which of these concepts resonates most with you and why?

THE CENTRALITY OF RELATIONSHIP TO INTERCULTURAL MUSIC EDUCATION

How might we then transform the kind of contact zone which is our intercultural music classroom to become the kind of third cultural space and cultural interface described above? As a music educator, I bring a background of ethnomusicology to my practice and classroom. I began working as a 'white-settler-colonial' ethnomusicologist in 1993 with the Yanyuwa, Garrwa, Mara and Kudanji Aboriginal community at Burrulula in the Northern Territory of Australia. As a discipline, ethnomusicology places itself firmly in the interstices between cultures and endeavours to 'approach music as a social process in order to understand not only what music is but why it is: what music means to its practitioners and audiences, and how those meanings are conveyed' (Society for Ethnomusicology, 2016). Each day I set up my Nagra reel-to-reel tape recorder, carefully balanced my notebook on my knees, ensured that my camera was at the ready and sat with Yanyuwa, Garrwa, Mara and Kudanji song women and song men to record and document the musical traditions from this region of Aboriginal Australia. As performers sang, I furiously scribbled down the beginnings of music notation for the songs I was hearing and did my best to take note of any other 'extra-musical' information about the performances singers wanted to share.

At that time, I imagined I was doing what a 'good' ethnomusicologist should. However, I quickly learned that there was much more to understanding music 'cross-culturally' than pressing 'record' and making transcriptions – what was missing from my practice was relationship. I realised that framing my work as 'cross-cultural' meant that it was 'always already' about us and them rather than a dialogue at the in-between. I saw clearly the unequal and neocolonial power relationships I was enacting as white-settler-colonial 'researcher' with Yanyuwa, Garrwa, Mara and Kudanji performers as 'researched' and decided that this was not the way I wanted to work. It did not sit well with me ethically, largely because of this colonial relationship.

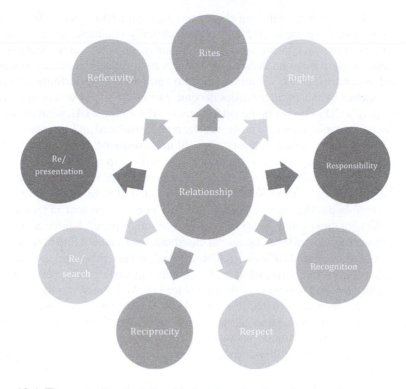

■ **Figure 13.1** The centrality of relationship to intercultural music education.

An important part of my journey towards intercultural practice is my location not only as a white-settler-colonial ethnomusicological researcher at Burrulula, but also as a family member. When I arrived at Burrulula I was married (and still am) to a Yanyuwa man and was immediately given a place in the Yanyuwa kinship system as his wife. We now have two children and my work with our family continues; however, I firmly embrace, rather than seeking to erase, the 'personal-is-political-is-pedagogical' underpinnings in my practice. Grounding myself in 'relationship' is the one way in which I am able to negotiate this complex space.

Placing relationship at the centre of my work allowed other words and concepts crucial to any intercultural musical encounter to come into play, and, by coincidence, they too begin with 'r' (see Figure 13.1). Let's discuss each 'r' word in turn and draw your attention first to *rites*. Here I am asking us to think deeply about the cultural contexts of the songs, dances, instruments, genres and ceremonies which make the journey into our classrooms. What kind of intercultural performance is it that we are seeking to create? Whose musical cultures are we bringing together as an encounter and what kinds of social, cultural, political and religious meanings does such music hold? How might I understand these musics as sound, concept and behaviour (after Merriam, 1964); and, further, how are they historically constructed, socially maintained and individually experienced (Rice, 1987)? How will I ensure that the musics have 'safe passage' in terms of ensuring that the complexities of their cultural embeddedness is not subject to a process which Murray Schafer (1977, p. 90) called 'schizophonia', that is, the splitting of sound from its original source? What is the kind of intercultural music education rite I might perform as a result?

Once we begin thinking about rites, asking questions about the *rights* of the peoples whose music we are attempting to interculturally encounter arises. Here I am invoking notions of power, control, agency and authority in relation to the makers of music – their rights as knowledge holders, as creators, as performers and artists, as traditional owners and as culture bearers. What kind of control and agency do performers have over the ways and means by which their musics become part of the sound waves in our classrooms? Do we play a CD or do we invite performers in? If we play a CD, what do, and can, we know about the way in which the music was recorded, produced and commercialised and the kind of control, agency and authority afforded to performers? If we invite performers in, what kind of control, agency and authority are we willing to make possible?

The flip side to talking about performers' rights is of course the way in which we exercise *our* rights as music educators. What kind of right is it exactly? And what kind of personal-is-political-is-pedagogical thinking does it represent in terms of who we are in relation to 'own' and 'other' in an intercultural space? I have already spoken of my white-settler-colonial positioning in the educational spaces I find myself in and this, in turn, holds particular kinds of white-settler-colonial powers, privileges and rights. When I reflect back on how and why I came to be an ethnomusicological researcher at Burrulula, the singular reason I was there in the first place is linked directly to the kinds of white-settler-colonial power and privilege I held and still hold to *be there* – particular kinds of social, educational, economic and cultural capital which are linked intimately to my subjectivity as a white-settler-colonial in Australia. The question, which now sits uneasily in the air between us, is: What is your location in relation to particular kinds of powers, privileges and subjectivities?

Case study 13.3: Practising inclusive pedagogies creatively

A music teacher is asked by his school principal to teach a weekly music lesson with recently arrived refugee children who are enrolled in the Intensive English Unit at his school. The principal has heard that singing songs in English can be an effective way for students of a non-English-speaking background to very quickly acquire some speaking proficiency in the language of their new country. The music teacher is concerned. While the music teacher is confident that he has a contemporary and popular repertoire of songs he can draw upon for the IEU students, he is not quite sure what kind of intercultural pedagogy he should be performing and whether or not the teaching and learning approach he might use in a Western context will necessarily align with, and therefore have the same impact for the learning of students from other countries. He understands that it is important for 'new arrivals' to 'assimilate' but the music teacher is uncomfortable about seeming to ignore the 'home' language of each student. The music teacher wishes he had more time to get to know each student – to know about their countries of origin, to know about the musics they practice and experience in their home countries – and laments that even knowing each student's name would be a start. But the IEU music class begins tomorrow and there is no time to 'know'. The music teacher sighs and stacks a class set of 'Sing with Me: Hit Songs from 2010' to take with him tomorrow.

Activity 13.5 A consideration of rights and privilege

In contemplating yourself in this scenario, what concept of 'rights' does it invoke?
What do 'rights' mean to you as a music educator?

How might you describe your subject location in your classroom in relation to
the kinds of social, educational, economic and cultural capital you have access to?

How does this play out in your intercultural work as a teacher?

Following on from our consideration of rights and rites leads us to think about *re/presentation*, that is, the way in which we represent and re-present musics of other cultures in our classroom, and, further, how we bring them into conversation with our own. In representing the musics of other cultures we are often engaged in a process which ethnomusicologist Carol Robertson refers to as the 'translation of information from one set of cultural realities to another'. She uses the metaphor of 'midwifery' to describe the significance of this task and her following explanation has an important message for us as music educators in relation to our intercultural work:

> The ethnomusicologist is often engaged in a dance of midwifery. She can coach or nurse the tradition she studies into public perception, but she may not excise its limbs when they do not move to the rhythms of the scholarly world. She is not the parent of the tradition; she is merely the facilitator. Yet how she brings the tradition into the light may determine its survival and acceptance. This is an awesome responsibility.
>
> (1995, p. 123)

The act of re/presentation is significant, then, because it has an enormous role to play in the kind of musical learnings we make possible for our students when they encounter music of another culture, and, further, the ways in which they might engage in a broader social, cultural and political relationship with the people and communities from which the music comes. Anthropologist Henrietta Moore (1997, p. 127) suggests that there are four important questions we need to ask ourselves if, when, and each and every time we decide that we are going to open the door and enter into a dialogue between our own and other musical cultures:

1   What sort of representation?
2   By whom? For whom?
3   Under what circumstances?
4   To what ends? For what purposes?

In order to ask these questions, as music educators, we need to do our re/search; indeed, we need to become 'teacher-researchers' of the music cultures we're entering into dialogue with. We need to become the kind of educational practitioner we imagine ourselves to be, that is, someone who continually strives to gain deeper understanding of what kind of teaching and learning we are performing, how we might perform it and why are we performing it in that particular way. We do this because we care about the impact it has on our students and our sense of being learners alongside them. We do this – perhaps – because we care about the ways in which the representations we make of the musics of other cultures contribute to social acceptance, racial tolerance and a world where differences are respected and valued.

Crucial to the centrality of relationship to intercultural music education is a mode of relating to 'self' and 'other' grounded in *respect*. If we understand this word to mean to look at a person with deep admiration for their abilities and qualities and with due regard for their feelings, wishes, rights and worldviews, then respect underpins all of our work in this space. It demonstrates that we are prepared to enact a certain amount of 'cultural humility' (Oetzel, in Alexander et al., 2014, p. 15) in order to learn about others and ourselves and it requires flexibility, mindfulness, empathy and commitment (Arasaratnam, in Alexander et al., 2014, p. 16).

A natural consequence flowing from a grounding of respect is *recognition*. In an intercultural classroom, recognition is acknowledgment that each culture enters into the teaching and learning space with a unique and distinct set of cultural ways of knowing, being and doing. They may or may not be the same, similar or in alignment with one another but a 'politics of recognition' asks all of us to recognise, accommodate and respect the difference. Recognition, then, can be an important means to understand and respond to difference.

It is our ability to respond that the next 'r' word attends to. A question I continually ask myself in my own work as an ethnomusicologist and educator, is what kind of *responsibility* do I take on and hold when I place myself at the 'in-between' of intercultural teaching and learning? There is a certain type of ethical and moral obligation which sits in the folds of respect, relationship, re/presentation and re/search that is inherently linked to the roles we might play as music educators in mediating the transference and counter-transference of power, knowledge and authority across, between and through our musical-cultural differences. For me, my ability to respond to such an ethical obligation has always centred on the ways in which I engage with the colonial difference between my Yanyuwa, Garrwa, Mara and Kudanji family and myself. It means always asking uncomfortable questions about the white power and privilege I hold to engage in such acts of re/presentation, and whose interests I am actually serving – whose musical-cultural ways of knowing, being and doing are at the centre? Why does this matter to me and how do I perform such *mattering*?

One of the immediate flow-on effects, which comes from thinking about our responsibilities in intercultural teaching and learning contexts, is a desire to perform *reciprocity*. As soon as respect and recognition become part of our praxis as music educators, we begin to search for ways to enable the teaching and learning relationship to become one whereby everyone involved in the intercultural encounter stands to benefit in some way. We seek to give back that which we take and ensure that our powers, privileges and rights are shared equally, in dialogue and in a spirit of collaboration rather than appropriation.

Finally, a respectful relationship, in an intercultural music education classroom, necessarily involves us in an ongoing process of *reflexivity*. Reflection, reflective practice and reflexivity are particular kinds of 'r' processes that have always held much promise in education (and in the social sciences more broadly) for exploring and exposing the positioning and politics of some of the related 'r' words I have already spoken about such as research, the researcher and acts of representation (e.g. Britzman, 1995; Chaudry, 2000; Davies, 1999). Being reflexive teachers in intercultural music education means that we are willing to consider ourselves *in relation to* others and ask *critical* questions about the powers, privileges and politics which underpin those relationships. Indeed, Stephen Brookfield argues that:

> Becoming aware of how the dynamics of power permeate all educational processes helps us realize that forces present in the wider society always intrude into the classroom. Classrooms are not limpid, tranquil reflective eddies cut off from the river of social, cultural and political life. They are contested arenas – whirlpools containing the contradictory crosscurrents of the struggles for material superiority and ideological legitimacy that exist in the world outside.
>
> (1995, p. 9)

Becoming attentive, through a reflexive approach to the ways power is working in our classrooms, is one of the most *powerful* ways we can begin to work more democratically and cooperatively, and in an intercultural classroom, this is a significant imperative.

Activity 13.6 Asking the questions

Go back and look over each of the 'r' words. Which has the most meaning and relevance for you and why?

WAYS FORWARD TO INTERCULTURAL MUSIC EDUCATION CLASSROOM PRACTICE

In closing this chapter, I realise that I have asked many more questions than I have provided answers for – and I hope that in and of themselves these prompt a different way of engaging with difference in your intercultural music education classroom. The following 'ethos' framework (Department of Education and Training, 2016) is one I have found useful in 'puzzling out' the kind of personal-is-political-is-pedagogical intercultural music educator I imagine and would like myself to be – and I share it here with you in the hope that it might do the same for you. The *ethos framework* has three parts – personal, classroom and whole-school – and together they provide a way to navigate the contact zone of the intercultural music education classroom and enact the circle of 'r' words I have explored. One of the first steps we need to undertake as music educators is to consider our *personal ethos*. Here we need to ask what are the understandings, assumption and perceptions, experiences and knowledges I bring with me into my classroom about 'own' and 'other' cultures? What impact does this set of awarenesses have on the ways I might perform intercultural music education and to what ends? The second step is to consider how our personal ethos is reflected in the classroom. Our *classroom ethos* relates to the curriculum, pedagogies and processes we use to engage in music education 'midwifery' and respectfully value, represent, include and privilege our own and other cultures in the cultural interface in which we find ourselves. The final part to the ethos framework is *whole-school ethos* and this relates to the ways in which our school community – from principals to parents to heads of programs to administration staff – commits to and enacts a philosophy of interculturality. Each of you will take on board the ideas presented in this chapter in your own way, for each intercultural music education moment is exactly that – a moment. It is a moment, however, to break with business as usual and enact something different within the differences; and I leave you with this promise of hope from critical educator bell hooks: 'the classroom with all its limitation, remains a location of possibility' (1994, p. 207).

REFERENCES

Bhabha, H. K. (2004) *The Location of Culture*. London: Routledge.

Greene, M. (1995) *Releasing the Imagination: Essays on Education, the Arts, and Social Change*. San Francisco, CA: Jossey-Bass.

hooks, b. (1994) *Teaching to Transgress: Education as the Practice of Freedom*. New York, NY: Routledge.

Nakata, M. (2007) *Disciplining the Savages: Savaging the Disciplines*. Canberra, ACT: Aboriginal Studies Press.

TEACHING CREATIVELY IN CREATIVE LEARNING COMMUNITIES

Pamela Burnard

Current research shows a strong positive relationship between successful professional learning communities and creating a positive school culture. All of the chapters in this book explore creative learning opportunities on offer to primary school teachers in the development of an effective professional learning community. Individually and socially constructed values and beliefs guide teachers no matter where they work or in what endeavour. In schools, the learning culture and the creative learning community[1] interact to make up the context of the specific work place setting where teachers can focus, engage and develop their practice of teaching creatively. As Wenger puts it:

> Education, in its deepest sense and at whatever age it takes place, concerns the opening of identities – exploring new ways of being that lie beyond our current state. Whereas training aims to create an inbound trajectory targeted at competence in a specific practice, education must strive to open new dimensions for the negotiation of the self. It places students on an outbound trajectory toward a broad field of possible identities. Education is not merely formative – it is transformative.
>
> (Wenger, 1998, p. 263)

All of the chapters in this book represent thinking about the importance for attention to relationships and the possibilities for transforming primary music teaching (and learning). In reflecting on Wenger's definition of 'education' as where theory enriches practice, throughout this book we see 'the opening of identities' resonating well with the realities of children's experience and questions about everyday life in classrooms, and for teachers' ideals and aspirations about their own creativity to be released and realised through engagement in meaningful learning communities.

Teachers and children develop trust through engagement in meaningful learning communities. Teachers and children are at the heart of this process, and creativity in education is in part determined by the cultural surroundings in which the school is located, in terms of the multiple musical styles and influences encountered, whether at home, through the media or beyond. If it is to relate to the social constructions of childhood that are prevalent in the society of which schools are part, and if it is to make sense culturally, then children's music making and musical practices have to be seen in relation to this wider context. In teaching and learning creatively (exploring, producing, experimenting and innovating), and in valuing creative musical work, it is the responsibility across the whole community for teachers to include parents and all of those across the community at large, because it is important to hear and engage with children's work and to become familiar with it as a valid part of their learning activities and culture.

To be precise, 'what counts' as music and making informed judgements about creativity plays a major part in determining the teachers' practice and must ensure the creative involvement of the teacher. Creative teachers are not happy to be bound to 'one way' to teach. Creative teachers need to act as creative role models themselves who value the creative dimensions of their own musical lives and make connections between their personal responses to experience children's music and their teaching. The issues addressed in this book reflect this meshing of socio-cultural factors, as well as deriving from our own experience as teachers, teacher educators and researchers who are centrally concerned with music in primary schools and teachers' confidence to teach music creatively.

So, what is it to be a creative teacher? Stenhouse (1985) argues that teachers' development and self-awareness are essential requirements for effective education. Being a primary school teacher who does music daily with her/his class is, in a sense, little more than being profoundly and completely oneself. But to practice this belief, to be oneself, necessitates self-knowledge, self-exploration and creativity.

Although music and teaching, as with music and learning, are closely interrelated, they tend to be respectively the province of one or other of these two disciplines and distinguished as different kinds of knowledge. How teaching music takes place in primary schools should be concerned with understanding practice and ascribing value to the things that are learned and learned creatively. In this book we have emphasised the involvement of the teacher in classroom endeavour and leadership practice in roles as composer, improviser and performer as having a momentum of its own in addition to a field of influence in building the learning community.

Where Wenger's work makes its most original contribution to socio-cultural theory, and links so profoundly to the type of creative teaching practices emphasised in this book, is in his promotion of individual identity (and here I am thinking of the teacher) and its relationship with community (the children). Socio-cultural understanding of identity supports the notion of a confluence of the individual and the group. The connectedness of human activity (such as music making in all its forms) defines one in terms of the other, and vice versa. As Wenger puts it:

> Building an identity consists of negotiating the meanings of our experience of membership in social communities. The concept of identity serves as a pivot between the social and the individual, so that each can be talked about in terms of the other.
>
> (Wenger, 1998, p. 145)

The idea of a learning community developing dimensions of 'practice' as the property of a community (see Figure 14.1) has been coined the term 'community of practice' which is a useful theory or way of understanding the social practices developed in classrooms through the values, actions and interactions of teacher and learners. *Joint enterprise* refers to what is negotiated in terms of what counts as music and creativity. *Mutual engagement* refers to doing things creatively together, to relationships and social complexity and to community

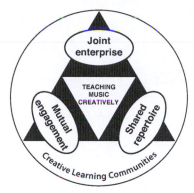

■ **Figure 14.1** Dimensions of creative practice in creative learning communities (Wenger, 1998, p. 73).

maintenance and engagement. *Shared repertoire* refers to the values, skills, actions, tools and passions that are shared between members.

The idea is to develop communities of practice where teacher and children co-construct ways of teaching and learning music, where creativity is a path and process of moving, as well as a quality of space for negotiating the meanings of learning in social communities. The participation of teacher in various roles – as composer, improviser, artist, critic and audience – is greatly esteemed as a core element of the emotional and learning relationship between educators and children (i.e. of the creative learning community), for which it is hoped that teachers will appreciate more fully their potential to teach music creatively and teach for music creativity.

NOTE

1   Creative learning is defined by Biddulph (2017) as a type of learning which 'manifests in opportunities of risk through which children search for imaginative possibilities, informed and valued by the particular social cultural context within which these opportunities occur. Creative learning pedagogies embrace spaces of intercultural uncertainty within which children's agency is fostered, where fluid (and often divergent) creative responses are nurtured and where awareness of the diverse diversities in the way creative learning manifests is explicitly encouraged'.

FURTHER READING

Biddulph, J. (2017) *The Diverse Diversities of Creative Learning at Home: Three Case Studies of Ethnic Minority Immigrant Children*. PhD thesis, Cambridge University.

Craft, A. (2015) *Creativity, Education and Society: Writings of Anna Craft*. Stoke-on-Trent: Trentham Books.

Higgins, L. (2012) *Community Music: In Theory and in Practice*. New York, NY: Oxford University Press.

BIBLIOGRAPHY

Abbs, P. (2003) *Against the Flow: Education, the Arts and Postmodern Culture*. London: Routledge Falmer.

Addo, A. O. (1997) Children's idiomatic expressions of cultural knowledge. *International Journal of Music Education*, 30, 15–24.

Airasian, P. W. and Russell, M. (2007) *Classroom Assessment: Concepts and Applications* (6th edition). New York, NY: McGraw-Hill.

Akuno, E. A. (2005) *Issues in Music Education in Kenya: A Handbook for Teachers*. Nairobi: Emak Music Services.

Akuno, E. A. (2009) *Indigenous Kenyan Children's Songs: An Anthology*. Nairobi: Emak Music Services.

Alexander, B., Arasaratnam, L., Avant-Mier, R., Durham, A., Flores, L., Leeds-Hurwitz, W., Mendoza, S. L., Oetzel, J., Osland, J., Tsuda, Y., Yin, J. and Halualani, R. (2014) Defining and communicating what 'intercultural' and 'intercultural communication' means to us. *Journal of International and Intercultural Communication*, 7(1), 14–37.

Alexander, R. J. (ed.) (2010) *Children, Their World, Their Education*. Final Report and Recommendations of the Cambridge Primary Review. London: Routledge (especially pp. 239–45, 471–4, 496–500).

Anttila, E. (2007) Children as agents in dance: Implications of the notion of child culture for research and practice in dance education. In L. Bresler (ed.) *International Handbook of Research in Arts Education*, Springer International Handbooks of Education (Volume 16, Section 8, doi:10.1007/978-1-4020-3052-9-59). Dordrecht: Springer, 865–79.

Arnot, A., McIntyre, D., Pedder, D. and Reay, D. (2004) *Consultation in the Classroom*. Cambridge: Pearson Publishing.

Aróstegui, J. and Ibarretxe, G. (2016) Intercultural education and music teacher education: Cosmopolitan learning through popular music. In P. Burnard, E. Mackinlay and K. Powell (eds.) *The Routledge International Handbook of Intercultural Arts Research*. Abingdon, UK: Routledge.

Barks, C. (1995) *The Essential Rumi*. San Francisco: Harper.

Barrett, M. S. (1996) Children's aesthetic decision-making: An analysis of children's musical discourse as composers. *International Journal of Music Education*, 28, 37–62.

Barrett, M. S. (2005) Musical communication and children's communities of musical practice. In D. Miell, R. MacDonald and D. J. Hargreaves (eds.) *Musical Communication*. Oxford: Oxford University Press.

Barrett, M. S. (2006) Inventing songs, inventing worlds: The 'genesis' of creative thought and activity in young children's lives. *International Journal of Early Years Education*, 14(3), 201–20.

Benson, F. (2012) *Thrown in the Deep End: Informal Learning in a Primary Music Classroom*. Unpublished honours thesis, University of Sydney. Available at http://hdl.handle.net/2123/8857

Bhabha, H. K. (2004) *The Location of Culture*. London: Routledge.

Biddulph, J. (2017) *The Diverse Diversities of Creative Learning at Home: Three Case Studies of Ethnic Minority Immigrant Children*. PhD thesis, Cambridge University.

Bishop, J. C. (2014) 'That's how the whole handclap thing passes on': Online/offline transmission and multimodal variation in a children's clapping game. In A. N. Burn and C. O. Richards (eds.) *Children's Games in the New Media Age: Childlore, Media and the Playground*. Farnham, UK: Ashgate, pp. 53–84.

Bishop, J. C. and Curtis, M. (2001) *Play Today in the Primary School Playground*. Ballmoor, Buckingham: Open University Press.

Black, P., Harrison, C., Lee, C., Marshall, B. and Wiliam, D. (2004) Working inside the black box: Assessment for learning in the classroom. *Phi Delta Kappan*, 86(1), 9–21.

Black, P. and Wiliam, D. (1998) *Inside the Black Box: Raising Standards Through Classroom Assessment*. London: King's College University.

Blair, D. V. (2007) Musical maps as narrative inquiry. *International Journal of Education & the Arts*, 8(15). Available at www.ijea.org/v8n15

Boal-Palheiros, G. and Hargreaves, D. (2001) Listening to music at home and at school. *British Journal of Music Education*, 18(2), 103–18.

Boden, M. (2005) *The Creative Mind: Myths and Mechanisms*. London: Routledge.

Bresler, L. (2002) *Out of the Trenches: The Joys (and Risks) of Cross-Disciplinary Collaborations*. Focus Areas Report, ISME World Conference and Music Festival. Bergen, Norway: International Society for Music Education, pp. 53–71.

Britzman, D. (1995) 'The question of belief': Writing poststructural ethnography. *International Journal of Qualitative Studies in Education*, 8(3), 229–38.

Brookfield, S. (1995) *Becoming a Critically Reflective Teacher*. San Francisco, CA: Jossey Bass Publishers.

Brophy, T. (2000) *Assessing the Developing Child Musician*. Chicago, IL: GIA.

Brown, A. R. and Dillon, S. (2007) Networked improvisational musical environments: Learning through online collaborative music making. In J. Finney and P. Burnard (eds.) *Music Education with Digital Technology*. London: Continuum, pp. 131–41.

Bruner, J. (1996) *The Culture of Education*. Cambridge, MA: Harvard University Press.

Burn, A. (2011) *Children's Playground Games and Songs in the New Media Age, 2009–2011*. Project Report. Available at http://projects.beyondtext.ac.uk/playgroundgames/uploads/end_of_project_report.pdf

Burn, A. N. and Richards, C. O. (2014) *Children's Games in the New Media Age: Childlore, Media and the Playground*. Farnham, UK: Ashgate.

Burnaford, G., Aprill, A. and Weiss, C. (2001) *Renaissance in the Classroom: Arts Integration and Meaningful Learning*. Mahwah, NJ: Lawrence Erlbaum.

Burnaford, G. (with Brown, S., Doherty, J. and McLaughlin, H. J.). (2007) *Arts Integration Frameworks, Research and Practice: A Literature Review*. Washington, DC: Arts Education Partnership.

Burnard, P. (2000) How children ascribe meaning to improvisation and composition: Rethinking pedagogy in music education. *Music Education Research*, 2(1), 7–23.

Burnard, P. (2002) Investigating children's meaning making and the emergence of musical interaction in group improvisation. *British Journal of Music Education*, 19(2), 157–72.

Burnard, P. (2004) Pupil-teacher conceptions and the challenge of learning: Lessons from a Year 8 creative classroom. *Improving Schools*, 7(1), 23–34.

Burnard, P. (2006) The individual and social worlds of children's musical creativity. In G. McPherson (ed.) *The Child as Musician: A Handbook of Musical Development*. Oxford: Oxford University Press, pp. 353–74.

Burnard, P. (2008) Special Issue on Creativity, policy and practice discourses: Productive tensions in the new millennium. UNESCO Observatory E-Journal, *Multi-Disciplinary Research in the Arts*. Retrieved from http://education.unimelb.edu.au/about_us/specialist-areas/arts_education/melbourne_unesco/observatory_of_arts_education/the_e-journal/volume_1_issue_3

Burnard, P. (2012) *Musical Creativities in Practice*. New York: Oxford University Press.

Burnard, P. and Biddulph, J. (2013) Music. In R. Jones and D. Wyse (eds.) *Creativity in the Primary Curriculum* (2nd edition). London: David Fulton, pp. 130–148.

Burnard, P., Grainger, T. and Craft, A. (2006) Documenting possibility thinking: A journey of collaborative enquiry. *International Journal of Early Years Education*, Special Issue on Creativity and Cultural Innovation in Early Childhood Education, 14(3), 243–62.

Burnard, P. and Hennessy, S. (2009) *Reflective Practices in Arts Education*. Dordrecht, The Netherlands: Springer.

Burnard, P. and Kuo, H. (2015) The individual and social worlds of children's musical creativities. In G. McPherson (ed). *The Child as Musician: A Handbook of Musical Development* (2nd edition). Oxford: Oxford University Press, pp. 486–99.

Burnard, P., Mackinlay, E. and Powell, K. (2016) *The Routledge International Handbook of Intercultural Arts Research*. Abingdon, UK: Routledge.

Burnard, P. and Younker, B. A. (2002) Mapping pathways: Fostering creativity in composition. *Music Education Research*, 4(2), 245–61.

Butler, R. (2008) Evaluating competence and maintaining self-worth between early and middle childhood: Blissful ignorance or the construction of knowledge and strategies in context? In H. W. Marsh, R. G. Craven and D. M. McInerney (eds.) *Self-Processes, Learning and Enabling Human Potential*. Charlotte, NC: Information Age Publishing, pp. 193–222.

Campbell, P. S. (1991) The child-song genre: A comparison of songs by and for children. *International Journal of Music Education*, 17, 14–23.

Campbell, P. S. (1998) *Songs in Their Heads: Music and Its Meaning in Children's Lives*. Oxford: Oxford University Press.

Campbell, P. S. (2002) The musical cultures of children. In L. Bresler and C. Thompson (eds.) *The Arts in Children's Lives: Context, Culture and Curriculum*. Netherlands: Kluwer, pp. 57–69.

Campbell, P. S. (2010) *Songs in Their Heads: Music and Its Meaning in Children's Lives* (2nd edition). New York: Oxford University Press.

Campbell, P. S. and Wiggins, T. (eds.) (2013) *Oxford Handbook of Children's Musical Cultures*. New York, NY: Oxford University Press.

Carle, E. (1969) *The Very Hungry Caterpillar*. New York: Puffin.

Centre for the Use of Research and Evidence in Education (CUREE). (2009) *Building the Evidence Base: Learner's Survey Final Report*. Coventry: CUREE.

Chaudry, L. N. (2000) Researching 'my people,' researching myself: Fragments of a reflexive tale. In E. St. Pierre and W. Pillow (eds.) *Working the Ruins: Feminist Poststructural Research and Practice in Education*. New York, NY: Routledge, pp. 96–113.

Child, L. (2000) *I Will Not Ever NEVER Eat a Tomato*. London: Orchard Books.

Clarke, S. (1998) *Targeting Assessment in the Primary Classroom*. London: Hodder and Stoughton.

Cohen, V. and Trehub, S. (1999, April) *The Kinaesthetic Source of Musical Schemes: Infants' Reaction to Descending Versus Ascending Tonal Patterns*. Presented at the International Research in Music Education Conference, University of Exeter, England.

Coll, H. and Finney, J. (eds.) (2007) *Ways Into Music: Making Every Child's Music Matter*. Matlock, UK: The National Association of Music Educators.

Consortium of Institutions for Development and Research in Education in Europe (CIDREE). (2005) *Cross-Curricular Themes in Secondary Education*. Available at www.cidree.org.

Cooper, P. and McIntyre, D. (1993) Commonality in teachers' and pupils' perceptions of effective classroom learning. *British Journal of Educational Psychology*, 63, 381–99.

Craft, A. (2005) *Creativity in Schools: Tensions and Dilemmas*. London: Routledge.

Craft, A. (2015) *Creativity, Education and Society: Writings of Anna Craft*. Stoke-on-Trent: Trentham Books.

Craft, A., Cremin, T. and Burnard, P. (eds.) (2007) *Creative Learning 3–11 and How We Document It*. Stoke-on-Trent: Trentham, pp. 65–75.

Craft, A., Cremin, T., Burnard, P. and Chappell, K. (2007) Teacher stance in creative learning: A study of progression. *Thinking Skills and Creativity*, 2(1), 37–55.

Craft, A., Cremin, T., Burnard, P. and Chappell, K. (2008) Possibility thinking with children in England aged 3–7. In A. Craft, T. Cremin and P. Burnard (eds.) *Creative Learning 3–11 and How We Document It*. Stoke on Trent: Trentham Books.

Creative Partnerships. (2005) *The Rhetorics of Creativity: A Review of the Literature*. Arts Council: London.

Cremin, T. (2009a) Creative teachers and creative teaching. In A. Wilson (ed.) *Creativity in Primary Education*. Exeter: Learning Matters.

Cremin, T. (2009b) *Teaching English Creatively*. Abingdon, UK: Routledge.

Cremin, T., Burnard, P. and Craft, A. (2006) Pedagogy and possibility in the early years. *Thinking Skills and Creativity*, 1(2), 108–19.

Csikszentmihályi, M. (1997) (First publ. 1996) *Creativity, Flow and the Psychology of Discovery and Invention*. New York: Harper Perennial.

Custodero, L. A. (2007) Origins and expertise in the musical improvisations of adults and children: A phenomenological study of content and process. *British Journal of Music Education*, 24(1), 77–98.

Davies, C. (1986) Say it till a song comes (reflections on songs invented by children 3–13). *British Journal of Music Education*, 3(3), 270–93.

Davies, C. (1992) Listen to my song: A study of songs invented by children aged 5–7 years. *British Journal of Music Education*, 9(1), 19–48.

Davies, C. A. (1999) *Reflexive Ethnography: A Guide to Researching Selves and Others*. New York, NY: Routledge.

De Nora, T. (2000). *Music in Everyday Life*. Cambridge, UK: Cambridge University Press.

Department of Education and Training. (2016) *Embedding Aboriginal and Torres Strait Islander Perspectives in Schools (EATSIPS)*. Available at http://indigenous.education.qld.gov.au/eatsips/framework/Pages/default.aspx

DfE (2011) *The Importance of Music: A National Plan*. London: The Crown.

Dodd, L. (1983) *Hairy Maclary from Donaldson's Dairy*: New York: Puffin.

Dowden, T. (2014) Challenging, integrated, negotiated and exploratory curriculum in the middle years of schooling: Designing and implementing high quality curriculum integration. *Australian Journal of Middle Schooling*, 14(1), 16–27.

Eisner, E. W. (2004) What can education learn from the arts about the practice of education? *International Journal of Education and the Arts*, 5(4), 1–12.

Emberly, A. (2009) *'Mandela Went to China . . . and India Too': Musical Cultures of Childhood in South Africa*. Unpublished doctoral dissertation, University of Washington.

Espeland, M. (1987). Music in use: Responsive music listening in the primary school. *British Journal of Music Education* 4(3), 283–297.

Espeland, M. (1991). *Music in Use: Selections of Music for Schools*. Stord, Norway: Stord Lærarhøgskule.

Fautley, M. (2009) Assessment for learning in music. In J. Evans and C. Philpott (eds.) *A Practical Guide to Teaching Music in the Secondary School*. Abingdon, UK: Routledge, pp. 63–72.

Fautley, M. and Savage, J. (2011) Assessment of composing in the lower secondary school in the English National Curriculum. *British Journal of Music Education* 28(1), 51–67.

Finney, J. and Burnard, P. (2007) *Music Education with Digital Technology*. London: Continuum.

Finney, J. and Burnard, P. (eds.) (2009) *Music Education with Digital Technology* (2nd edition). London: Continuum.

Fleishman, P. (2000) *Big Talk: Poems for Four Voices*. Somerville, MA: Candlewick Press. Illustrated by Beppe Giacobbe.

Franklin, M. (2000) Overcoming music phobia. *Orbit*, 31(2), 32–3.

Gaunt, K. D. (2006) *The Games Black Girls Play: Learning the Ropes From Double-Dutch to Hip-Hop*. New York: New York University Press.

Gentry, J. R. (1982) An analysis of developmental spelling in GNYS AT WRK. *The Reading Teacher*, 36(2), 192–200.

Giglio, M. (2010) *Creative Activity in Musical Education Contexts in Schools: Forms of Collaboration Between Pupils and Actions of the Teacher*. Unpublished doctoral thesis, University of Neuchatel.

Giglio, M. (2012) Creating a 'space' for class discussion about collaborative creativity: The point of view of teachers. In G. Mota and A. Yin (eds.) *Proceedings of the 24th International Seminar on Research in Music Education*. Thessaloniki, July 8–13, 2012, pp. 81–8.

Giglio, M. and Perret-Clermont, A.-N. (2010) A teaching sequence granting space to the students' collaborative creation in the music classroom: Some observations. In G. Mota and A. Yin (eds.) *Proceedings of the 23rd International Seminar on Research in Music Education*. Changchun: North East Normal University, pp. 96–101.

Gillies, R. M. (2007) *Cooperative Learning: Integrating Theory and Practice*. London: Sage.

Ginsburg, M. (1974) *Mushroom in the Rain*. New York: Simon & Schuster.

Gipps, C. (1999) Socio-cultural aspects of assessment. *Review of Research in Education*, 24, 355–92.

Glover, J. (2000) *Children Composing 4–14*. London: Routledge.

Goff, R., and Ludwig, M. (2013) *Teacher Practice and Student Outcomes in Arts-Integrated Learning Settings: A Review of Literature*. Washington, DC: American Institutes for Research.

Gradel, M. F. (2001) *Creating Capacity: A Framework for Providing Professional Development Opportunities for Teaching Artists*. Washington, DC: The John F. Kennedy Center for the Performing Arts. Available at www.kennedy-center.org

Green, L. (2008) *Music, Informal Learning and the School: A New Classroom Pedagogy*. Aldershot, UK: Ashgate.

Greene, M. (1995) *Releasing the Imagination: Essays on Education, the Arts, and Social Change*. San Francisco, CA: Jossey-Bass.

Greher, G. and Ruthmann, S. A. (2012) On chunking, simples, and paradoxes: Why Jeanne Bamberger's research matters. *Visions of Research in Music Education*, 20. Available at www.rider.edu/~vrme/v20n1/

Hale, C. L. and Green, S. K. (2009) Six key principles for music assessment. *Music Educators Journal*, 95(4), 27–31.

Harrison, C. (2007) Music for all – how do we make it a reality? In H. Coll and J. Finney (eds.) *Ways into Music: Making Every Child's Music Matter*. Solihull, West Midlands: National Association of Music Educators, pp. 5–12.

Harwood, E. (1987) *The Memorized Song Repertoire of Children in Grades Four and Five in Champaign, Illinois*. Unpublished doctoral dissertation, University of Illinois.

Harwood, E. (1998a) Music learning in context: A playground tale. *Research Studies in Music Education*, 11, 52–60.

Harwood, E. (1998b) Go on girl! Improvisation in African-American girls' singing games. In B. Nettl and M. Russell (eds.) *In the Course of Performance: Studies in the World of Musical Improvisation*. Chicago: University of Chicago Press, pp. 113–25.

Hennessy, S. (2000) Overcoming the red-feeling: The development of confidence to teach music in primary school amongst student teachers. *British Journal of Music Education*, 17(2), 183–96.

Hennessy, S. (2009) Creativity in the music curriculum. In A. Wilson (ed.) *Creativity in Primary Education*. Exeter: Learning Matters, pp. 134–47.

Higgins, L. (2012) *Community Music: In Theory and in Practice*. New York, NY: Oxford University Press.

Higgins, L. and Campbell, P. S. (2010) *Free to Be Musical: Group Improvisation in Music*. Plymouth, UK: Rowman and Littlefield.

hooks, b. (1994) *Teaching to Transgress: Education as the Practice of Freedom*. New York, NY: Routledge.

Howell, G. (2007, August 15) Musical alphabets. *Music Work*. Available at http://musicwork. wordpress.com/2007/08/15/musical-alphabets/ (accessed 30 August 2012).

Howell, G. (2009) From imitation to invention: Issues and strategies for the ESL music classroom. *Musicworks: Journal of the Australia Council of Orff Schulwerk*, 14(1), 61–5.

Howell, G. (2009, April 2) Teaching the alphabet dance. *Music Work*. Available at http:// musicwork.wordpress.com/2009/05/02/teaching-the-alphabet-dance/ (accessed 30 August 2012).

Howell, G. (2011) 'Do they know they're composing?': Music making and understanding among newly arrived refugee and immigrant children. *International Journal of Communities Music*, 4(1), 47–58.

Irwin, R. L. and Chalmers, F. G. (2007) Experiencing the visual and visualizing experience. In L. Bresler (ed.) *International Handbook on Research in Arts Education*. New York, NY: Springer, pp. 179–93.

Jackson, J. (ed.) (2014) *The Routledge Handbook of Language and Intercultural Communication*. New York: Routledge.

Jones, P. and Robson, C. (2008) *Teaching Music in Primary Schools*. Exeter: Learning Matters.

Kafai, Y., Peppler, K. and Chapman, R. (2009) *The Computer Clubhouse: Constructionism and Creativity in Youth Communities*. New York: Teachers College Press.

Kind, S., de Cosson, A., Irwin, R. L. and Grauer, K. (2007) Artist-teacher partnerships in learning: The in/between spaces of artist-teacher professional development. *Canadian Journal of Education*, 30, 839–64.

Koopman, C. (2005) The justification of education in the arts. *Journal of Philosophy of Education*, 39(1), 85–97.

Laurence, F. (2007) Let the bird fly free: Making music with children. *Ways into Music: Making Every Child's Music Matter*. Matlock, UK: National Association of Music Educators, pp. 10–19.

Laurence, F. (2010) Listening to children: Voice, agency and ownership in school musicking. In R. Wright (ed.) *Sociology and Music Education*. Farnham: SEMPRE, pp. 243–62.

Lave, J. and Wenger, E. (1991) *Situated Learning: Legitimate Peripheral Participation*. Cambridge: Cambridge University Press.

Lill, A. L. (2015) *Informal Learnings: Young People's Informal Learning of Music in Australian and British Schools*. Unpublished doctoral thesis, University of Sydney. Available at http://hdl.handle.net/2123/13683

Ludwig, M., Marklein, M. B. and Mengli, S. (2016) *Arts Integration: A Promising Approach to Improving Early Learning*. Washington, DC: American Institutes for Research.

Lum, C. H. (2008) Home musical environment of children in Singapore: On globalization, technology, and media. *Journal of Research in Music Education*, 56(2), 101–17.

Malloch, S. and Trevarthen, C. (2009) *Communicative Musicality: Exploring the Basis of Human Companionship*. New York: Oxford University Press.

Marsh, K. (1995) Children's singing games: Composition in the playground? *Research Studies in Music Education*, 4, 2–11.

Marsh, K. (1999) Mediated orality: The role of popular music in the changing tradition of children's musical play. *Research Studies in Music Education*, 13, 2–12.

Marsh, K. (2006) Cycles of appropriation in children's musical play: Orality in the age of reproduction. *The World of Music*, 48(1), 8–23.

Marsh, K. (2008) *The Musical Playground: Global Tradition and Change in Children's Songs and Games*. New York: Oxford University Press.

Marsh, K. (2013) Music in the lives of refugee and newly arrived immigrant children in Sydney, Australia. In P. S. Campbell and T. Wiggins (eds.) *Oxford Handbook of Children's Musical Cultures*. New York: Oxford University Press, pp. 491–509.

Marsh, K. (2016) Creating bridges: Music, play and well-being in the lives of refugee and immigrant children and young people. *Music Education Research*, 19(1), 60–73.

Marsh, K. and Dieckmann, S. (2016) Interculturality in the playground and playgroup: Music as shared space for young immigrant children and their mothers. In P. Burnard, E. Mackinlay and K. Powell (eds.) *The Routledge International Handbook of Intercultural Arts Research*. Abingdon, UK: Routledge, pp. 358–68.

Marsh, K. and Young, S. (2006) Musical play. In G. McPherson (ed.) *The Child as Musician: A Handbook of Musical Development*. Oxford, UK: Oxford University Press, pp. 289–310.

McPherson, G. (2006) *The Child as Musician: A Handbook of Musical Development*. Oxford: Oxford University Press.

Merriam, A. P. (1964) *The Anthropology of Music*. Chicago, IL: Northwestern University Press.

Mills, J. (1993) *Music in the Primary School*. Cambridge: Cambridge University Press.

Mills, M. (2009) Capturing student progress via portfolios in the music classroom. *Music Educators Journal*, 96(2), 32–8.

Minks, A. (2006) *Interculturality in Play and Performance: Miskitu Children's Expressive Practices on the Caribbean Coast of Nicaragua*. Unpublished doctoral dissertation, Columbia University, New York.

Minks, A. (2008) Performing gender in song games among Nicaraguan Miskitu children. *Language and Communication*, 28(1), 36–56.

Minks, A. (2013) Miskitu children's singing games on the Caribbean coast of Nicaragua as intercultural play and performance. In P. Campbell and T. Wiggins (eds.) *Oxford Handbook of Children's Musical Cultures*. New York, NY: Oxford University Press, pp. 218–31.

Moore, H. (1997) Interior landscapes and external worlds: The return of grand theory in anthropology. *The Australian Journal of Anthropology*, 8(2), 125–44.

Moyle, A. M. (1978) *Aboriginal Sound Instruments*. Canberra, ACT: Australian Institute of Aboriginal Studies.

Murphy, R. (2007) Harmonizing assessment and music in the classroom. In L. Bresler (ed.) *International Handbook of Education and the Arts*. Dordrecht, Netherlands: Springer, pp. 361–379.

Murphy, R. and Espeland, M. (2007) *Upbeat: Teacher's Resource Book*. Dublin: Gill and MacMillan.

Nakata, M. (2007) *Disciplining the Savages: Savaging the Disciplines*. Canberra, ACT: Aboriginal Studies Press.

Nettl, B. (1960) Musical cartography and the distribution of music. *Southwestern Journal of Anthropology*, 16(3), 338–47.

Nixon, D. T. and Akerson, V. L. (2002) *Building Bridges: Using Science as a Tool to Teach Reading and Writing*. ERIC: ED465616.

Odena, O. (ed.) (2012) *Musical Creativity: Insights From Music Education Research*. Surrey, UK: Ashgate Publishing.

Office for Standards in Education (OFSTED). (2008) *Assessment for Learning: The Impact of National Strategy Support*. Report No. 070244. London: Author.

Ogden, H. C. (2008) *Vivid Moments Long Remembered: The Lifetime Impact of Elementary School Musical Theatre*. Unpublished master's thesis, Queen's University, Kingston, ON.

Ontario Ministry of Education. (2009) *The Ontario Curriculum, Grades 1–8: The Arts*. Toronto, ON: Author.

Organisation for Economic Co-operation and Development (OECD). (2008) OECD/CERI International Conference: *Learning in the 21st Century: Research, Innovation and Policy*. Assessment for Learning Formative Assessment. Paris: OECD.

Owen, N. (2011) *Placing Students at the Heart of Creative Learning*. London: David Fulton.

Parsons, M. (2004) Art and integrated curriculum. In E. Eisner and M. D. Day (eds.) *Handbook of Research and Policy in Art Education*. NAEA. Mahwah, NJ: Lawrence Erlbaum, pp. 775–94.

Pound, L. and Lee, T. (2011) *Teaching Mathematics Creatively*. London: Routledge.

Pratt, M. L. (1992) *Imperial Eyes: Travel Writing and Transculturation*. London: Routledge.

Rabkin, N. and Redmond, R. (2004) *Putting the Arts in the Picture: Reframing Education in the 21st Century*. Chicago, IL: Columbia College.

Rao, D. with Pearson, B. (2005) *Circle of Sound: Voice Education: A Contemplative Approach to Singing Through Meditation, Movement and Vocalization*. London: Boosey and Hawkes, pp. 54–7.

Reese, S. (2003) Responding to student compositions. In M. Hickey (ed.) *Why and How to Teach Music Composition: A New Horizon for Music Education*. Reston, VA: MENC, The National Association for Music Education, pp. 211–232.

Rice, T. (1987) Toward the remodeling of ethnomusicology. *Ethnomusicology*, 31(3), 469–88.

Riddell, C. (1990) *Traditional Singing Games of Elementary School Children in Los Angeles*. Unpublished doctoral dissertation, University of California, Los Angeles.

Robertson, C. (1995) The ethnomusicologist as midwife. In R. Solie (ed.) *Musicology and Difference: Gender and Sexuality in Music Scholarship*. Oakland: University of California Press, pp. 107–24.

Robinson, K. and Azzam, A. M. (2009) Why creativity now? A conversation with Sir Ken Robinson. *Educational Leadership*, 67(1), 22–6.

Rosen, M. (1989) *We're Going on a Bear Hunt*. London: Walker Books.

Rudduck, J. (1999) Teacher practice and the student voice. In M. Lang, J. Olson, H. Hansen and W. Bunder (eds.) *Changing Schools/Changing Practices: Perspectives on Educational Reform and Teacher Professionalism*. Louvain, Belgium: Garant Publishers, pp. 41–54.

Rudduck, J. and Flutter, J. (2004) *How to Improve Your School: Giving Pupils a Voice*. London: Continuum.

Rudduck, J. and McIntyre, D. (2007) *Improving Learning Through Consulting Pupils*. London: Routledge.

Rudduck, J., Wallace, G. and Day, J. (2000) Students' voices: What can they tell us as partners in change? In K. Stott and V. Trafford (eds.) *Boys and Girls in the Primary Classroom*. Buckingham: Open University Press.

Rudduck, J., Wilson, E. and Flutter, J. (1998) *Sustaining Pupils' Commitment to Learning: The Challenge of Year 8*. Cambridge: Homerton Publications.

Russell, J. and Zembylas, M. (2007) Arts integration in the curriculum: A review of research and implications for teaching and learning. In L. Bresler (ed.) *International Handbook of Research in Arts Education*. Dordrecht, NL: Springer, pp. 287–302.

Russell-Bowie, D. (2009) Syntegration or disintegration? Models of integrating the arts across the primary curriculum. *International Journal of Education and the Arts*, 10(28). Retrieved from http://www.ijea/v10n28/

Ruthmann, S. A. and Dillon, S. C. (2012) Technology in the lives and schools of adolescents. In G. McPherson and G. Welch (eds.) *Oxford Handbook of Music Education* (Volume 1). New York: Oxford University Press, pp. 529–47.

Savage, J. (2012) Those who can – play; those who can't – use music tech? How can teachers knock down the walls between music and music technology? In C. Philpott and G. Spruce (eds.) *Debates in Music Teaching*. London: Routledge, pp. 169–84.

Sawyer, K. R. (2004) Creative teaching: Collaborative discussion as disciplined improvisation. *Educational Researcher*, 33(2), 12–20.

Sawyer, K. R. (2011) *Structure and Improvisation in Creative Teaching*. New York, NY: Oxford University Press.

Schafer, M. (1977) *The Tuning of the World*. New York, NY: Alfred A. Knopf.

Sendak, M. (1970) *Where the Wild Things Are*. London: Random House.

Small, C. (1998) *Musicking: The Meanings of Performing and Listening*. Hanover, NH: Wesleyan University Press.

Smithrim, K. (1997) Free musical play in early childhood. *Canadian Music Educator*, 38(4), 17–24.

Society for Ethnomusicology. (2016) *What Is Ethnomusicology?* Available at www.ethnomusicology.org

Somekh, B. (2007) *Pedagogy and Learning with ICT: Researching the Art of Innovation*. New York: Routledge.

Spruce, G. (2001) Music assessment and the hegemony of musical heritage. In C. Philpott and C. Plummeridge (eds.) *Issues in Music Teaching*. London: RoutledgeFalmer.

Stenhouse, L. (1985) *Research as a Basis for Teaching*. London: Heinemann.

Swanwick, K. (1999) *Teaching Music Musically*. London: Routledge.

Swanwick, K. and Tillman, J. (1986) The sequence of musical development: A study of children's composition. *British Journal of Music Education*, 3(3), 305–39.

Thibeault, M. D. (2012) Music education in a post-performance world. In G. McPherson and G. Welch (eds.) *Oxford Handbook of Music Education* (Volume 2). New York: Oxford University Press, pp. 517–30.

Thomas, V. & Paul, K. (1987) *Winnie the Witch*. Oxford, UK: Oxford University Press.

Thomson, P. and Gunter, H. (2006) From 'consulting pupils' to 'pupils as researchers': A situated case narrative. *British Educational Research Journal*, 32(6), 839–56.

Upitis, R. (1990a) *This Too Is Music*. Portsmouth, NH: Heinemann.

Upitis, R. (1990b) Children's invented notations of familiar and unfamiliar melodies. *Psychomusicology*, 9, 89–106.

Upitis, R. (1992) *The Compositions and Invented Notations of Children*. Portsmouth, NH: Heinemann Educational Books.

Upitis, R., Abrami, P. C., Brook, J., Troop, M. and Catalano, L. (2010) Using ePEARL for music teaching: A case study. In G. Pérez-Bustamante, K. Physavat and F. Ferreria (eds.) *Proceedings of the International Association for Scientific Knowledge Conference*. Seville, Spain: IASK Press, pp. 36–45.

Upitis, R., Smithrim, K. and Soren, B. (1999) When teachers become musicians and artists: Teacher transformation and professional development. *Music Education Research*, 1(19), 23–35.

Vass, G. and Chalmers, G. (2015) NAPLAN, achievement gaps and embedding indigenous perspectives in schooling: disrupting the decolonial option. In B. Lingard, G. Thompson and S. Sellar (eds.) *National Testing in Schools: An Australian Assessment*. Abingdon, UK: Routledge, pp. 139–51.

Webster, P. (1990) Creativity as creative thinking. *Music Educators Journal*, 76(9), 22–8.

Welch, G. F. (2003) The importance of singing. In A. Paterson & E. Bentley (eds.) *Bluebirds and Crows: developing a singing culture in and out of school*. Matlock, UK: The National Association of Music Educators (NAME), pp. 2–5.

Wenger, E. (1998) *Communities of Practice: Learning, Meaning and Identity*. New York: Cambridge University Press.

Wiggins, J. (2010) *Teaching for Musical Understanding* (2nd edition). Rochester, MI: Center for Applied Research in Musical Understanding.

Wiggins, J. (2011) When the music is theirs: Scaffolding young songwriters. In M. S. Barrett (ed.) *A Cultural Psychology of Music Education*. Oxford: Oxford University Press, pp. 83–113.

Willett, R. (2014) Remixing children's cultures: Media-referenced play in the playground. In A. N. Burn and C. O. Richards (eds.) *Children's Games in the New Media Age: Childlore, Media and the Playground*. Farnham, UK: Ashgate, pp. 133–51.

Young, S. (2007) Digital technologies, young children, and music education practice. In K. Smithrim and R. Upitis (eds.) *Listen to Their Voices: Research and Practice in Early Childhood Music*. Waterloo, ON: Canadian Music Educators' Association, pp. 330–43.

Younker, B. A. (2003) The nature of feedback in a community of composing. In M. Hickey (ed.) *Why and How to Teach Music Composition: A New Horizon for Music Education*. Reston, VA: MENC, The National Association for Music Education, pp. 233–242.

INDEX

Page numbers in *italic* indicate a figure or table on the corresponding page.